About the Authors

David Bellin is Director of Graduate Studies in the Department of Computer Science at North Carolina A&T State University. He also consults internationally on object analysis and technical training with organizations such as Macy's, Universidad Nacional Autonomia de Mexico, and the United States government. He has received a Congressional Fulbright Award in computer science and an IBM Corporation University Partnership Award.

Susan Suchman Simone is the President of Information Fountain Incorporated, specializing in technical writing and training. She has taught classes for Yourdon, Incorporated and North Carolina State University and has developed training materials for companies across the country including Chase Manhattan Bank, New York Life, and Banamex.

The CRC Card Book

The Addison-Wesley Series in Object-Oriented Software Engineering

Grady Booch, Series Editor

David Bellin and Susan Suchman Simone, *The CRC Card Book*
0-201-89535-8

Grady Booch, *Object Solutions: Managing the Object-Oriented Project*
0-8053-0594-7

Grady Booch, *Object-Oriented Analysis and Design with Applications, Second Edition*
0-8053-5340-2

Grady Booch and Doug Bryan, *Software Engineering with Ada, Third Edition*
0-8053-0608-0

Dave Collins, *Designing Object-Oriented User Interfaces*
0-8053-5350-X

Martin Fowler, *Analysis Patterns: Reusable Object Models*
0-201-89542-0

Wilf LaLonde, *Discovering Smalltalk*
0-8053-2720-7

Lockheed Martin Advanced Concepts Center and Rational Software Corporation,
Succeeding with the Booch and OMT Methods: A Practical Approach
0-805-32279-5

Ira Pohl, *Object-Oriented Programming Using C++, Second Edition*
0-201-89550-1

David N. Smith, *IBM Smalltalk: The Language*
0-8053-0908-X

Daniel Tkach and Richard Puttick, *Object Technology in Application Development,
Second Edition*
0-201-49833-2

Daniel Tkach, Walter Fang, and Andrew So, *Visual Modeling Technique: Object
Technology Using Visual Programming*
0-8053-2574-3

David Bellin
Susan Suchman Simone

The CRC Card Book

ADDISON-WESLEY

An imprint of Addison Wesley Longman, Inc.

Reading, Massachusetts   Harlow, England   Menlo Park, California
Berkeley, California   Don Mills, Ontario   Sydney
Bonn   Amsterdam   Tokyo   Mexico City

Many of the designations used by manufacturers and sellers to distinguish their products are claimed as trademarks. Where those designations appear in this book, and Addison Wesley Longman was aware of a trademark claim, the designations have been printed with initial capital letters.

The publisher offers discounts on this book when ordered in quantity for special sales.

The author and publisher have taken care in preparation of this book, but make no expressed or implied warranty of any kind and assume no responsibility for errors or omissions. No liability is assumed for incidental or consequential damages in connection with or arising out of the use of the information or programs contained herein.

For more information, please contact:

Corporate & Professional Publishing Group
Addison Wesley Longman, Inc.
One Jacob Way
Reading, Massachusetts 01867

Library of Congress Cataloging-in-Publication Data

Bellin, David, 1951–
    The CRC card book / David Bellin, Susan Suchman Simone.
        p. cm. -- (The Addison-Wesley series in object-oriented
  software engineering)
    Includes bibliographical references and index.
    ISBN 0-201-89535-8 (alk. paper)
    1. Object-oriented programming (Computer science) 2. Application
  software—Development. I. Simone, Susan Suchman, 1948.
  II. Title. III. Series.
QA76.64.B437   1997
005.1'17--dc21   97-8250
                                           CIP

0-201-89535-8

1 2 3 4 5 6 7 8 9 -MA- 0100999897

First printing, May 1997

Contents

Chapter 1   1

CRC: A Problem-Solving Technique

Chapter 2   19

OO Concepts and Vocabulary

Chapter 9 **165**

Case Study 3: Traffic Control

Chapter 10 **185**

Implementing CRC in Smalltalk

Figure List

Foreword

by Ward Cunningham

Many minds must work together to design a modern computer system. There was a time when an individual could know enough to write a whole program. Those days are past. Today we find that to be valuable software must be comprehensive, integrating all aspects of a problem. Designing and building such software requires teamwork. This book describes how knowledgeable people can work together to solve software design problems using CRC cards: ordinary index cards that become props in a performance that explores the behavior of yet-to-be-written computer programs. Here you will get a glimpse of the discussion that takes place as teams grapple with emerging ideas, trade-offs, and finally, decisions. This book also explains the psychology of these group activities, so that you can understand why they work and then reproduce them with your own teams.

The CRC card sits at the center of every team activity described in this book. CRC cards represent a thing, an object, a part of an object-oriented program. Every object in the program is there for a purpose. It has responsibilities, which it meets by collaborating with other objects. A CRC card is a handy way to keep track of assigned responsibilities for each class of objects. That's what CRC stands for: Class, Responsibilities, and Collaborations.

The authors of this book, David Bellin and Susan Simone, use two group problem-solving techniques: brainstorming and role playing. Although the approaches are well-known, this book describes both as they are applied to design with CRC cards. They illustrate the techniques they describe by including the team dialog as it might be heard in an actual design session. These conversations make the material fresh and accessible. But remember: this is not a novel. Every sentence of the dialog is there to make an important point. Any team learning to use CRC cards would be wise to read the dialog that accompanies each point several times—once before conducting their first meetings, and again after they have seen some of the social dynamics that occur. The first reading will set expectations. On a second or third reading, the dialog will yield examples of useful social interactions, as well as serving as an index for the analytic material in the book.

Of course, to make the dialog work, the authors must tell more of a story about the design situations behind the examples. The Cyber-Trading system and the Fashion Pro computer-aided-design environment provide case studies of computer systems on a scale that requires design by a team. This makes the discussion of concepts concrete. Insights abstracted from the details of these design situations will stay with the reader a long time. The book closes with one more example, this time worked out all the way to code. This portion is like a second book. You can see how design decisions are made, and then see how those decisions play out in the final product.

I first proposed CRC cards as a way to experience what was unique about the then-new discipline of object-oriented programming. The technique's emphasis on responsibility and collaboration was meant as a direct counterpoint to classification, which was attracting too much attention from designers and methodologists of the day. I borrowed the idea of using index cards for software design from a HyperCard style guide. The thought of asking people to solve problems together, and to verbalize their thoughts while doing so, was suggested by the process of collecting "protocols" in usability-testing experiments. My first group designs were conducted the morning after I made the first CRC cards. Working with the cards has always been a social activity.

I've been pleased to see other authors take the CRC ideas and integrate them into more complete methods. Every such effort makes the cards more valuable. But not every author understands the social side of design as completely as the authors of this volume. David and Susan capture an often-neglected side of CRC in an engaging way and have added their own considerable experience to the CRC card method in the process. I am grateful to both for producing a book on CRC that I can recommend to anyone who wants to understand not only how to use the CRC method, but also the dynamics of the team approach to software design. If your goal is better software design, this book will help you achieve it.

Ward Cunningham

Foreword

by Kent Beck

Ward's introduction summarizes this book quite well, so I won't bother to do that at all. Instead, I'll tell a little story of the days before CRC and talk about how the contents of this book relate to the story.

Ward and I had the luxury of working in a research lab together, one that expected ideas, not products, and one that frankly didn't know quite what to do with two strong-minded thinkers, one of them just a punk (that's me). We wrote lots of Smalltalk code together, and we walked a lot and talked about our experience.

I started out just looking over Ward's shoulder as he programmed. In a few weeks I was able to spot typing errors before he did, becoming the world's most complicated and expensive spell checker. After a few months, though, Ward and I evolved a style in which we worked intensely and intimately with our problem, our development environment, and each other.

We recognized that we made a huge investment to get to our level of congruence. We talked about what we were doing at all levels, from how best to work Smalltalk's text editor to how best to handle requirements gathering. Every action, every day, was fair game for reflection and refinement.

On one of our walks, near the end of my tenure at Tektronix, Ward and I got to talking about how to reproduce our experience for other people. We knew that most folks would balk at spending six months just getting to know optimal sequences of menu commands for common tasks (and rightly so). We set ourselves the goal of reproducing the experience of shared understanding, of shared exploration, of communicated insight for others without requiring a lengthy apprenticeship.

While I was at Tek, we never found a way to share "thinking with objects." It was a few months after I had moved on that I got Ward's excited phone call, telling me that he had "got it." He described CRC cards to me. I didn't quite understand, but I knew enough to go with him. The next chance I got I invited him down to talk about and demonstrate his invention. I was struck, then as now, by the simplicity and power of his expression of our shared dream.

Which brings me back to this book. David and Susan have captured much of the spirit of sharing, thinking, and communicating that CRC was originally invented for. By focusing on the people aspects of CRC, they get at what CRC is really good for—getting people to talk, to understand, and to share their understanding of what a system is to do and how it is to do it. It is a significant contribution to the literature, not just of CRC, but of what it means for teams to develop objects, really what it means for teams to develop.

Kent Beck
First Class Software, Inc.
Boulder Creek, California

Preface

Applying the object-oriented paradigm in the development of software applications requires the individual developer and the application team to think and act quite differently than one would in approaching a procedures based project. Object-oriented projects follow a new software development life cycle, one that is both iterative and incremental, a cyclic spiral of analysis, design, and deployment. In this new application-development process, determining and defining properly the classes that are central to the desired system at the beginning of the life cycle is critical. Thorough analysis of the problem and good design up front saves time, and money and helps ensure a successful end result.

Although proponents of the object paradigm often say that identifying objects is a simple and intuitive process, a number of noted experts admit that this is not always true! Particularly with larger-scale applications, omitting a formal analysis of the base classes necessary to the application and the related analysis of their responsibilities and collaboration is certain to lead to missed schedules, blown budgets, and frayed nerves. The solution is to use the CRC process to determine the classes necessary to the system as part of the design process for the application. CRC (classes, responsibility, and collaboration) cards can be used to visualize and test different class-based models during the design phase. It is a proven technique used and advocated by leading methodologists.

The CRC Card Book demonstrates the use of the CRC methodology in a realistic team setting, covering the full range this methodology from initial identification of classes to the production of code based on these classes. At this writing, there are two other books on or incorporating coverage of CRC. Rebecca Wirfs-Brock wrote *Designing Object-Oriented Software* many years ago. It remains the classic definition of responsibility-driven design, but does not discuss the application of the technique in the team-oriented setting in which large-scale applications are developed. Nancy Wilkinson's book, *Using CRC Cards*, focuses specifically on the C++ programming community and likewise does not include any illustration of the team approach to class discovery.

The approach of the CRC Card Book is to cover the CRC method from start to finish, demonstrating its application in three different, detailed case-study examples while supplying tips and pointers throughout. The book demonstrates how real teams can use the CRC technique to accomplish a variety of tasks, including:

- Initially discovering classes
- Selecting the core classes
- Acting out class relationships and scenarios
- Refining the project requirements
- Furthering project management
- Serving as a guide to the design of code (in C++, Java, and Smalltalk)

This book is a useful tool for those applying the CRC technique. The tips, tricks, and pointers included are drawn from real-world experience, and all the various tables and lists presented in the text, are collected together in an appendix. The case studies are provided to help you visualize how the guidelines developed in the descriptive chapters might be applied in a real-life situation. All three case studies are based on real systems and are presented in a dramatized style to help you understand how to use the method better. Also included are two examples of how our third case study, the control of automobile traffic intersections, might look when in Smalltalk, C++, and Java. The source code from these chapters is available from Addison-Wesley at http://www.awl.com/cp/bellin-simone.html.

THE CRC CARD BOOK IS ORGANIZED AS FOLLOWS:

Brainstorming

We place special emphasis on the dynamics of team work, and how these dynamics are applied to the successful use of CRC. The first team strategy we suggest is brainstorming. We show how this applies to the task of finding classes and listing scenarios.

Role Plays

The second team strategy we recommend is role play. CRC cards provide a uniquely dynamic way of testing out your conception of the system and evaluating potential paths of collaboration. Role plays get everyone involved and invested in the system.

Case Studies

Three case studies are provided to help you visualize how the guidelines developed in the descriptive chapters might be applied in a real-life situation. All three case studies are based on real systems. They are presented in a dramatic, novella style to demonstrate more clearly how personalities and organizational culture come into play when a group is using the CRC technique. This is especially important in the context of brainstorming and role play. We hope that this approach not only will clarify the use of the method, but will provide a little entertainment along the way!

Implementations in Code

We also provide two examples of how our third case study, the control of automobile traffic intersections, might look when a programmer uses CRC cards as the basis for coding in Smalltalk, C++, and JAVA. Three experts in each language community joined with us to write this unique material.

Managing Object Analysis

Following the examination of role playing in the CRC method, we discuss the overall demands of managing an object-oriented project, along with suggestions as to useful metrics for monitoring the process, and for including legacy software in OO systems. We also provide some ideas for the transition from informal modeling with CRC cards to the use of a full-blown, formal methodology such as Schlaer-Mellor or the Unified Modeling Language. The final case study in the book provides additional insight into the application of these techniques.

Transition to Methodologies

In this concluding chapter we discuss the limitations of CRC cards and examine several popular and more comprehensive object-oriented analysis and design methodologies.

CRC Roadmap

Every chapter is full of useful tips, tricks, and pointers drawn from the real world. In addition to the various tables and lists in the text, we've collected these together in an appendix with pointers back into the book, so you can find things quickly when you need them.

Get to Work!

In *The CRC Card Book*, we have tried to distill a wide range of experiences and training tips for the use of CRC. We hope that some of it applies to all of you, and that all of it applies to some of you. Above all, remember, let CRC make your team work fun!

Acknowledgments

A host of wonderful people in and outside of the software community provided inspiration and assistance to this book. Naturally, the analysts, programmers, and users who participated in our developing process of brainstorms and role play deserve special thanks. So, too, do the first proponents of the idea of using Class, Responsibility and Collaboration cards: Ward Cunningham and Kent Beck. Upon finally meeting them at the object-oriented programming conference known as OOPSLA, we were wonderfully pleased to find them as creative and people oriented as we had hoped they would be!

Many reviewers read the manuscript and made incisive and helpful suggestions, including the following: Bruce Anderson, Steve Berczuk (Corechange), Ward Cunningham (Cunningham & Cunningham, Inc.), Richard Dué (Thomsen Dué and Associates Limited), Henry A. Etlinger (Rochester Institute of Technology), Don Gotterbarn (East Tennessee State University), David Gregory (BCS), Chris Jacobson (GemStone Systems, Inc.), Jeremy Raw (Independent Consultant, Durham, NC), Arthur J. Riel (Vanguard Training), Richard Scott, Doug Smith (Object Toolsmiths), Charles Snyder (Rational Software Corporation), Sandeep Singhal (IBM T.J. Watson Research), and Rebecca J. Wirfs-Brock (ParcPlace-Digitalk, Inc.).

At Addison-Wesley, it was our pleasure to work with the demanding, but reasonable, senior editor Carter Shanklin. Along with his overall guidance, editorial assistant Angela Breunning and production editor Melissa Lima provided excellent support throughout the myriad details that actually result in the final product. Bob Donegan, senior marketing manager, has provided many pleasurable chats and informal guidance over many years of shared coffee at trade shows.

And finally, but certainly at least as important, we would like to thank our three co-conspirators who implemented the traffic-intersection card design in the OO language of their expertise. These are Dr. Cay Horstmann (Java), Larry Smith (Smalltalk), and Jeremy Raw (C++). In reviewing their code, you'll see the unique creativity of each of these recognized experts. Their assistance is invaluable.

Thanks to you all!

Chapter 1

CRC: A Problem-Solving Technique

Systems analysis is the process of understanding a real-world situation so that we can construct automated support. CRC stands for Class, Responsibility, and Collaboration. The use of CRC cards facilitates the process of discovering the real-world objects which make up a system and its public interfaces. The CRC process assists analysts and users in mapping the collaborations among classes, defined by the responsibilities each has in the system being modeled. Although many marketers of object-oriented approaches to software development claim that objects are an intuitive, natural way of understanding systems, in real projects it is a challenge to identify the right ones. The CRC Card technique provides a solution.

Class, Responsibility, and Collaboration cards were first introduced by Kent Beck and Ward Cunningham in 1989 at a conference on "Object-Oriented Systems, Languages and Applications." The card technique immediately attracted attention as an easy-to-use, portable method for getting at the difficult problem of discovering and defining classes. Grady Booch, Ed Yourdon, Rebecca Wirfs-Brock, Adele Goldberg, and many other noted software developers now endorse the method as a means to get started analyzing the system domain. The book *Designing Object-Oriented Software*, by Rebecca Wirfs-Brock, remains perhaps the best detailed documentation of what has come to be called the "responsibility-driven" design technique. Nancy Wilkinson has written briefly about her experience with CRC at AT&T in her book *Using CRC Cards*. In *The CRC Card Book*, which you are holding, we pick up where they left off. We look deeper into just why CRC cards are so helpful and, understanding why, how analysis teams can make better use of the technique.

In this chapter, we discuss the problem-solving concepts which can be used to meet the challenge of discovering and defining classes. We discuss the skills which embody those concepts, and show how groups can use CRC cards to draw out these skills. We present a model for the use of CRC cards that emphasizes productive thinking (brainstorming) and teamwork (role play). Finally, we propose project management guidelines for the facilitation of CRC in an object-oriented project, looking at the notions of life cycles, evaluation metrics, and methodology choices. All of these concepts are developed in more detail in subsequent chapters.

THE CRC CARD

Without letting the cat out of the bag—we do want you to read the whole book—it may be helpful to preview CRC cards while we are thinking about problem solving. CRC stands for Class, Responsibility, and Collaboration. CRC cards are index cards (or computerized versions of same!), which are used to record suggested **classes**, the things they do, their **responsibilities**, and their relationship to other classes, **collaboration**. As you write down the names of the classes and think about what things a class must know about itself (knowledge responsibility) or do (behavior responsibility), you can see how the class that you are defining interlocks with other classes in the system. You can see how to reinforce the idea of encapsulation or polymorphism (more on this in Chapter 2) by moving responsibilities from one class to another and then introducing collaboration between classes.

Note that the visual nature of the CRC cards, and their physical aesthetic, is an important catalyst to problem solving. By moving the cards around on a table, you can trip new ideas, just as you might in rearranging the letters of an anagram searching for a new word. For this reason, even projects that use automated support for recording CRC cards will benefit from using printed, individual cards for brainstorming and role playing.

Even more important than the basic tasks, writing the cards and looking at the relationships between classes, the CRC card technique is valuable because you are working with other people. Whether or not you are someone who likes to work in groups, you will find that brainstorming by many minds and role playing the cards is a fruitful technique for moving from reproductive thinking—staring at padlocks and gates or your own personal set of CRC cards—to productive thinking—realizing that you can vault over the wall or use a novel class and responsibility allocation.

While we are on the subject of teams, it is important to appreciate the flexibility of CRC cards. They can be used to drive down to a very detailed level by a technical team looking forward to design and even by programmers (as you will see in the chapters on using CRC with C++ and Smalltalk). More important, whether the end use is technically oriented (program design), in the analysis phase of a project CRC cards allow users and systems people to work together using the same tool to describe the system. We have reinforced our commitment to the power of this quality in the CRC card technique by including users in all of the demonstration analysis teams in our case examples.

CRC Is Fun!

There is a myth, true or false, that loners are attracted to computer systems by the opportunities that they afford for solo flyers. Everyone who has spent any time at all in the field has a collection of famous stories of geniuses and gurus who work day and night conquering the vast deserts of technical challenge we call systems development. The world of computing is also rife with stories about systems that are quirky or secretive, the products of independent, even idiosyncratic solo flyers who bequeath to their less gifted heirs inscrutable codes following all sorts of unrecoverable logic. In other words, common knowledge tells us that systems cannot and should not be developed as a solo endeavor, but nobody wants to get stuck on a team. It just isn't any fun.

The CRC card technique offers some relief in this department if it is used right. Brainstorming and seeing problems open up is rewarding. If facilitators see this and take advantage of it, CRC can loosen up a group and help develop a dynamic that ties team members together and unifies their approach to a problem. The role play, where people take on the roles of classes and literally act out the system, can be a high-energy way to review ideas and test solutions. Differences in perspective can be a source of knowledge and of humor. Having fun can actually speed up the work.

This may seem like an unusual claim, because although they have a complicated chore to do (spurring the human mind to insight), CRC cards are pretty simple (see Figure 1-1). Most people use 3×5 inch index cards (5×7 inch cards if you want to write

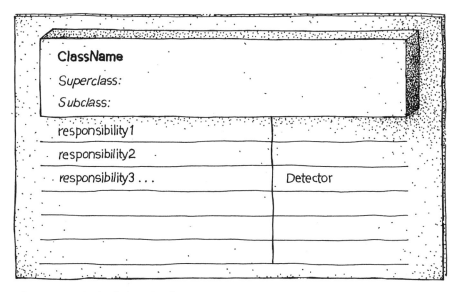

Figure 1-1 **A Blank CRC Card**

large, but don't get tempted to create power classes that do everything but pay your bills). Each card represents a class in the system. On the card, you write down the name of the class, its responsibilities, and what other classes it will work with to carry out those responsibilities. How can such a simple system be challenging and fun to use?

The answer is that, at the same time that they are a comprehensive way of noting information about classes, CRC cards are rooted in a process in which a team of people comes together to play with ideas. It is an informal technique that minimizes tension and boredom. First, because the cards are easy to work with, users and systems people can speak as equals. Second, because everyone is involved in writing things down, reading them back, and acting them out, no one has time to be bored. One of the fundamental prerequisites for successful teamwork is embedded in the technique: active learning. Instead of reading or listening to someone else's report and approving, improving, or rejecting it, members of the CRC card analysis team are all doing something that contributes to the system model and, as they do it, they are all learning something. It may still be difficult to come up with the right set of classes, and the work can be hard, but, as everyone knows, misery loves company!

PROBLEM SOLVING AND INSIGHT

In order to understand what to do with CRC cards, when and where to use the technique, it is helpful to establish a common understanding of why we need such tools in the first place. This has a lot to do with the nature of the human mind and the way that we go about solving problems. CRC cards do not "tell" the analyst what classes to choose or how they interlock. CRC cards are a catalyst, increasing the likelihood that the analyst will be able to come up with a good solution.

Since the time of the ancient Greeks, scientists and philosophers have debated the question of how the human mind is able to solve problems. This search is fueled by the belief that thinking distinguishes us from other forms of life. Superior problem solving is critical to what it means to be a person. Aristotle explained the way we think by using a model in which the mind works by association, by connecting up one thing to another until a solution is achieved. Locke and Hobbes shaped modern scientific thought by modifying the associative model to include the idea of trails of associations. As a problem solver works through alternatives, she is drawn to certain choices because the associations leading to those choices are stronger. Commenting on this nineteenth-century view of problem solving, renowned psychologist E. L. Thorndike described the approach of his scientific peers as "trial and error and accidental success." The stronger the method of trial and error, the more likely the success!

Anyone who has worked on a software project has probably had many personal experiences that supply anecdotal support to Thorndike's definition. For many of us this proof is so impressive that we may feel time spent on drawn-out analysis is wasted. Ultimately, a process of trial and error in coding will drive the process. Analysts hold their ground, shouting prophecies about the consequences of this problem-solving technique that neglects careful investigation and statement of the problem. They warn that no one can solve a problem without knowing what it is. The fate of systems that neglect analysis are doomed to fates such as high-cost maintenance and endless strings of enhancements. These forces line up on opposite sides of the software development barricades wielding CASE tools, lines of code, specification requirements, and new generations of programming languages in a war of words with no winner.

The resolution to this war between analysts and coders is not to declare one side a winner, but to understand why they are at odds. The analysis part of problem solving fulfills a particular set of parameters that cannot be duplicated or replaced during design or coding. During analysis, the problem solver is searching for a new way of understanding the problem that will lead to insights into its solution. Insight is a mysterious process. It is the accidental success that can be the foundation of deliberate successes for the rest of the project. These insights, flashes of understanding, vivid connections to the problem, become the basis for a system model that becomes the roots of the rest of the project.

Because insight is at the heart of the objective of analysis, success often means breaking away from old associations and seeing things in a new way. This does not mean that association and familiar connections have nothing to do with problem solving in analysis, but they are not the driving force. This is especially true if we want to move from a system concept based on procedural models and languages to one based on object-oriented models and languages. We want to open ourselves up to new ways of thinking because we are going to use new kinds of solutions. We want to use new concepts to free us of old methods. We want to maximize and promote that amazing quality of human thought called insight.

A Parable of Insight

There is an ancient Chinese fable that goes like this: Four men are walking across a field. They come to a great wall with a massive gate that is locked by a thick chain and a padlock. Three of the men attempt to pry the padlock open using anything they can find. They pound it with rocks, burn it in a fire, and beat it with a log to no avail. They finally collapse in front of the gate exhausted and defeated. Just at this moment, they hear a noise and see the fourth man emerging from the forest. He is holding a long shoot of fresh cut bamboo. He runs toward the wall, plants his pole in the ground and vaults over it.

The moral of the tale is that the fourth man had not solved the problem of the padlocked gate. He quickly sees that getting through the gate is a camouflage. The essential problem is not the padlocked gate; it is how to get to the other side of it. He has solved the problem by redefining it, creating a new and solvable problem. How many of us have had the experience of trying to implement a project that feels like a massive padlock? How many of us have had that nagging thought, "There must be a better way!" We call a person who has the fourth man's problem-solving talent a genius. But what is a genius? When the apple fell on Newton's head, what happened? Wasn't it a moment of insight in which he gave up an old way of seeing the problem and understood it in a new way? Isn't this what happened to Galileo as he watched from the top of the tower of Pisa? Isn't this what made Copernicus so sure the Earth orbited the sun?

In this book, we are not going to make the claim that CRC cards will transform everyone into a Newton or an Einstein, but they will move you in the right direction. However, there is one condition. Insight rarely visits human minds unless the people involved are aware of what they are trying to do. Gestalt psychologists call this metacognition. Metacognition describes a situation in which the people trying to solve the problem understand what it is they are trying to do. They recognize that they are engaged in a process that draws on logical association. They are also aware that the solution is not necessarily self-evident.

If we apply the idea of metacognition to analysis, one implication is going to be that teams of analysts who are aware of their method are more likely to have new ideas. Tools that support and facilitate this kind of problem solving are therefore very valuable. In fact,

Figure 1-2 **Problem-Solving Insight**
Source: "An Einstein Centennial Post Card" by Sidney Harris,
What's So Funny About Science?, William Kaufman, Inc.

almost any analysis tool becomes much more powerful when the people who are using it understand what they are trying to accomplish. If the tool is designed to be a catalyst to new ideas, the team must be both patient and open to unexpected ideas. If the tool is simply used as a form of annotation of old ideas, the likelihood of new insights will be sharply decreased. CRC cards are no exception. The more you understand how they work, the more likely they are to work for you.

CRC CARDS AS A METACOGNITIVE PROCESS

Studies of metacognition show that two groups of people will have different degrees of success solving the same problem if one group has first been trained in problem solving and reasoning prior to being presented with the problem. People who are self-conscious about their problem-solving strategies do better than people who depend on unconscious response or "getting lucky." Trained problem solvers who know how the technique they are using is supposed to work are much more likely to be successful and will achieve success more quickly. This means that using CRC cards involves more than knowing where to write things down. It means that the full power of the technique depends upon a team of problem solvers who not only know what they are supposed to do, but have some idea of how to solve complex problems.

For these reasons, we have developed an approach to understanding the CRC card technique that involves learning about two key problem-solving facilitation strategies: brainstorming and role play. You will also see that our approach depends on teamwork. Although CRC cards can help a single analyst working on a small system, larger, more complex problems are much more easily resolved by a group. Brainstorming and role-play strategies maximize the advantages of group work, which in turn maximizes the advantages of using the CRC card technique.

Brainstorming is a strategy that has been used in all sorts of situations from advertising teams looking for a new "concept" to improvisational theater groups working through a new idea. You could say that it has its roots in jazz, in the revolution that led jazz musicians to incorporate untested playing into formal performance. The assumption behind this leap is that, for reasons undetermined, the human mind has the capacity to draw in unexpected brilliant connections when "thinking" is the least deliberate. In addition, when this kind of mental exploration goes on in a group, individual members may be carried beyond what they can do on their own into unexpected levels of accomplishment. Putting this in a more mundane context, when a team of analysts get together to work out a system, trading ideas in a fast and uninhibited way (using brainstorming) yields a better result than the deliberate work of one individual.

This same assumption applies to the use of role play in the CRC card technique. After using brainstorming to come up with the elements of the system and some possible arrangements, the team uses a play-acting technique to test different scenarios. The team poses a set of "what if" scripts and then acts them out. Each person on the team literally takes on the role of a class and, using the CRC card as a script, acts out the system. The value of this strategy is that the act of pretending to "be a class" and figuring out what you have to do triggers the same responses as brainstorming. Playing with the cards triggers unanticipated insights. Role play does this successfully because it makes team members active participants. Instead of "paying attention" while reading or listening, the team members are engaged directly in the role play, and that engagement spurs insight.

It is our belief that working in teams, promoting creative thinking, and using open-ended strategies such as brainstorming and role play will maximize the added value of using CRC cards in a project. Without these strategies, CRC cards are often no more than another kind of notation of known information. With these strategies CRC cards encourage restructuring of perspective, invite insights, and yield CRC card sets that truly embrace object-oriented principles. The CRC cards serve as a catalyst to the fundamental, first-step problem that confronts any object-oriented project: finding classes.

THE CHALLENGE OF FINDING CLASSES

Although some object-oriented gurus have spoken about the naturalness of seeing the world as made up of classes and objects, real-life practitioners may beg to differ. Over and over again, the results of analysis arrive at the door of the designer looking like the same old thing. There are classes, but the way in which they are defined, the allocation of responsibilities, and the paths of collaboration look a lot like a functional specification dressed up in an object-oriented gown. In other words, what we get is not a bamboo pole solution, but

Figure 1-3 **The Orchestra Conductor Model**

a padlocked gate. The designer is not told, "Make me something that I can use to get over the wall!" She is told "I don't care how you do it, but get this padlock off this gate!"

Another barrier to insight when trying to find classes is that there is a tendency to lock into old names and old ways of seeing the world. Psychologists refer to this as fixation or a mental block. If we keep thinking in terms of databases and functions that can be performed on those databases, it can be very hard to come up with classes that take advantage of the most powerful elements of object-oriented languages such as polymorphism and inheritance. (These terms are explained in Chapter 2.) A common manifestation of this problem is the "object-oriented" model in which a conductor class stands in front of an orchestra of worker classes. The conductor signals each of the musicians individually (see Figure 1-3). How different is this from a control module or a transaction center on a structure chart? Not different enough! Instead of an orchestra, we want to see something more like a jazz ensemble in which each of the players knows his or her role and, by responding to messages from the other musicians, can follow, drop out, or solo (see Figure 1-4).

The phenomenon of mental blocks is another element of thinking that has been studied by psychologists and pondered by writers and scientists for ages. We've talked about insight, but what about its opposite? What is it that causes that same mind to sometimes "get

Figure 1-4 **The Ensemble Model**

stuck"? One study of the problem of fixation looked at the way people solve puzzles, in particular word puzzles called anagrams. These cases are interesting because we are given the problem in one form, a string of words in a particular order, and must solve the problem by reordering the letters in order to form a completely new word. Studies show that problem solvers work much more quickly if the original string of letters does *not* form a word. Using words, presenting the problem in the form of a solution, a meaningful sequence of letters, and then asking people to rearrange the letters results in longer solution times and less frequent success. Even something as simple as having the nonsense strings pronounced before the problem solving begins can result in slower work and lower rates of success. The more signs that the problem is self-evident (a padlock on a gate), the more difficult it is to reformulate it and come up with a solution.

If we are going to be successful at solving the problem of finding and naming classes, using CRC cards (or any other method), we must understand both (1) the goal of the task and (2) what we can do to stimulate productive thinking.

So, let's begin at the beginning with the first issue, which is our goal of discovering and naming classes. We should begin by defining what we mean by a class. How is a class different from an object? Why is it advantageous to begin the analysis with a discussion of classes instead of objects? Is this just a semantic issue? Or is there something fundamentally different about objects and classes that makes a discussion of classes a better way to begin thinking about the system?

A class is a category, an expression of the commonality of characteristics that encompasses a number of particular incarnations—or, to put it in object-oriented terms, a generalized description that may be instantiated in a number of different specific cases or objects. For example, in a warehouse system that controls the movement of product, we might talk about a class called Vehicle. All of the equipment used to move stuff around the warehouse is considered to be of the class Vehicle. However, there may be a number of different vehicle objects that are by no means identical. There are forklift objects and truck objects. They are different, but are bound by a commonality we call belonging to a class. There may even be subsets of Vehicle, AutomatedVehicle and NonAutomatedVehicle. All members of the class Vehicle are defined. All members of the subclasses share those defined characteristics even though they may be distinguishable by additional information (e.g., different means of executing start or stop). All Vehicle objects (forklifts, trucks, carts) and all instances of Vehicle Objects (forklift VN#34897) are governed by the profile defined for the class.

In Chapter 2 we review some of the basic object-oriented development concepts, but for now, this distinction should suffice to show that classes are important because they drive the analysis at a level of abstraction that inhibits the tendency of people to get wrapped up in particulars. The old saying that a person may lose sight of the forest for the trees is based on an all-too-familiar truth. Human beings have a strong tendency to think in particulars. We want to know, "What does it mean to be an Account in a Banking System?" but we answer the question by discussing the particulars of a myriad of specific types of accounts. We want to think about the Account class, but we get lost in the specifics of one instance or another of the Account object.

A critical problem for an analysis team setting out on an object-oriented development effort is going to be utilizing information that is often delivered in a very specific form (given procedures, databases, processing methods, etc.) captured by looking at existing system documentation, interviewing people as they do a job, talking to people about a new product or service they are planning to deliver, and converting it into a network of collaborating classes. This involves abstract thinking. Abstract thinking means taking all of that specific information you are picking up and translating it into a model that captures *what* is going on without prejudice of *how* it has been done. It means looking at the *things* of an activity and attempting to see what they have in common. It means looking at things that are often arranged in one order (procedures and activities) and discovering how they can be rearranged in a new structure (classes and objects). CRC cards will not do this thinking for you, but by focusing the discussion on classes, using the language of classes, and supporting that language with a visual aid (the cards themselves), CRC can stimulate the insights that are critical to successful object-oriented systems.

The second issue, how to stimulate productive thinking, is built into the way in which we use the CRC cards to experiment with various answers to the question of classes. The process is going to be (1) a group process and (2) an iterative process. Many minds will yield many ideas for solutions, and the first solution is not likely to be the final solution. You will have to go through several batches of CRC cards before you have an accurate and useful picture of the system. The first few sets of cards may even be assembled in a very mechanical way, but, sooner or later, often when you are most frustrated or absolutely sure that you cannot think of another way to "see" it, the pieces will suddenly fit together in a new way and you will have your object-oriented system specification.

Making CRC Work: Project Management Guidelines

CRC cards depend on two key working strategies: group work and iteration. Project management guidelines should reflect and respect this. To make CRC cards work, analysis teams and managers should focus on these key items:

Team building
Inclusion of application experts
Coordination with a formal methodology
Careful selection of a pilot project
Careful design and coding

Later chapters will address all of these topics in more detail, but let's look at each one briefly, in order to understand the context in which the CRC card technique is being applied.

Team Building

We want to make sure that anyone who is going to use the CRC card technique pays attention to the importance of the internal dynamics of group work and to the softer side of the way in which teams function. If brainstorming, role play, and other forms of insight-facilitating strategies are going to be used, the people participating in the team must feel free to express ideas. They must feel free to not only contribute the brilliant insight that puts the group over the top, but to toss out ideas that may prove unusable. The process will only work if everyone feels free and safe about making contributions.

Developing the right "feeling" among team members can be difficult, especially where users may distrust technical staff, or technical staff may feel impatient with the users' way of talking about their work. However, if you are going to use a creative team-based technique, notions about "right" and "wrong" can become an enemy to progress. They can stall the group or censor good ideas. Sometimes, without realizing it, if we are intimidated by a group, we cut off our own ideas and label them as stupid, foolish, off the mark, or otherwise not worthy of mention. This habit of censorship can be so strong that it becomes subconscious. It is exacerbated by the tendency of people in a group to take on roles: leaders, watchers, talkers, listeners.

To avoid this, we emphasize the work of the facilitator in CRC card sessions. This person is not only a leader who has experience with the technique, but someone who has a sharp eye for group dynamics. The facilitator is the one who sets the tone for the group by using inclusive techniques like round robins to let everyone know they are equal as contributors. The facilitator can also use mechanical responsibilities, like dividing up the classes before a role play, that help to ensure that everyone's voice is heard.

Of course, if the facilitator is going to be able to do a good job, the team members have to be selected with an eye to success. Each member should be on the team for a reason, because they contribute a sphere of expertise that is complementary to that of the other members. This applies to personalities as well. Ignoring characteristics that affect behavior in a group will not buy you success if you are using a team approach such as CRC cards. Forcing a solo flyer who would rather figure it all out alone, huddled over a glowing tube, Jolt cola in hand, onto a team that is user based and exploratory may be a poor choice. CRC cards are, ultimately, a way to get work done, not a way to change people.

In *The CRC Card Book,* we have tried to illustrate the kinds of choices a manager must make by describing the characters on each team in our case studies. Notice as you read these that there are two elements at work. First, managers choose their teams based on a combination of skills and personality. Second, people are unpredictable. Often, a person who is usually very quiet, someone who does their work alone and rarely speaks up in meetings, may turn out to be a good team player. Brainstorming and role play are meant to draw people out. So choose your teams with caution and build them carefully, but don't rule out the unexpected.

Inclusion of Application Experts

There seems to be an intellectual divide in the world of systems development. At the same time that there is general agreement that users are the ultimate measure of acceptance or failure, there is also a sense that users are an obstacle to development. If only there were no users to complain, all systems would be perfect! This attitude is played out perfectly in a scene in Tracy Kidder's *The Soul of a New Machine*. After a long and arduous development effort, the technical team arrives at the New York coliseum where they witness a crowd of customers clustered around their machine. Listening, they see that their work is destined to be pearls before swine. The team is shocked. These users have no appreciation for the beauty of the technology they are about to buy and will, inevitably, put it to the wrong use.

Kidder makes his point well, without sparing us a moment of the heroic effort of the technical team, feeding our awe of them and their achievement. However, his message is clear. Nothing gets used for its sheer technical beauty. It is appreciated because it meets the users' needs. For this reason, above all, we need a way to include users in systems analysis that brings them into the process. Interviewing users is helpful, but it is not inclusive. It still leaves the users outside of the doors of development. Bringing users into CRC card sessions opens the doors. If we get it wrong, we get it wrong together.

There is another reason to include users in CRC card sessions. Object-oriented development has certain characteristics that support the added value of early user input. In the "before-OO" world, data was examined independently of the procedures which affected it. Analysis models often described the flow of work as separate from data. Multiple models, each assigned to capture different "parts" of a procedurally based system, were constructed. In the "after-OO" world, the base concept of a class and the encapsulation of data in objects fuses all of the elements of a system. Procedural information (user work flows, etc.) are not separate from information allocation. It all gets discussed at the same time.

What this means is that a team that is conversing about "user stuff" is mapping the core of the system. CRC cards are not a powerful technique because they magically map conversation into technical specifications. They are powerful because they provide a framework for a class-driven, object-oriented discussion of applications in a format that is both understandable to users and useful to technical people. As you will see in the chapters on coding, although CRC cards on large projects should be supported by a broader methodology, they are not a "throwaway" tool. CRC cards capture user-talk directly in a medium that is a valuable input all the way through the development life cycle.

Coordination with a Formal Methodology

A technique is a procedure for performing specific tasks. CRC cards are a technique that supports the task of defining the elements of a software system: the basic classes, what each class does, and how they all collaborate together. However, the CRC card technique is not a methodology. A methodology deals with the logical principles underlying the organization of a system, usually accompanied by a specific notional scheme and a set of techniques.

It models complexity through multiple views that each convey an aspect of the system under development. In a large project, there should be a master strategy guided by a methodology such as the Unified Method (Booch–Rumbaugh–Jacobson) or Shlaer–Mellor.

Understood in this context, CRC is a useful technique for capturing application concepts, and for modeling the basic framework of a system because it can be used in conjunction with any larger-scale methodology. Especially in the case of larger applications, project management entails the selection of a broader strategy for coping with the complexity of aspects involved in the system. You may even think of the methodology as an umbrella that encompasses a multiplicity of techniques, one of which applies to the task of finding classes.

This also points to the importance of addressing large projects in terms of a logical segmentation. In *The CRC Card Book*, we have chosen to carve out the application domain and, within that domain, to subdivide development in such a way that the CRC card team is looking at a domain of fairly limited scale. In this sense, we are in agreement with the idea of system domain discussed by Shlaer–Mellor, where they treat applications, architecture, and operations as discrete domains and use the information model and state diagrams to represent reasonably discrete subsets of the system.

In the case studies, we stay within the application domain to make the information equally accessible to users, managers, designers, and programmers. We have been careful to carve out limited subsystems or project phases for the CRC card sessions we discuss. This is important and should be supported by whatever methodology you use. CRC cards do not work for massive numbers of classes. The limits of the human mind radically reduce the effectiveness of any analysis effort if the domain under discussion is too broad. The same restriction of scale applies to good results from object-oriented design. Use a methodology to support the definition of domains that are reasonably discrete (perhaps no more than 12 principal classes) and to map the CRC information for those domains together. This is the best way we have found to scale CRC methods to very large systems.

CRC cards do not have enough notational power to document all the necessary components of a system. They cannot provide a detailed view of the data in objects, they do not give implementation specifics, and they cannot provide an adequate view of the states through which objects transition during their lifetime. CRC cards provide only limited help in the design activities of making strategic trade-offs in the factoring of functionality. And, CRC cards alone provide only a little help in specifying things such as how users will give and receive data (interface design), interprocess communication functionality, algorithm design, data structures, performance, or resource utilization. Although CRC cards done well can assist, for many of these matters, it helps to use a full-scale methodology.

In the chapter on methodologies, we do not select any particular methodology as better or worse from the point of view of either object-oriented development or project management. Instead, we try to show you some of the ways in which the information captured on the CRC cards can be translated into models that are used by popular methodologies. At the same time, we do recommend that you select a methodology. Use CRC cards to get at the difficult problem of finding classes, but do not count on them to do the work of capturing all of the modeling information you will need to fully execute a large-scale system.

Careful Selection of a Pilot Project

Another important management decision will be the careful selection of a pilot project. If your organization is new to object-oriented development, the key to acceptance is going to be your ability to use object orientation for its strengths. For example, object-oriented technology is particularly strong in applications areas that involve a heavily graphical user interface component. This does not mean that there must be a graphical interface in order to use OO successfully, but it does set up a flag indicating that the strengths of OO in comparison to other methods will be most obvious in this kind of project. If you want to win a high level of acceptance in the organization, it's best to have a pilot project that highlights the differences between the new approach and the old way of doing systems.

There is going to be a steep learning curve when you move into the arena of object-oriented projects. Even with a good warm-up technique such as CRC, the route from start to finish will be arduous. Plan the project on a scale where team members can see some return on their learning investment. In addition to the rewards of a project with a large graphical user interface, factors that can be turned to advantage include domain definitions that work on a scale of twelve or fewer classes, project teams that are small and clearly focused, and a time frame of six to nine months for completion.

It is also very valuable to collect information about your process from the very beginning. Whatever pilot you choose, keep track of the measures that can be used for historical comparison of results. In the chapter on project management, we discuss a few ideas for metrics that offer a way to assess progress and effectiveness. Remember that the reason for doing a pilot project is to learn before tackling an entire system. That learning depends on a historical record of what you have done before, so that you can evaluate what works best, and what does not. Set up measurement techniques during the pilot and build on them later. Object-oriented development is relatively new, so reliable outside benchmark data is limited. Be ready to take advantage of your own track record, as you accumulate the metrics data which is its record.

Careful Design and Coding

Is everyone in computing looking for a silver bullet? Sometimes it feels that way. Similarly, everyone on the selling side is tempted to tout their product as the real, yes, finally, silver bullet. CRC cards are not a silver bullet. Implementing object-oriented systems is by no means a trivial process. This book focuses on the early steps in creating systems, the analysis of the classes basic to them. We stress the creative process of analysis. We talk about how much energy can be tapped by using a technique that gets people involved. But, when the cards are all done and you are ready to move on, you still face the challenge of deriving a language-specific design from the analysis, for coding.

One valuable management strategy for addressing the transition from analysis to design is the concept of frameworks. In his book *Design Patterns for Object-Oriented Software Development,* Wolfgang Pree has written extensively on the use of application frameworks and includes many detailed examples of how this affects the quality of coding. Analysis of coding on the meta-level can lead to a stronger, more truly object-oriented coding strategy. Again, as in the case of methodologies, rating and selecting a coding strategy is beyond the scale of this book, but it is an important consideration that should be a self-conscious element for any object-oriented project. No matter how good your analysis and how insightful the results of the CRC card sessions, design and coding must be driven by its own rationale, and that rationale should directly address the characteristics and strengths of the object-oriented language you are using.

The major language platforms currently used are C++ and Smalltalk. Runners-up include ADA-95 and Eiffel. Many would add to the list Actor, Delphi, CLOS, Object-COBOL, Visual BASIC, and about a dozen others. Using any of these languages, CRC card analyses can be the basis of early prototypes in organizations which use the prototyping or incremental-build life cycles. We do not recommend CRC cards as the basis for detailed design work, or for use without a methodology if you are working on complex applications.

A discussion of language trade-offs is a book in itself; however, we are partial to C++, Java, and Smalltalk. To give you a better idea of how a programmer might use CRC card input, we have included a chapter in which a programmer expert in each takes a set of CRC cards for one of our cases and makes a number of design and coding decisions. In both cases, the leap from the CRC cards to examples of code is just that: a leap. There is a lot of intervening thought that will be supported by a methodology in a large-scale project. Nonetheless, these sample coding chapters will help you see the link between the CRC card technique and the final product: code.

SUMMARY

CRC cards are a wonderful invention that can support any object-oriented development effort regardless of scale, methodology, or language. They can be used for new systems, and for the discovery of ways to add new enhancements to existing applications. CRC cards assist in the incremental and iterative style so important for developing sound systems. A good manager will not ask them to do too much. Remember to scale the domain and be people-aware when you put together the project team. Encourage interaction between users and technical people, and respect the commitment you make during analysis. Use brainstorming to encourage creative problem solving. Use role play as a proactive testing method that feeds into more productive thinking. Keep an open mind, and always remember that iteration is at the core of the process. Do not be afraid to revise and rework ideas. CRC cards make this kind of trial-and-error work possible and encourage that important accident called insight.

In the next chapter, we review some of the basic concepts of object-oriented development and lay the groundwork for learning about CRC. If you feel confident about these ideas, move ahead to the chapters on finding classes and role play. When you are done reading, try out the technique. For newcomers, we hope that you will find that CRC is just the thing you needed to break out of old patterns and enter the new world of objects. For veterans, we hope that CRC offers another strategy that you can add to the bag of tricks, one that will help you on your own, and, more importantly, will help you work productively with others on your object-oriented projects.

Chapter 2

OO Concepts and Vocabulary

Before you work with CRC cards, it will be helpful to establish some basic definitions for the terms and concepts of object-oriented development. If you are already familiar with the vocabulary, you may want to skip to the last section of the chapter where we illustrate the terms in a short example. There is also a brief bibliography at the end of the book for readers who want a more detailed discussion of object-oriented concepts.

The topics covered in this chapter include a brief introduction to the idea of objects, the relationship of objects to classes and the concept of instantiation, inheritance and the use of superclasses and subclasses, polymorphism, and the value of abstract classes. Finally, there is a brief example in which we use the vocabulary to address a potential object-oriented development project.

THINKING ABOUT THE WORLD AS OBJECTS

Let's say that your organization has decided to move over to an object-oriented approach. This decision is going to entail a shift in perspective from the very start of development. The first question you ask about the system is *not* going to be, "What processing must this system do?" Instead, you will be asking, "What entities are involved?" The world you model during analysis is not going to represent a succession of capabilities so much as it is going to view the world as a network of "things" that can do stuff and that know stuff about themselves. We call these "things" objects.

Talking about objects involves a shift in paradigms. Under the new rules, the first areas of concern during analysis are going to be (1) the identification and definition of objects, (2) the assigning of responsibilities for knowing and doing to objects, and (3) the description of interactions between objects (called collaboration).

The vocabulary used to talk about this new perspective revolves around the objects. Systems are made up of objects, or as Grady Booch puts it, of "tangible entities with some well-defined behavior." This is why so many claims are made for the intuitiveness or natural-ness of using an object-oriented approach to solving systems development problems. People ordinarily see their world in terms of "things" or entities. They also see the objec-tives of their work and their thought in terms of the subjects that they are working with or thinking about. Talking about objects is a familiar way of discussing a system.

Another thing that we do is see objects in terms of appropriate contexts. Putting this in object-oriented terms, every domain of concern has a set of objects that we associate with it. If I am thinking about keeping track of airplane flight bookings, I think of flights, reservations, tickets, payments, etc. If I am working on a factory, I will be thinking about orders and widgets, parts and components. This is a very natural and concrete place to start if I want to understand what is going to be the central concern of my automated system.

Encapsulation

Another characteristic of an object that you need to keep in mind as you define the system is that each object must determine its own behavior, and each object knows certain information about itself. This is called *encapsulation,* or information hiding, and it is one of the strongest qualities contributing to the effectiveness and efficiency of object-oriented technology. If a second object needs to know information that belongs to the first object, it must request that information. Only an object knows things about itself. The object needs to know certain things about itself in order to behave correctly. The object can *collaborate* with other objects in order to carry out its assigned behavior, sharing responsibility for actions.

Because encapsulation applies to behavior as well as knowledge, an object has certain behaviors, things it can do. These are called *methods*. When we describe the object Computer-Terminal, it not only knows the status of its screen, but may also be assigned the ability to revert to a blank screen. This ability is called a *responsibility*. The behavior of an object is therefore said to be encapsulated. Only the object knows how to execute its own behavior.

Another way of talking about the collaboration between objects is to think of them as objects that request services from other objects and objects that fulfill requests for service. The petitioning object is often referred to as the client and the petitioned object as the server. When a client object makes a request (sends a message to another object), the client or message sender does not need to know anything about how the receiving object will com-ply with the request. Thus the methods of the receiving object are invisible to the sending object; that is, methods, like data, are *encapsulated*.

David Taylor uses a drawing of objects as doughnut-like shapes to show their capacity to encapsulate behavior and data. In the illustration of Taylor's object model in Figure 2-1, you can see that there are two types of information. First there are sections drawn on the circle of the doughnut which represent the methods or the behaviors this object knows how to do. Inside the doughnut is the data, the knowledge available to the object.

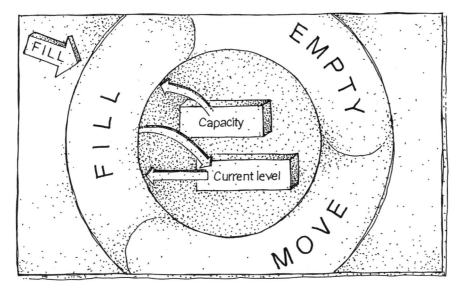

Figure 2-1 **Encapsulation of Knowledge and Behavior**

The object in Figure 2-1 is a container for fluids, which can fill itself, empty its contents, and move to another location. If another object needs a fluid filled into the container to meet its responsibilities, it must transmit the message "fill", but it does not know anything about the inner workings of the container. The requester (sender) does not know how the receiver (Container) will do the work. The receiving object verifies its ability to perform a "fill", and completes the requested action. If the receiver object doesn't know how to perform the requested action, or which other object to collaborate with for help, it will report back to the sender, saying something like, "Do not understand what you want me to do." The Container is also the only object that knows its capacity. If the volume is too much, it will send back a request telling the sender that it cannot accept the fluid. The requester of the action never sees the data inside the doughnut.

Taylor's model of the object as a doughnut reinforces the essence of software based on the collaboration of objects. All actions and all knowledge are conceptualized as the allocation of capabilities for doing and knowing to objects. As a result, during analysis, we are going to look for a way to represent the system in terms of clients and servers, objects that send requests and objects that can act in response to requests. And it may be the case that an object is a client in some collaborations, and the server in others.

Instantiation: Classes and Objects

The objects in a system are related, on a concrete level, to real-world entities. However, in analyzing systems we also think in terms of abstractions, or **classes** of objects. For example, the object in Taylor's model is not identified by a unique name. As far as we can tell from the figure, the system involves some sort of device for filling containers with fluids. Let's call that object a Container. The object Container is very general in what it does. If this is a system for a large chemical plant, there may be a number of Containers, each with a unique serial number.

The next step in object-oriented thinking is easy and follows the kind of thinking we do every day. If there are a bunch of these Containers, each with its unique serial number, we could say that they are all similar to such an extent that they constitute a *class*. Without even discussing any particular Container, we can discuss what it will do, and therefore how it is distinguishable from other objects in our system. During analysis, we are going to talk first about classes and establish the knowledge and behavior that govern all instances of that class. Then we will know that any object that is truly of that class must conform to this profile. Otherwise, it is a member of another class.

In summary, moving from abstract to concrete, the class denotes the general characteristics and behavior, or, as Grady Booch describes it, the "common structure and common behavior" shared by many instances of objects of that class. We have the class Container and all objects in that class will share the designated knowledge and behavior. If an object Container #123456 is asked by some other object in the system (the sender or client) to move some materials from one side of the warehouse to the other, it will look to its class for the specification as to whether or not it knows how to do this. Even though Container #135879 is painted red and has a different serial number, it will conform to the same class definition as Container #123456. They are two different objects in the real world, but both are *instantiations* of the same class in the system.

Classes are crucial to object-oriented analysis. They make it possible to describe the system in global terms without worrying about the implementation. The analyst can determine that there is a class (Container) that has certain knowledge (current level, capacity) and behavior (Fill, Empty). As you will see, CRC cards are useful during analysis because they help the project team think about the objects in the system domain in terms of classes. They help people who may be caught up in the details of difference that dominate the concrete world translate their knowledge into a useful abstraction.

Inheritance: Classes, Superclasses, and Subclasses

We just saw the value of creating abstract groupings of classes which share common functionality. Abstract classes are used during analysis to organize and refine knowledge and behavior in the system. The idea of describing requirements in terms of generalizations that can be made more specific is applied iteratively as you move from system analysis to design. For example, in some cases, there may be a high level of shared behavior or knowledge that applies to a whole class, but there are also behaviors or knowledge that are unique to subsets of those classes.

We now have to reiterate the process of analyzing difference and similarity within a defined class. For another example, take the case of a robot AutonomousVehicle. We may realize that there are numbers of objects that conform to the class but are also quite different from one another. For instance, in one part of the warehouse they use a lot of mechanisms that lift things using a cranelike arm, while, across the floor, we see a little autonomous robot with a camera eye looking at parts. After discussing this equipment, the analysis team comes up with two subclasses, the CameraVehicle and the CraneVehicle. All the AutonomousVehicles are one of these two and, because of their differences, cannot be fully defined without addressing these distinctions.

The class AutonomousVehicle now becomes a *superclass,* and we will call CameraVehicle and CraneVehicle subclasses. Figure 2-2 shows a simple diagram used by OO analysts to show this relationship. It is called a *hierarchy.* Classes lower down on the hierarchy *inherit* all of the behaviors and knowledge of their parent superclasses, and may have additional behaviors or knowledge of their own.

The two subclasses, CameraVehicle and CraneVehicle, inherit all of the behaviors and knowledge of the superclass AutonomousVehicle, but they may have unique behaviors or

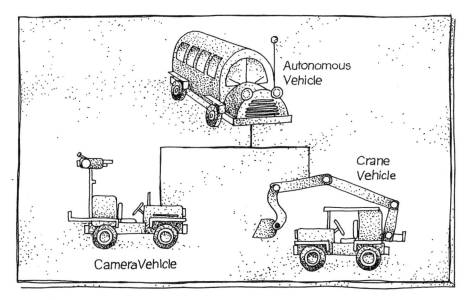

Figure 2-2 **Hierarchy of Superclass and Two Subclasses**

knowledge as well. For example, the CameraVehicle may need to know things about changing contrast or angles, whereas the CraneVehicle has no such knowledge. They may also be able to do different things, in other words, have some behavior distinct from the other subclass.

This distinction between the superclass and its children is important when CRC cards are written. The team must decide which characteristics belong at the generalized level (superclasses), and which apply at a more specific level (assigned to a particular subclass). It is also important to remember that the reason for defining a superclass is to emphasize and lock in similarity. Watch out that the subclasses do not become so complicated in their push for difference that they render the impact of similarity at the superclass level immaterial.

A good way to understand more about class hierarchies is to use the browser in an OO programming tool. The system library provides predefined classes for mathematical functions, user interfaces, data structures, and other common elements. By moving up and down the hierarchy, you can see how certain methods are specified at the superclass level, and then inherited by subclasses. This division of responsibility results in higher-level classes that can be reused to provide a baseline of knowledge and behavior for any new subclass. Similarly, subclasses can add new capabilities (new methods), without any change in the superclass. This gives object-oriented systems great flexibility and increases the potential for software reuse.

Abstract Classes

Before we move on to working with the CRC cards, the idea of abstract classes should be understood. Because behavior and knowledge can be inherited, it is often useful to think about the definition of a superclass in the context of similarity, common knowledge, and behavior, even if no such purely defined object will ever exist. In other words, it is useful to think about superclasses that may never be *instantiated* in the real world. We use them to understand commonality on a abstract level, and to define it, even though it may never be instantiated in such a pure form.

What happens is that the superclass encompasses shared knowledge and behavior, whereas subclasses articulate distinct adaptations. Look at the example of the Document class in Figure 2-3. There is never going to be an entity that is a document as such. Any document that is created and saved must be a TextDocument, a GraphicsDocument, or a SpreadsheetDocument. The Document class is an abstract class. It captures commonality, but, because of inheritance and polymorphism, does not lock in the subclasses. Save can be defined at a high level, as a behavior of the abstract class. As new subclasses are added, they automatically inherit this common behavior. The work is done at the level of definition of the abstract class and does not need to be repeated.

You can see immediately that the problem-solving skills discussed in the introductory chapter are going to come into play here. It is not enough just to say what a single element of the system must know or do; you must also learn to conceptualize an abstract commonality. The more you can see the essence of the problem on an abstract level, the more you

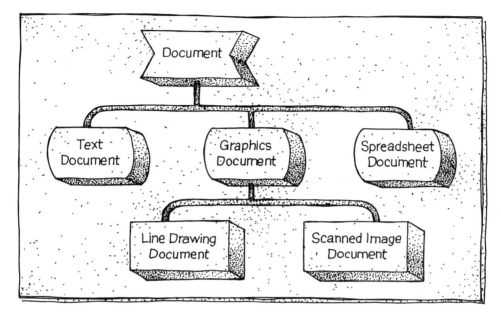

*Figure 2-3 **Document: An Example of Abstraction***

will be able to create hierarchies in which the definition of the superclass really does provide a core or baseline of knowledge and behavior that can be reused without redefinition.

Finally, before leaving the idea of hierarchies, consider the way in which class names can reinforce the concept of an abstract class. In the report preparation system, Document is no longer going to be used casually as a stand-in for a combination of things. Instead, Document will be a specified superclass that is never instantiated. Any instantiated section of the report will belong to one of the subclasses: TextDocument, GraphicsDocument, or SpreadsheetDocument. When you write the CRC cards, you will see that careful naming can be a big help in understanding relationships between classes, especially within a hierarchy.

Polymorphism

One of the powers of object-oriented languages is that they allow you to use common method names which are executed differently depending upon which object is the receiver (server). This is called *polymorphism*. Polymorphism simplifies the problem of similarity and difference that we discussed earlier by allowing you to use one name for the same essential behavior from the point of view of the sender (client) even though similar but distinct receivers may execute them differently.

Here again, the browser can help us see how this works. Go into the browser and look at the methods for several classes. Without much hard searching, you will notice that the same method, that is, the same name for a behavior, is frequently found in different classes.

This means that from the point of view of an object sending a message to an object in any one of those classes, there is an essential similarity in the requested behavior from the point of view of the sender. However, because of polymorphism, from the point of view of the receiver, the method may be carried out differently.

One example of this that we encounter regularly without even getting inside an object-oriented system browser is the concept of "save" in a business system. If we want to prepare a report, we develop an entity called a Document. This Document is a combination of different kinds of information: spreadsheets, text, graphics, etc. When we talk about classes we could approach the problem by saying that there is a superclass Document. Individual portions of the report, sections, files, or whatever they are called in a particular technology, can then be identified as subclasses of the superclass Document and named: SpreadsheetDocument, TextDocument, and GraphicsDocument.

As the writer develops the report Document, he or she will want to save the work. Sometimes this will involve saving text; other times it may be a spreadsheet or a graph. In the superclass Document, there is a behavior called Save. Polymorphism enlarges the scope and complexity of this allocation. As a result of polymorphism, if the superclass Document recognizes the message "Save", so do each of its subclasses that inherit this method. Moreover, when we actually implement the system, each subclass supplies its own "Save" method. Figure 2-4 shows how this might look when it is mapped out.

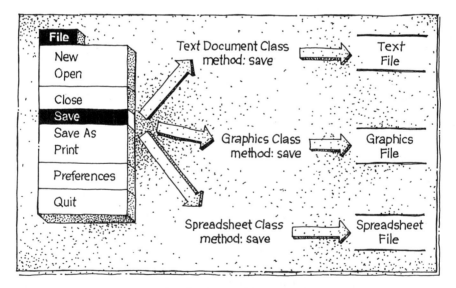

Figure 2-4 ***Save: An Example of Polymorphism***

Polymorphism adds a unique dimension of power to object-oriented systems. It is the quality that makes the structure of inheritance more than a shell. It is possible to have inheritance without polymorphism. C++ turns polymorphism on and off to allow for minimization of run time. However, without polymorphism, inheritance is not very useful. The objective is to simplify communication by having a different implementation behind a common interface. The common interface makes it easy to describe the system during the analysis phase using the concept of inheritance and applying it to superclasses and subclasses, while polymorphism ensures that the design will be able to take full advantage of these relationships. We can just send the "size" message to any shape, and it will know how to respond, instead of our needing rectangleSize, ovalSize, and circleSize messages. In other words, it becomes easier to change the system to incorporate new classes.

Frameworks and Patterns

Another concept that can help you find classes is the idea of design patterns and frameworks. Based on architectural concepts, frameworks are, in essence, blueprints for building. In the case of a house, the blueprint provides a general plan for the house showing major design objectives such as the partitioning of the space, the use to be made of each area, and general relationships between elements of the house (the living room, sleeping areas, cooking and eating, etc.). Now, if we say that a house is a system, you can see that the blueprint serves to show frameworks that attach together as interrelated elements. In object-oriented systems we say that frameworks are collections of classes which belong together.

The analysis of existing patterns can help us to see new frameworks. Existing frameworks can lead you to the identification of collections of classes that can be reused with little modification. One element of the framework that helps in this identification process is what we call a pattern. If you develop a good pattern vocabulary, you can spot frameworks and see how they apply to your system. Instead of reinventing successful patterns, you can take advantage of them. The more you work with object-oriented systems, the larger your pattern vocabulary will be, and the more easily you can use frameworks and patterns to evaluate and group classes for a new system without starting from scratch. Researchers have found that this can substantially lessen the magnitude of the development effort.

The generalizations that underlie frameworks help us to see classes in terms of groups. In many cases, the classes in a given system will fall into four common groups. In later chapters we discuss this in more detail, and some of the case studies demonstrate how actual teams can use patterns in their work.

A CASE IN POINT

The concepts used in object-oriented development involve a shift in thinking, but this is not as difficult as the profusion of new terms may make it seem. Ideas such as inheritance and polymorphism actually correspond to the way in which people who use systems talk about their needs! As a case in point, let's consider the discussion that is taking place in the fast-food industry about the automation of order-taking. As you read the next paragraph, think about things that stand out as objects in the new system. What are the classes to which these objects belong?

Walking into a McDonald's or a Burger King may seem fast enough already, but new ideas are in the cards. In an article "Restaurants and Computers Speed-up Soup to Nuts," in *The Wall Street Journal* (Oct. 25, 1995), the writer describes the effort of various chains to develop self-service terminals. Instead of placing orders with people, customers will soon key in their orders or use touch screens to select food items. On the screen they will be able to access food by type (main course or dessert). They will also see lists of specials and package meals.

After choosing their meal, the customer will be given an order number which is shown to the cashier, who can then look up the amount they must pay. While some customers may prefer the old-fashioned people-to-people route, proponents of the system hope that the computers will make waiting time fun by keeping customers busy. And, as Joaquin Pelaez of Taco Bell points out, "The beauty of this is that the customers will see specials and promotions at the same time that they place their orders." In other words, instead of talking, daydreaming, or just looking around, waiting customers are being readied for their most important role: buying lots of food.

Looking over this discussion with our object-oriented glasses on, it is interesting to note that the objects involved stand out, while the exact mechanics of the procedural side remain indeterminate. The new version of the order-entry system will have to handle objects (food such as burritos and tacos) that fall into several classes. First, there are FoodItems in general. FoodItems can be divided into "kind-of" subclasses such as MainCourse, Beverage, and Dessert. Second, there are Orders. Orders breakdown according to subclasses that could be called RegularOrder, SpecialOrder, and PromotionOrder. FoodItems can be "part-of" the Orders, although they are not in the Order class, since they are kinds of FoodItems, not kinds of Orders!

Let's use an inheritance hierarchy to visualize what is going on here. Figure 2-5 shows the hierarchy of the classes identified so far. Note that a kind of FoodItem, such as a Dessert, can also be *part* of a SpecialOrder. During analysis, arranging classes in hierarchies and understanding "kind-of" or "part-of" relationships between classes helps convey similarity and difference to designers in a way that can support their use of concepts such as polymorphism. Don't be afraid to delve into these relationships, in all their complexity. They are the reality that the system must support!

Once you have developed a view of the system with this schema for classes, any new food that is going to be sold through the automated order-entry system can be identified as an object that belongs to one of the classes on the hierarchy. If it belongs to that class, it should be able to inherit class characteristics from the superclass. Otherwise, there is a

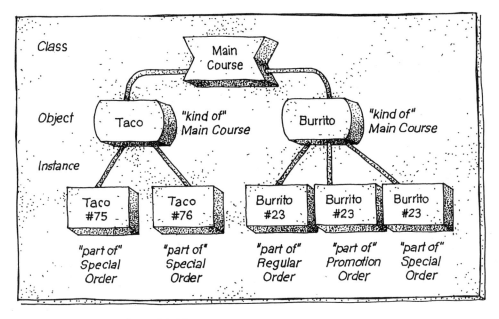

Figure 2-5 **Fast Food: An OO View**

problem with the class structure. If I want to sell "Flautas," they will be placed in the hierarchy as a MainCourse and, perhaps to promote the new product, offered as part-of a Special. This means that many of the behaviors of a Flauta have already been addressed by FoodItem and MainCourse and can be reused. During analysis, the system development team has to be careful to anticipate class behavior, but once the pattern has been described, individual objects can be integrated rapidly.

Polymorphism reinforces the flexibility and ease which comes from viewing systems as interconnected classes. If there is a method called "SetPrice" that is used to adjust pricing, that method can be named as a responsibility for the FoodItem class. If a subclass has to implement that method in a slightly different way, the name of the method will still be the same. Only the programmer who works on the code needs to hammer out the details of the different implementations. For the analyst and for the user, the concept of "SetPrice" is the same, even when the implementations differ.

Encapsulation comes into play when we begin to ask questions about the data. Instead of envisioning a common file in which all prices are stored, the price of each item is "hidden" inside that item. A FoodItem knows its price. When an Order (another class in the system) must calculate its total, it will do so by requesting (as a client) the correct price from the FoodItem (the server in this case). Similarly, if we want to have the system create a Menu at the beginning of each sales cycle, Menu will collaborate with FoodItems to get price data. We can streamline the description by saying that Menu collaborates with FoodItem. FoodItem, as the superclass, has the responsibility to "know price" which is inherited by the subclasses. For the purposes of analysis, we do not need to worry about how particular subclasses implement their methods.

This is a very simple example. The case studies later in the book will give you some more involved examples. What is important at this point is not the details, but to show the way in which thinking in terms of classes guides the discussion to an object-oriented solution which makes sense.

SUMMARY

In this chapter, we reviewed basic concepts and vocabulary used in object-oriented development. First, we talked about objects and the way in which encapsulation makes object-oriented approaches to systems different. Next, we discussed relationships between objects and classes, and inheritance, the way in which classes can be arranged into hierarchies. This led to a brief description of polymorphism and the unique capabilities of object-oriented systems to maximize reuse. Finally, we discussed the role of abstraction, and its importance to successful use of the object-oriented approach. The closing section of the chapter illustrates these concepts in a short "fast food" example.

Now that you are familiar with the basic concepts used in object-oriented development, it's time to apply them when defining the requirements for a more complex system. In the next section of the book, you will see how CRC cards make this easier. Even without knowing the details of how inheritance and polymorphism are implemented, teams of users and analysts can map out system requirements by using CRC cards. The cards ensure that they have a common understanding, and that they agree upon what the system will look like. How they brainstorm to do this is the subject we turn to next.

Chapter 3

Getting Started with CRC

Now that you understand the basic vocabulary used in object-oriented development and the fundamental problem-solving issues involved in the analysis phase of an object-oriented project, it is time to look at the CRC card itself and the strategies that you can use to come up with a good set of classes. The process begins with the selection of a project team with an appropriate mix of skills. The next step is an open-ended approach to finding classes based on brainstorming first and winnowing out later.

In the course of the chapter, we provide a set of guidelines for doing this work. As you saw in the introductory chapters, choosing and defining classes is going to be one of the most important things that you do in an object-oriented project. CRC cards are an aid, a catalyst in the process because they are easy to use and encourage interaction. Even so, what you get out of your CRC card sessions will depend upon what you put in. The guidelines we suggest are not rules, but they should maximize the problem-solving interactions that make CRC card technique so popular.

You will notice that brainstorming strategies are at the heart of our approach to using CRC cards. We believe that the thing that makes CRC card sessions worth adding to your project calendar is the high level of creative interaction they support. This "two heads are better than one" and "genius is the product of many minds" philosophy is critical. Yes, one person working alone can make good use of CRC cards, but the cards' real power is that they help a group of people become a problem-solving team.

WHO WRITES CRC CARDS?

The most significant advantage of the CRC card approach is its adaptable, informal style. CRC cards are ideal for the early stages of analysis when a team composed of users, analysts, and designers is trying to articulate a comprehensive model of the system. At this

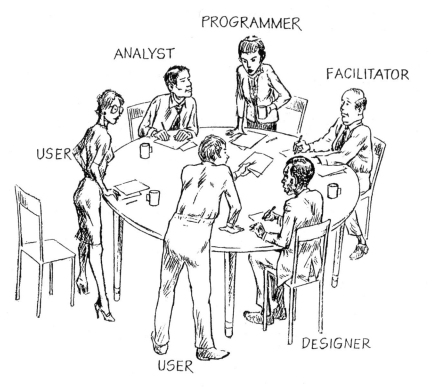

Figure 3-1 **The CRC Card Team**

stage, users contribute expertise in the language of the domain. The analysts and designers are the learners. At the same time, the analysts and designers are working to translate what they learn about the domain into a model that anticipates the basic assumptions of object-oriented technology. CRC cards provide an easy-to-use, nontechnical medium through which users can describe the domain. CRC cards anticipate the nature of object-oriented systems by capturing the domain in a vocabulary of classes and responsibilities.

For this reason, the best way to write CRC cards is as a team (see Figure 3-1). Rather than sending each team member off to interview users and write his own CRC cards, use the process of writing the CRC cards as a catalyst and a focus for teamwork. Meet as a team and work as a team to understand the system, and to formalize the project vocabulary. Writing the CRC cards is not a mechanical activity; it is a process in which a number of people with a variety of roles and points of expertise work together to articulate the characteristics of the system.

Two Is Only Company; Ten Is a Crowd

The ideal size for the CRC card team is five or six people. A group of this size is large enough to contribute a variety of perspectives and thinking styles, but small enough to attend to its purpose. Since the CRC card set that is developed must be singular in its representation of the system, the group has to be able to arrive at a consensus, a picture of the system that every member of the group can accept. If there are more than six team members, some differences may only be resolvable by vote and majority rule. This is not a good situation, because it leaves some members of the development team dissatisfied and predisposed to accept a system they feel ignores critical items. Obviously, this is not a good solution.

Larger teams often end up taking the advice given by people respected for their experience and track record, and this is the reason why an experienced person should be included on all teams. There is no substitute for experience (even when you're in the middle of obtaining some!).

A small team of two or three people may not have the diversity of views or the range of knowledge to analyze anything but a "toy" system. CRC cards can be used by individuals or a small team. They are certainly useful to anyone trying to collect details about the classes in a new system, and the discussion in this chapter will be useful for these small groups. However, many of the questions we have been asked, about how to use CRC cards effectively, deal with the complexity of applying them to a larger project. All of the things that we say about the team approach to CRC can be adapted to a smaller project and an individual analyst, but we will frame our discussion in terms of larger projects and a five- or six-member team. This is the optimal situation for CRC role play, a significant part of the CRC card approach described later in the book.

The team should be composed of one or two Domain Experts, two analysts, an experienced OO designer (one of whom will often be the lead programmer), and someone specifically chosen to be the group's facilitator and leader. We've found each of these roles to be crucial to success, so let's review next what each team member is supposed to contribute.

Domain Experts: Don't Forget the User

The core of the team that writes the cards are the domain experts. These are users who bring both vocabulary and practical knowledge to the analysis effort. Filling out the CRC cards does not require expertise in programming or even design from every member of the team. The CRC cards are useful because they make it easy for users to plug in what they know, while using the idea of classes to organize their domain knowledge. It can even be said that users are at a distinct advantage because they are not worried about code or object concepts. They respond to classes as a clever model that helps them express their requirements in a way that is meaningful to the people who are building systems for them.

We do offer one word of caution in the selection of the users who will work on the CRC card team. Seek out individuals who know the guts of the domain and work with it every day. It is fine to use CRC cards to show a group of managers what is going on and to demonstrate that the team understands the system, but managers' distance from day-to-day operations makes them less valuable for writing out the CRC cards. At the same time, do not get tangled up in the details of how particular things are handled. Pick a user who has an overview of what is going on, and who is familiar with operational requirements.

In addition, don't be afraid to choose people whose personalities fit the work of analysis. During the first stages of development, the team members should be people who enjoy problem solving and who like to investigate and explore. Look for domain experts who bring a variety of perspectives and a wide breadth of knowledge to the team. Look for individuals who want to see the system grow.

Good Analysts Are Good at Making Connections

The title "systems analyst" refers to the role of the person on the team. Whether these team members come from a technical background or concentrate on the user side of systems development, they need to work with the facilitator to guide the group toward establishing a clear scope and a comprehensive analysis of the system. So, whether or not the analysts have had experience on an object-oriented project, they should be interested in developing a keen understanding of the basic concepts: inheritance, polymorphism, and encapsulation. The more familiarity they have with object-oriented libraries and the language to be used on the project, the easier it will be for them to appreciate the contribution of CRC to the expression of system requirements in terms of collaborating classes.

At the same time, what distinguishes the role of an analyst from that of the designer is a focus on user needs. For the analyst, CRC cards are an excellent preliminary form of documentation: one that is user friendly and yet based on the concept of classes. The analysts help the users solve the problem of system definition by sorting out elements of the domain into classes. They do this by asking questions and drawing out connections. If the CRC cards are incomplete, it is probably not because the domain experts don't know what they want, but because the analysts have not asked enough questions. The great thing about the CRC cards and the role play is that they make question-asking natural and easy.

A Good Designer: Seen, but Not Often Heard

In some ways, during analysis the designer is the least significant person in the group! There should be at least one member of the team who knows where the project is going from a technical point of view, but their technical knowledge is contributory, not critical, to the success of the CRC technique. The main value of having designers participate in the CRC card sessions is that it is important for someone to see the project through from start to finish. This can be a significant factor in system acceptance and system completeness. Hearing the users discuss their domain and transform it into the language of CRC brings the designer closer to key requirements.

Another reason for including designers in the CRC process is to maximize the ability of the development project to take advantage of rapid prototyping. Early delivery of partial sections of the system is an invaluable factor in favor of object-oriented development. The designer on the CRC team listens to the domain experts formulate their needs in terms of classes and respond to the comments and questions of the analysts. Thus, the designers are building knowledge that they can use to try out implementation ideas for prototypes of the system.

There is a distinct advantage for the team if some members are fluent in object-oriented implementation. The designer keeps implementation in mind, as an object expert during the analysis discussions. While being cautious not to intimidate team members new to classes and objects, an expert designer can interject questions that the users and analysts might not think to ask. As the CRC cards are filled in and tested through role play, the designer can begin to see what priorities and complexities will put pressure on the design.

Choose Your Facilitator with an Eye for Quality

It can help the group work more smoothly if there is a member of the team who knows a lot about object-oriented systems, but whose role is to facilitate discussion rather than decide on technical questions. This facilitator may be an outside consultant in a small organization new to object-oriented systems, or, in a larger organization, an in-house expert. The key role of the facilitator is to concentrate on the task of focusing the group on the work at hand.

In our examples, we have concentrated on situations where the teams are new to object-oriented development, because we would expect that many of our readers are also new to the field. However, if you are in an organization with considerable object-oriented development experience, you may want to use a rotation system where the role of the facilitator is assigned to a different person for each CRC card session or for a set of sessions. In either case, be sure that the facilitator is good at listening and making tactful comments. Whoever assumes the role of the facilitator temporarily abdicates the role of working member to concentrate on guiding the group.

If you are not in an organization with experienced object-oriented project veterans, limited in-house expertise can be leveraged when local mentors are assigned to projects as advisors. If you don't have in-house gurus, a facilitator who is also a project consultant can be an effective solution. As an expert, this person has the credibility to lead the group. At the same time, as a consultant, he or she is not personally invested in company politics. Such an individual can help the group avoid pitfalls such as "procedural talk," set up guidelines for the CRC sessions, and resolve differences.

Organizations new to object-oriented systems should be on the lookout for people who have facilitator potential. Candidates for the role of facilitator not only must have technical know-how, but must be sensitive to group process and be able to teach. The facilitator is integral to the success of the CRC card technique. A facilitator with tact and knowledge can make a big difference in how comfortable neophytes feel with the new perspective. CRC sessions that go well can be a big selling point in an organization where, enthusiastic or not, people are unsure of their ability to master the world of object-oriented technology.

Finally, during the CRC sessions, differences of opinion regarding class responsibilities and paths of collaboration must be resolved to everyone's satisfaction if the system is going to be accepted. However, this is not going to be true if the facilitator acts as a decision maker who "rules" on disagreements. Good facilitators use their expertise to help the group see the advantages and disadvantages of each possibility in order to arrive at a satisfactory choice as to which representation of the system makes the most sense. Good facilitators help the team to accomplish high-quality work in a comfortable working environment.

READING THE CRC CARD

Now that you have your CRC card team, it is time to look at the CRC card itself. You will see immediately that the cards have been designed to promote clarity. While it may take a while to decide which way to write the CRC cards and how they fit together, the information on the cards is unambiguous. Reading the CRC card is very straightforward. The cards are annotated in an explicit notation that is easy to understand.

Figure 3-2 shows a generic CRC card. You can use regular file cards, or you can use computer software. Either way, you are going to see the same thing. The card is divided into several main areas: the class name, the responsibilities, and the collaborators on the front of the card, and a definition (optional) and attributes (optional) on the back of the card. The class name is written at the top of the card. Below it, on the left-hand side of the card, there is a list of the things that class must do: its behavior (responsibilities). On the right-hand side of the card, there is a list of collaborators, other classes that are asked to do things so that this class can fulfill its responsibilities.

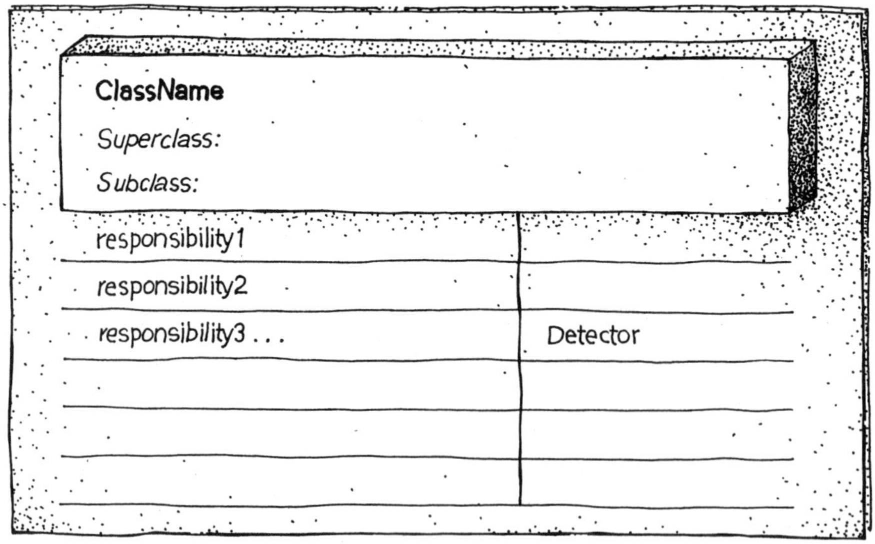

Figure 3-2 **A Blank CRC Card**

If you use index cards, it may work best if you choose a smaller card size (3×5 in. or 4×6 in.). Larger index cards are good for people with large handwriting, but they also provide a temptation to fill up space. The goal of the CRC card is to paint a picture of a class that has high cohesion, that sticks to a clear task. Filling up space on a big, empty index card does not necessarily mean that all of the responsibilities listed on the card belong together. In fact, if the 5×7 inch card is full, you may have a class that is doing too much.

Another logistical consideration involves the use of software to support the CRC card process. The value of computer support is that (1) nobody has to read handwriting and (2) the cards are all together in one place. This second issue can be important if there is a larger project with multiple subareas of the system being studied together or in sequence. However, the need to lay the physical cards down on a table and move them around as you discuss collaboration means that even computer-supported CRC card sessions must produce hardcopy of the cards, so that they can be moved around, held up in the air, etc.

Going back to the CRC cards, there are a number of things that you need to know about reading them. First, every card will eventually have a class name and at least one responsibility, although at the early stages blank cards can be useful. Some classes may have several responsibilities. The rest of the fields on the card are optional and depend upon the results of the analysis. If a class is part of a hierarchy, it may have a superclass or subclasses. But not all classes will be part of a hierarchy. If a class depends upon other classes to help it carry out its responsibilities, it will have collaborator(s) written on the line opposite the responsibility that is supported by the collaboration. Some classes may not need to collaborate, so there will be nothing on that side of the CRC card.

The back of the CRC card may be filled in or left blank. The back of the card is used to list attributes of the class and to write a class description. If you know attributes, you may jot them down on the back of the card so that you won't forget them, but they are not going to affect your ability to make use of the CRC card technique or to conduct a CRC role play. If it makes it easier to remember what you mean, write a definition on the back of the card. Again, this description will not affect your ability to role play with the cards.

Some CRC card users have found that using the back of the card for attributes can be distracting and even misleading. If an attribute is significant from the point of view of systems analysis, it will show up on the front of the CRC card because it will be the subject of a knowledge responsibility. For example, an Account class might have "know balance" as one of its responsibilities. So, it is acceptable practice to use the back of the card to record descriptions and attributes, but beware of so-called attributes that really belong in the category of knowledge behavior on the front of the CRC card. You should always be able to explain why a class should "know." The discussion later in the chapter should help you make this distinction more easily.

BRAINSTORMING: A DISCOVERY TECHNIQUE

The next subject we have to tackle is how to come up with the information that gets written down on the CRC cards. First of all, remember that the strength of CRC cards is that they are an excellent technique for taking advantage of the group process in problem solving. The old cliché "two heads are better than one" is not an empty adage! As we pointed out in the introductory chapter, the notion that computer systems development is work for one mind, locked alone in a room dogging its way through the problem, has not proved very effective.

Unfortunately, from the beginning of their computer education, programmers and designers are often left alone to suffer in silence. A premium is placed on the idea of "genius," the great mind that wraps itself around the problem and comes up with a solution unaided and without distraction. This may be an attractive and romantic view of problem solving, but it is not practical. In the real world, where systems are increasingly complex and interdependent, it is the teams, not the individuals, which come up with the best solutions.

Group problem solving works by making it possible to throw together a variety of ideas, compare them, and synthesize unanticipated solutions. With CRC cards, a group of people throw together their ideas about what a system should do, compare them, and synthesize them into a set of classes recorded on CRC cards. Moreover, this is not a random process. There is a method for doing it: problem solving through postulation, evaluation, and selection. The first step in this process is brainstorming.

Description of Brainstorming Principles

Our first claim is that several people can generate more ideas than one person working alone. However, in order for this to happen, each person must feel free to explore ideas, make suggestions, be creative, and have fun. That means that the group has got to start working by suspending judgment and encouraging involvement. Strong notions about "right" and "wrong" can censor good ideas. Sometimes, without realizing it, we even cut off our own ideas and label them as stupid, foolish, or off the mark. This habit of censorship can be so strong that it becomes subconscious. In a brainstorming session, the group, guided by a set of principles, combats the censorship and frees team members to propose any alternative from the most logical to the most absurd. In this way, brainstorming at the beginning of the CRC card process can lead to sets of CRC cards that bring a new perspective to the problems and tasks at hand.

Principle #1: All Ideas Are Potential Good Ideas

The first principle of brainstorming is based on the importance of breaking down any tendency to censor before you speak. This principle is related to the golden rule of brainstorming: "Treat every suggestion as if it were your own." When the team is in brainstorming mode, anything goes. This means that anything you think of that comes up in response to the question at hand should be offered up to the group as an idea. Don't decide for the group whether your idea is "dumb" or "brilliant." Don't decide for yourself that someone else's idea is "dumb" or "brilliant." All ideas are equal, because all ideas have the potential to lead to an unanticipated solution.

This principle has proved difficult for many of us who are working in an environment where there is pressure to produce results quickly. Tossing out ideas and even getting a little foolish can feel a lot like wasting time. Yes, if the group gets too carried away or if one person gets out on a limb, time may be wasted. But the facilitator is in the group to check this kind of behavior. Members of the team should not have to worry about ideas before they present them to the group. Yes, the list of candidate classes, for example, may have a number of suggestions that get dropped, but cutting out the ideas that do not pan out will take a lot less time than trying to make the system work if something gets forgotten.

Principle #2: Think Fast and Furiously First, Ponder Later

The next principle of successful brainstorming relates to the pace of the group. If each person waits quietly for a good idea, the creative juices won't flow. Studies have shown that when people in a group take turns in quick succession, one person triggers another. Especially when you are trying to break out of old patterns and see new possibilities, deliberation first can be very inhibiting. Save careful consideration for later.

For example, if you are trying to come up with a list of classes in a system, use a meeting structure that supports brainstorming. Assign a scribe to write the ideas on a flip chart. Then everyone should toss ideas (possible classes) out as quickly as they can. Obviously, as the list gets longer, the pace of suggestions slows. Let the group members pressure themselves to keep going. This push forward operates as another device to free the creative mechanisms and to dislodge ideas hiding out in the subtle corners of inhibition.

Principle #3: Give Every Voice a Turn

Anyone who has spent much time on project teams or in business meetings knows that people come in many flavors. Some of us are predisposed to talk all of the time; others are reluctant to talk at all. Words per minute is, however, a poor measure of thought. To prevent old habits from interfering with brainstorming, try using a rotation. Start with one person and then go around the table, each person contributing one idea. This pattern should continue until team members are truly forced to "pass" because they are out of ideas. When everyone passes, brainstorming is winding down.

Note that the rotation and the option to "pass" insures that the eager beavers are not the only ones talking. Remember principle number one, "All ideas are potential good ideas." Make sure that this value is respected. Let people make "far out" suggestions as they dry up on the obvious. Don't censor now. It will be easy to eliminate ridiculous items later.

You should also be aware that the brainstorming part of the CRC card session is at the beginning of the process, so it can set a mood that lasts for the duration of the project. If people who tend to keep quiet, to be shy about participating, experience acceptance when they speak early on, they will be much more likely to be regular contributors throughout the project. Establishing an inclusive atmosphere is an important part of the facilitator's responsibility right from the beginning of the project.

Principle #4: A Little Humor Can Be a Powerful Force

Humor helps convert a random group of people into a cohesive team. Laughing together creates a bond between people. Laughter dispels tensions and signals a shared perspective. Reaching for new ideas at a rapid clip pushes everyone to take a chance. Ironically, it can be those desperate and ridiculous items on the list of prospective classes that put everyone on the same wavelength. In this way, brainstorming can open doors and break down barriers. As a result, the group automatically establishes a baseline of trust and interdependence that makes it easier to debate the serious issues sure to arise later.

Using Brainstorming to Find Classes

Now we are ready for the real work of finding classes. In this section of the chapter we will suggest a step-by-step approach to creating a set of candidate classes for your system, and narrowing that list down to a group of core classes that you will use to begin to work with the CRC cards. As you read through the four steps, remember that each team and each project is different. Don't be afraid to adapt to the personality of your team and your project. At the same time, be wary of abandoning systematic teamwork. The four steps were chosen because they have proved successful for groups using brainstorming in a wide variety of situations. They are meant to be guards against common problems in group dynamics, so take advantage of them to keep your group working in top form from the very beginning.

Step 1: Review Brainstorming Principles

Begin the first work session by reviewing the four brainstorming principles. It is a good idea to write them on a board or post them on a wall in the room where the team is working. Although the ideas are not complicated, they are easy to forget when the real work of finding classes begins. Just seeing these guidelines written on the wall can help people remember to put aside personal style and work with the team.

Step 2: State Session Objectives

When you are ready to start brainstorming classes or start using brainstorming to address another analysis problem, the facilitator should take the time to state the objective for the brainstorming part of the meeting. The objective should be precise and fairly narrow—for example, "Today, we want to come up with a candidate class list" or "Let's come up with as many possible collaboration paths as possible with the classes we have defined so far." Write the objective at the top of the board or flip chart.

This is very important. Even if the work the team has to do seems obvious, writing down your objective provides an anchor. It is something that the group can focus on if discussion slides off track. For example, during systems analysis it is easy to get sidetracked recounting the details of current procedures and telling war stories. Some of that sort of talk can be helpful and very revealing, but it can also lead to long digressions that are not relevant to the new system. Users may also digress in this way to reinforce their own sense of knowledge and control in a situation where changes are immanent. Attacking or silencing someone who is caught up in an explanation of this sort can be embarrassing and even insulting. Drawing the group's attention back to the objective can provide a neutral way to get everyone back on track.

Step 3: Use a Round-Robin Technique

One of the most difficult aspects of teamwork is getting everyone in the room to work on equal footing. Both organizational differences (jobs, position, etc.) and personality can quickly and inadvertently lead to a core of speakers and a core of listeners. Moreover, the fact that the listeners are not talking does not mean they are not thinking or that they are in agreement. The best way to avoid this dynamic is to use a round-robin technique to solicit suggestions.

For example, if you are trying to develop a list of possible classes for a system, go around the table. As each member of the team contributes an idea, write it down on the board. The facilitator should do the writing since the other members of the team should be watching and thinking. If there is a team member who does not have enough information on a particular problem to contribute to the brainstorming, that person can act as scribe as a way to keep involved; however, if a team is chosen well, every member should be an important source of possible classes.

The goal of the round robin is to allow the group to move ahead at an even tempo but to give people enough time to think. Short pauses are fine, but breaks of more than 60 seconds can interrupt the momentum and ideas may be lost. To keep things going you can establish a "pass" policy. If someone is really stumped, they can "pass" for that round, but they should take their regular turn the next time around. The facilitator needs to be sensitive here. If someone is slower to speak, don't cut off their turn too soon. At the same time, keep things moving so that other people do not forget what they want to say. The brainstorming is complete when everyone in the group has to pass.

Step 4: Discuss and Select

This is when all of the ideas produced by brainstorming are discussed and winnowed down. Now that everyone's suggestions are down in black and white, bearing equal weight in importance, it is time to sift out the best items. Now is the time when the digressions ruled out by the facilitator during the round robin can be aired. However, there should still be a defined sense of purpose. Beware of sliding back instead of moving forward. Do not go through the list item by item inviting comment. You'll never get done this way and, more likely than not, you will find the group gets sidetracked, some members become restless, and focus dissolves.

Restate the objective for the brainstorming session. Next, ask for suggestions for the category of clear-cut winners, those items that everyone agrees are classes or responsibilities or whatever you are trying to identify. Put these on a separate list or mark them clearly. Next, address the items that do not fit at all. There will always be some because we have used the principle of accepting all ideas to avoid quenching or censoring good ideas, but, inevitably, some of those ideas will be easy to eliminate in the context of a complete list.

Finally, address the items that fall in between "yes" and "no." The best way to do this is to assign a limited time for discussion (5–10 minutes) and then take a voice vote on whether or not to include the item. If the group cannot decide, establish a consistent policy: either include all undecided items, or postpone inclusion until you understand the system better. There are advantages and disadvantages to both strategies. The strategy of inclusion may give you more to work with as you move on to the next analysis activity. The strategy of exclusion allows you to work with items that are definitely at the core of the system. When the team has developed a sharper sense of the system, it may be easier to evaluate the "maybe" items on the brainstorming list.

Now that you understand how brainstorming works, it is time to put it into practice for solving the problem of finding classes. First, you need to use brainstorming to come up with a broad list of candidate classes; then, you need to winnow that list down to a set of core classes that can be used to write an initial set of CRC cards. However, before you can brainstorm about candidate classes, you are going to have to do a little bit of research and information collection. Whether you are starting up a new system or reengineering an old one, there are a number of places you can search for classes.

THE CANDIDATE CLASS LIST: WHERE DO CLASSES COME FROM?

Some candidates for the role of a class in an object-oriented system will be obvious from the start. Others may be disguised by an ingrained procedural perspective brought to the work. For this reason, rather than trying to list classes methodically, it is more effective to use brainstorming. By following the brainstorming principles and going through the four brainstorming steps, a project team can come up with a more comprehensive list of classes in less time than an individual developer.

Brainstorming classes takes advantage of spontaneity, but it still requires preparation. Before beginning the brainstorming session, each member of the team should be assigned an investigative path, a set of things that they need to do to flood themselves with knowledge and ideas about the system. There are four common resources that can be assigned to team members, depending upon their level of technical expertise. These are the starting point. Anything that tells the team more about the system is a valid resource to use in preparing to brainstorm for candidate classes.

Read Over All Requirements Documents

The first resource for the CRC card team is the documentation that states the system requirements. In some cases, this will be a formal document. In other cases, it may be a much less formal service request conveyed in a memorandum. Don't overlook indirect sources. If there are meeting minutes or additional memorandums about the application or the work requirements of the group you are going to support, include these as well. Whatever documents you find, examine them and look for potential class names.

Selecting classes from written sources can be done mechanically by underlining all of the nouns and noun phrases. Convert them to singular nouns and add them to the candidate class list. Physical objects (printers, screen displays, etc.) also qualify as candidates. Tools that are used to interface with the system may also become classes in an object-oriented system. Figure 3-3 shows a memorandum regarding the development of an ATM (automatic teller machine) system with the nouns circled that might be classes. These are items that the team member charged with reviewing this resource can consider as possible classes to contribute when the team begins to brainstorm.

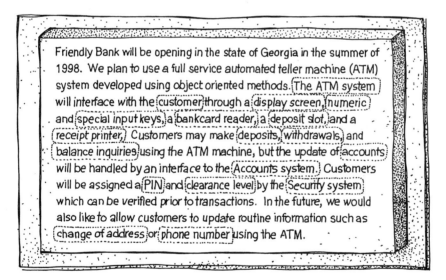

Figure 3-3   **Request for Service Memo for ATM System**

Look Carefully at Reports

Another source of class names are the reports generated by current operations and profiles for reports the user would like from the new system. These documents can be treated just like the written requirements: circle nouns and noun phrases, and then list them as singular class names. Many of the items in the reports will overlap with the requirements document. There should also be some additional items that will eventually help the team envision superclasses and hierarchies. For the moment, do not worry about the relationships between the candidate classes you find in reports. Just bring them to the brainstorming session and add them to the list.

You should also be aware that reports often include ghost classes or aliases, and items that are really only attributes, not full-fledged classes. We will discuss how to spot these later. For now, collect all the possible classes you can and bring them to the brainstorming session. Keep track of the actual reports and put them in a file. You may need them to decide which classes really are key to the system and which are not relevant and why. Old reports often contain categories of information that are needed to get around problems with old systems. You don't want to carry those forward into the new system. As you will see later, writing and role play with CRC cards will help you make better judgments in this area.

Conduct Interviews

Written requirements documents can never capture all of the subtle points of a system. Experienced users, who know the domain well, are a critical resource for defining classes and understanding how they can be linked together. The users selected to participate in CRC sessions should not only be familiar with the current system, but aware of innovations in their field that may be part of the new system.

The most effective way to capture this information is to include domain concept experts in the CRC sessions. On the other hand, if you want to keep the CRC card team down to a workable size, there may be important users who are not going to come to the CRC card sessions. They may represent small pieces of the system, or they may be physically unable to attend because of the geographical distribution of the organization. Whatever the reason, you need to include input from these users in your class candidate research.

Use the same attention to nouns and noun phrases that you used in the case of written documentation as you listen to users. Verbs and verb phrases can be used as you consider which object is responsible for the action discussed, and as you clarify just what collaborations are necessary to carry the action out. Try to tape interview sessions and then listen to them afterwards. You can even use sketches of information models, data flow diagrams, flow charts, or any other notation that lets you (1) capture what the user is saying in notation that will be meaningful later and (2) review your interpretation of what the user is saying with the user to be sure you have understood it correctly.

Brainstorming and follow-up discussion offer an important check on the information gathered during interviews. Seeing your notes on one user's perspective and the classes you spot in the context of the classes other team members suggest is a fast and easy way to uncover contradictions and to spot areas where you don't have enough information.

Examine Documentation and Files

Whether you are working with a legacy system or starting on a new system, someone on the CRC team should review the data resources that document the current system. This includes file layouts, relational database designs, and any information there is about repositories used by the organization for related systems. Again, you are looking for classes, for entities that are key to the system.

The team member who is looking at data resources may want to follow up with a set of interviews with people who use them on a daily basis. Encourage the users to talk about what they are doing and win their confidence. Remember, an analyst is not just a record keeper; a really good analyst is a detective.

In the spirit of detection, it may not be sufficient to look only at routine work. Find out if users are keeping records of their own. If there are limitations to the old system, each worker has probably developed private ways to gather information that they need to do their job. Photocopies and hard copy of information available on-line is also a signal that there are information connections that are needed to do the work, but which are not possible under the old implementation. Collect and annotate everything.

To select candidates from these sources, follow the same noun searching method used before. Again, don't worry about attributes and objects yet. These can be sorted out after the brainstorming stage.

SUMMARY

We've shown the brainstorming techniques you can use to come up with a good set of candidate classes. The process begins with the selection of a project team with an appropriate mix of skills. The next step is an open-ended approach to finding classes based on brainstorming first and winnowing out later. Next investigate responsibilities and collaborations.

We provide a set of pointers and tips for doing this work. Coming up with the potential classes is one of the most important things you do in an object-oriented project. CRC cards are an aid, a catalyst in the process. The guidelines we suggest are not rules, but they will maximize the group interactions that make the CRC card technique so popular.

Chapter 4

Selecting the Core Classes

If all of the team members have done their work well, the brainstorming session described in Chapter 3 can turn out a formidable list of candidate classes. Following our earlier rule of thumb for project size, if all of the candidate classes are core classes, the system is much too big. However, before you decide to search for subsystems, which can be an extensive analysis task in itself, there are some easy things you can do to analyze the candidate class list. Many of the classes may be duplicates. Other candidates may actually be attributes and not classes in themselves. Another thing you will have to do in order to evaluate the candidate classes is to clarify the scope of the system. Without a firm system boundary, it will be impossible to develop an accurate list of core classes. This section of the chapter offers guidelines for evaluating the items on the candidate class list and coming up with a good initial core class list.

To make this process easier to visualize, we will use an abbreviated version of an ATM system. We have chosen this example because it is an application that many of our readers will recognize, at least as users. The case studies in the later chapters will give you a chance to see how a group works on a project using the CRC cards. So, for now, we will simply give you the results of the steps in the process to serve as examples of the concepts. Let's begin with a candidate class list for the ATM.

The ATM system which we are going to develop is a simple one. Bank account holders may make deposits or withdraw cash from their checking and savings accounts using the ATM. They can make balance inquiries, but they cannot transfer funds from one account to another (even though this is desirable, the bank decided not to implement it). The ATM produces a printed receipt for the customer. Access is authorized through the use of a bank card and a personal code (PIN). With these requirements in mind, we have come up with a candidate class list. It is intentionally inclusive to demonstrate the kind of list you may develop as the result of a brainstorming session. Note that we have written the names of the possible classes using the same capitalization we used in the chapter on object-oriented technology basics, to help you get used to the notation from the beginning.

ATM Candidate Classes

ATM	CashDispenser
FinancialTransaction	ScreenMessage
BankCard	Display
BankCustomer	FundsAvailable
PIN	DepositEnvelopeFailure
Account	Balance
SavingsAccount	TimeOutKey
CheckingAccount	TransactionLog
Transfer	Amount
Withdrawal	AccountHolder
Deposit	Printer
BalanceInquiry	ScreenSaver
Receipt	Prompt
ReceiptPrinter	NumericKey
Keypad	Key
Screen	

There are a number of techniques you can use to work through the candidate class list and decide which are the items that best qualify as classes for which you want to write a CRC card. There is no simple formula for doing this. This is the point at which the team moves from brainstorming mode to analysis mode. You must look at each item on the list and ask, "Is this really a class?" "Does this class belong to the system as it is defined in this project?" "How do the classes on this list fit in together?" "What does the inclusion of one class tell me about the inclusion or exclusion of other classes?" These questions can be asked in any order, and answering one may send you back to reexamine the answers to another. What we offer in this section is not a chronological set of steps, but a number of approaches you can use to sort out your thinking about candidate classes and pick the core classes you want to include on your initial set of CRC cards.

IDENTIFY CRITICAL CLASSES

The first thing that you want to do with the full candidate class list is to break it down into categories. You may even want to start a new set of lists using three sheets of flipchart paper or three lists on a whiteboard. Actually, a whiteboard or some easily erasable surface should be a basic tool for this part of the CRC card session, so that it is easy to revise your thoughts and to see the impact of those changes. The objective of the process is (1) to find critical classes which will definitely be written on CRC cards, (2) to eliminate irrelevant items, and (3) to review the leftover classes, deciding whether to write CRC cards for them now and eliminate them later if they prove to have no significant role, or to put them on hold and see if they turn out to be critical later.

The best way to begin is to select those classes that are definitely critical to the system. These will probably be classes that relate directly to the main entities involved in the application. They will echo the core items in the vocabulary used to describe the system domain. They will show up as the preliminary candidates for an information model. They will be names of things that recur in almost every source used to create the candidate class list. You can also think about critical classes in terms of things that are going to undergo a change of state. For example, in the ATM system the critical classes will include Account, Deposit, Withdrawal, and BalanceInquiry. Note that an Account class will undergo a number of changes of state that are the result of system activity (open/closed/overdrawn).

At the other end of the spectrum, as you look over the list with an eye for critical classes, you will see that because the brainstorming encourages inclusion, some items on the list are going to prove irrelevant. As the team discusses the critical classes, their sense of what the system does is going to be sharpened. Place a mark beside each item that seems to meet the requirement "irrelevant" as easily as the first list of classes met the requirement "critical." In the case of the ATM list, some of the items that were elicited by the brainstorming but which, upon further review, fall outside of the system might include Printer, ScreenSaver, and Prompt. All of these class candidates have more to do with the user interface than the banking side of things, so they are not relevant even though they are part of the bigger picture that encompasses both banking and user interface.

Now you have two sets of classes, but there are a number of items on the candidate class list that do not fit clearly in either. These third-category items are going to be the focus of the rest of your class selection process. In order to sort them out and move them up to "critical" status or to discard them, you are going to have to clarify the system definition. In other words, sorting out the candidate class list is going to serve as the impetus and guide for some basic system analysis. In the case of the ATM, looking at the candidate class list, we are going to have to understand what we mean by ATM system before we can be sure what to do with the leftover classes. If the critical classes are not obvious, it may even be necessary to clarify system boundaries before developing a critical class list.

Clarify System Scope

One of the most difficult parts of many software projects is deciding exactly what job we are trying to do in a given development effort. The larger the project, the more important—and the more difficult—this becomes. Software development efforts are notorious for their record-breaking failures to meet promises for delivery. To some extent this can be blamed on work habits, complexity, or unexpected interruptions. Often, however, it is not that the project is late, but that the original effort has mushroomed in scope. This usually happens through slow and unobserved alterations in the original mission. If we put this in terms of the problem solving discussed in the opening chapter of the book, it means that the elements of the problem posed are changing even while the problem solvers are at work. Some people like to call this "chasing a moving target," but it is worse than that: the target itself is changing and, as often as not, expanding as we work.

A system scope diagram can be a vital part of the project definition. Let's look at the ATM system. What do we mean by the ATM project? Are we talking about the soup-to-nuts delivery that includes the software that handles the banking applications, the software that handles the user interface at each ATM, and the software that interfaces between them? Where does it begin and end? Are we responsible for updating account records in this system, or are we just capturing the activity? These questions or something similar should be familiar to anyone who has ever been involved in a development project. The system boundaries should be a product of deliberate decision making. If you are not sure about system boundaries, you will have a difficult time deciding which are your core classes.

We are not going to recommend or require any particular method for capturing system scope. However, it should be built on a foundation of the same vocabulary that is used to talk about classes inside and outside of the domain. As an example, we have drawn a scope diagram for the ATM system (shown in Figure 4-1). In this diagram you can see that we are treating the banking information capture as a separate project from the development

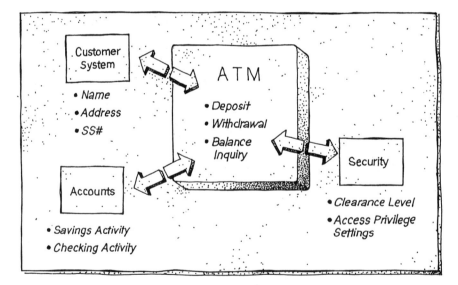

Figure 4-1 **Defining System Boundaries: The ATM Project Scope Diagram**

of the interface with the user. We have done this to simplify the scale of our example. If we were to decide that this is too trivial an undertaking, we could pull the Interface box inside our scope. The point of the discussion here is not to analyze criteria for determining system scope. The point is to insist that the sharper your thinking about the system boundaries is, the easier it will be to evaluate your candidate class list.

Now that you have clarified the system scope, the team should be able to go through the candidate class list and place each item in one of three categories:

1. Critical (must be included)
2. Irrelevant (outside the system scope)
3. Undecided (still a problem)

TAKE ADVANTAGE OF HOT SPOTS, FRAMEWORKS, AND PATTERNS

Another concept that can help you find classes and sort out the candidate classes is the idea of design patterns and frameworks. Based on architectural concepts, frameworks are, in essence, blueprints for building. In the case of a house, the blueprint provides a general plan for the house showing major design objectives such as the partitioning of the space, the use to be made of each area, and general relationships between elements of the house (the living room, sleeping areas, cooking and eating, etc.). Now, if we say that a house is a system, you can see that the blueprint serves to show frameworks that attach together as interrelated elements. In object-oriented systems, we say that frameworks are collections of classes that belong together.

The analysis of existing frameworks can help us to see new frameworks, collections of classes, among the members of the candidate class list. Existing frameworks can lead you to the identification of collections of classes that can be reused as collections with little modification. One element of the framework that helps in this identification process is what we call a pattern. If you develop a good pattern vocabulary, you can spot these frameworks and see how they apply to your new system. Rather than reinventing, you can take advantage of successful patterns. The more you work with object-oriented systems, the larger your vocabulary will be, and the more easily you can use frameworks and patterns to evaluate and group classes for a new system without starting from scratch. Researchers have found that this can substantially lessen the magnitude of the development effort.

The generalizations that underlie frameworks help us to see classes in terms of groups. In many cases, the classes in a given system will fall into four common groups:

Application Domain
Database
GUI (User Interaction)
External Interface (Interaction with Outside System)

Within each class group, there are nine common patterns of classes:

Clients
Servers
Things
Transactions
Locations
Interacting Systems
Interacting Devices
Collections
Containers

Analyzing the items on the ATM list, it will be apparent that many if not all of the ATM classes fall into one of the four class groupings. You can use this list to begin to identify which of the nine common patterns might apply to each class.

One way to make use of existing frameworks and patterns during systems analysis is to look for specific "hot spots" and to find classes on the candidate class list that are tied to each hot spot. Wolfgang Pree uses this approach to focus interviews with users on commonality and difference between applications. He suggests that analysts should ask users questions that lead to the identification of hot spots, to these points of difference expressed in the context of commonality. Pree explains, "Domain experts have to be asked: Which aspects differ from application to application? What is the desired degree of flexibility?" Once you know this, you can go on to identify patterns and frameworks that will help you see classes as important because of their participation in these hot spots. You will see later that hot spots also help you use hierarchies to sort out and select core classes.

For example, in the analysis of the ATM candidate class list, domain experts on the team might point out that the ability to withdraw cash is an important "hot spot." Although the ATM may have other uses, the reason for developing the technology is to allow withdrawals. They also explain that withdrawals take place in essentially the same way whether they are introduced through the ATM or by a teller. The ATM may be only the first in a series of innovations, so they want the withdrawal approach to be flexible enough to be used in the future when, perhaps, cash cards replace cash. Looking at the candidate classes, they identify several that may be touched by this "hot spot": Account, Withdrawal, Funds-Available, and BankCard.

Now that the team has identified a "hot spot," they can review the library of patterns to see if they have a generalized template to guide them in their understanding of the classes involved. In some cases, the existing pattern can be reused fully. In other cases, the team may reuse the general pattern, but it will have to be modified. Whatever the extent of the reuse, the existing pattern will make the addition of responsibilities and collaborations to the CRC card much easier.

Of course, many organizations are just beginning their object-oriented efforts and have no library of frameworks or patterns. There is no getting around the fact that this is a disadvantage, one of many reasons why early adapters of object-oriented technologies have a competitive advantage, a payback for their work as pioneers. Fortunately, many authors and software developers are now distributing models of object strategies which offer blueprints that give you class patterns that may be reused in your system. Looking at such patterns, you can apply them to the CRC cards you are writing and speed up the process of analysis. Patterns and frameworks that have been generalized for reuse in this way are usually called object meta-patterns. Let's see how this could apply to the team on the ATM project.

Let's say that the ATM team in our example does not have an in-house blueprint from which to draw, but they want to use frameworks and patterns to understand their classes better. To get started, they look at Peter Coad's book, *Object Models: Strategies, Patterns and Applications*. They have been trying to understand which classes are going to be involved in the authorization of withdrawals. On page 81 of Coad's book they see a meta-pattern #33, "Selecting interacting systems or devices," that looks as if it will help them understand the scope of the ATM system. This pattern can help the team decide which classes on their candidate list might be outside the scope, because they are part of systems that will interact with the ATM, but which are not part of their immediate development effort.

Using the meta-pattern, the team members decide that the interaction with the outside system can be modeled using a "system interactions class" which encapsulates the details of the communications. On the basis of this analysis, the team adds a new class to the ATM core class list, AuthorizeSystemInteraction. Remember that we felt that the candidate class list was exhaustive because of the time spent using brainstorming to develop it. However, you are going to find that new classes will materialize as you understand the system better. Often they are classes like AuthorizeSystemInteraction that grow out of research into patterns which takes place after the initial brainstorming session is over.

Using Coad's book, the ATM team is able to take advantage of patterns even though they are new to object-oriented systems and have no precedents in their own organization. The AuthorizeSystemInteraction class clarifies the interaction of the ATM with the bank's existing security authorization system, and the auditors will be content! This new class will also help them untangle the cluster of related classes, as you will see in the next discussions.

PHANTOMS AND GHOSTS, SURROGATES AND ALIASES

Phantoms and ghosts are candidate classes which appear at first to be classes, but turn out to be without substance. They are apparitions, images which appear as if in a dream, objects that don't belong within the system being analyzed. The best time to catch these phantoms is during the analysis of the scope diagram, but we can also offer a few pointers on how to spot potential ghosts as the team reviews the candidate class list.

First of all, look for classes that have to do with what is going on, but that are really pieces of outside systems with which yours just has to interface, but which you don't have to model. In the ATM system, this would include things such as BankCustomer and Printer or Keypad. In the case of the BankCustomer, we have a phantom class that is clearly present in the working of the system, but which is known to the system indirectly. Direct knowledge of the BankCustomer is knowledge that involves tracking the state changes (current, former, etc.) of the class, changes that are irrelevant to the system or which we "know" only indirectly through the validation of the PIN and/or the BankCard. So, it may be more accurate to start out with only BankCard on the core class list and to put BankCustomer on the "irrelevant" list. If the team has used the object meta-pattern discussed earlier, they may spot this even faster because they have already integrated the new class AuthorizeSystemInteraction into their core class list.

The list of undecided candidates may include a number of cases of false identity which are not ghost classes. They may instead be aliases: classes using an assumed name, really surrogates identical to an already identified important class. These duplicate classes usually arise from different words used by different divisions of an organization to refer to the same thing. Conversely, different divisions also may use the same words to refer to different things. If analysts have been thorough in collecting source documents and conducting interviews, these aliases (and antonyms, if you will) should show up on the candidate class list. They are usually not too hard to spot, but you may have to exercise some patient politics to get users to accept a common name for their classes.

Looking over the candidate class list for the ATM, we can spot an example. A BankCustomer and an AccountHolder are probably surrogates for the same class. We can either select one of the terms or create a new name. In the case of the ATM, we might want to choose AccountHolder as the most accurate name, because BankCustomer may be a legitimate entity in other systems—and could even be a class in another system with which our system will interface at a later date. Remember, if we are going to link up systems, each class name is going to have to be unique, so choose names now that will minimize conflicts later.

Another, less straightforward case of apparent duplication are the classes Balance and FundsAvailable. Some users in the bank may have adopted a policy-based vocabulary in which the two are synonymous, while elsewhere there are users who argue that not all of a customer's balance may be used for withdrawals, so we need two classes. If the latter is true, then we are going to have to say that Balance and FundsAvailable are different, because we want to choose the class names that are the most flexible and that may allow us to reuse classes in the future.

Sorting the candidate class list and finding the core classes is a first step in an iterative process. Be aggressive in narrowing down the candidate classes to a sharply focused core. You can always go back to the discard lists (undecided and irrelevant) if you find that the core classes you have selected are not sufficient to do the work of the system. If a class has been eliminated because it appears to be a phantom or a surrogate, the decision can be reversed if it proves incorrect as the analysis deepens and the CRC card set is road-tested during role play.

Distinguish Attributes from Classes

Now we are going to take that examination a step further, and ask what is the nature of these classes? What are they likely to do? And, as soon as we start to ask this sort of question, we see that some candidate classes are not classes at all. They are really sets of information which belong to a class (attributes of a class).

When we talked about surrogates and aliases, we decided that FundsAvailable and Balance should both be included because they convey different information. In the case of Balance, this term refers to the amount of money or assets in an Account. What makes Balance distinguishable from FundsAvailable is that they each may refer to a different amount or value. Balance and FundsAvailable are not classes in themselves. They are attributes of the Account class and, as such, may be assigned values at any time.

Another clue that these are attributes and not classes is that they cannot change states. Compare Balance to PIN. There may be a policy in the bank that says that each Account has a PIN just as it has a Balance, so if Balance is an attribute, isn't PIN also an attribute of Account? The answer might be "yes," but we have a complication. A PIN could also be a class which changes state. A PIN may be active, suspended, or invalid as a result of the enforcement of certain rules. If this is so, we are going to need a PIN class. If it is not true, then PIN could be treated as an attribute.

Here again we are going to make our best guess, and then test and revise as we work out responsibilities and collaborations. We may find out that we added PIN to the core class list, but that it turns out to function as an attribute because instead of continuing to exist in various states, a PIN is either assigned or an attribute with null value. There is no rule to use to tell whether to err on the side of including attribute-like classes or not. Try not to overload the core class list with dubious items, because this creates unnecessary work. On the other hand, you will probably find that classes that are really attributes will fall to the side quickly as you try to assign responsibility, because their only work will be to know their own value.

THE ANNOTATED CANDIDATE CLASS LIST

We have offered a variety of strategies for evaluating the members of the candidate class list. We have also emphasized that the goal here is to identify the first-cut CRC cards, which will be revised as we work with them. Accordingly, the candidate classes for the ATM have been sorted out into three categories: (1) core, (2) undecided, and (3) eliminated. We have also annotated each item on the noncore lists to show why it was not included in the core.

Core Classes
FinancialTransaction
Account

BalanceInquiry
Withdrawal
Deposit
BankCard
AuthorizeSystemInteraction

Undecided Classes
PIN (attribute)
SavingsAccount (attribute of Account)
CheckingAccount (attribute of Account)
ATM (ghost—system name)
FundsAvailable (attribute)
Balance (attribute)
AccountHolder (alias)

Irrelevant (outside scope, many are candidates for user interface system)
ReceiptPrinter
KeypadScreen
CashDispenser
ScreenMessageDisplay
DepositEnvelopeFailure
TimeOutKey
TransactionLog
Printer
ScreenSaver
Prompt

QUESTIONS TO ASK OF A "GOOD CLASS"

When you have finished analyzing the candidate class list and understand why you have eliminated classes, go back once more to the core class list. Using the following guidelines, examine each class. If necessary, make adjustments to the naming of the class. At this point, you should understand your core classes well enough to begin to see the system through an object-oriented lens, as a network of classes that collaborate in order to fulfill system requirements.

A good class will have the following characteristics:

Has a clear, unambiguous name easily recognized by domain experts
Has a name that fits in with other systems developed by your organization
Uses a singular noun for its name, not a plural
Begins with an uppercase letter

Has responsibilities
Remembers (has knowledge)
Is needed by other classes (collaborates)
Actively participates in the system

The last four items on the list add a new dimension to the analysis, the dimension of the roles of classes in relation to one another. We have not discussed this yet, but when you are doing your analysis with a full picture of the CRC card technique in mind, they will come into play. We will investigate these aspects of the core classes in the next part of the chapter. However, before we move on, let's review the actual use of the CRC card itself.

Writing Classes on the CRC Cards

When you have a satisfactory list of classes, a CRC card should be started for each class. Put the name of each of the core classes on the top line of a card. Note that the set of CRC cards for the ATM is still quite small. That is because some of the cards included in the final set will not be obvious to the team yet. For example, the core classes include the class BankCard. In the final set, it turns out that even the BankCard (magnetized and assigned by another system) is outside the scope of our project. It is the BankCardReader class that needs to be implemented by this development team. However, at this point, the analysis has not uncovered these details, so BankCard is included and there will be a CRC card for the class.

The team has now entered the class names on CRC cards, but hold onto the candidate class list. Mark items on the list as you rule them out or move them to the core list, but leave the original list intact. An item that seems to be irrelevant at the moment may show up later as a relevant class.

The team now has a set of cards. If the system is small, this will not take much time, but if the system is complicated, the team could spend quite a bit of time finding classes. The facilitator should be sensitive to the mood of the group. If the discussion of classes becomes too tedious, the group can get bogged down by details that will be easier to understand later. In a large system, it is sometimes a good idea to identify the main clusters and then to move on to assigning responsibilities for them. When necessary the candidate class list can be revisited. Additional candidates for the core can be selected and recorded on CRC cards as their role becomes clearer.

ASSIGNING RESPONSIBILITIES

Now that you have a set of core classes, the team can begin to work out the way in which those classes work together to comply with the requirements for the system. Many developers recommend the use of scenarios and role play for the discovery of responsibilities and collaboration. Others prefer to look at each class and write down a preliminary set of responsibilities, sketch in the collaboration, and test their solution with a role play. The deciding factor is often the complexity of the application and the familiarity of the analysts with the classes. If the application is easy to understand and the analysis team already has some idea of what needs to happen, they may find that it is easy enough to fill in responsibilities on the CRC cards before doing a role play. However, if the application is not clear, it may be very difficult to name responsibilities.

In this section of the book, we are going to move ahead with the explanation of what responsibilities are and how they fit on the CRC card. We will also explain how to add collaboration and look for hierarchies. Keep in mind that the rationale for this choice is largely dependent on the necessity to artificially separate elements of the CRC card technique in order to explain them. When you work on your project, you will have to be flexible. If writing down responsibilities and collaboration independent of the use of scenarios proves difficult, abandon the effort and move directly to the development of scenarios and role play described later in the book.

"WHAT and Not HOW"

The first thing that we want to emphasize about the use of CRC cards to assign responsibility is that the level of investigation must be *what* the classes need to do, *not how* they do it. Grady Booch sums this up when he warns, "When considering the semantics of classes and objects, there will be a tendency to explain how things work; the proper response is 'I don't care.'" This is especially important because polymorphism makes it possible to implement the same designated method differently, so you may end up losing much of the power of object-oriented languages if you create false semantic distinctions when naming responsibilities.

Let's go back and take another look at the ancient Chinese tale discussed in the first chapter (Figure 4-2). Remember that there were two approaches to the problem: in this case, one in which two men struggle with the padlock on the gate, the other in which a man evades the lock entirely by vaulting over the wall. Viewed from the perspective of what and how, the men rattling the padlock can be labeled "how" type problem solvers. They are asking themselves "How am I going to get the gate open?" The pole vaulter bypasses their dilemma entirely by asking "What do I want to do?" and answering "I want to get over the wall!" Once he has put the problem in these terms, he can go on to design an implementation that will succeed. His solution is not the only solution, but his problem is the only one that can realistically be solved.

With the word "What" in mind, you are ready to move on and work out the responsibilities for the classes on the core class list. These responsibilities come in two flavors: what a class must know about itself, and what a class must be able to do. In any given project, the team will be addressing both of these at once, but for the sake of clarity, let's divide them and look first at what is meant by responsibility for behavior.

Figure 4-2 **The Ancient Chinese Fable of the Locked Door**

Responsibility for Behavior

Most classes will have to do things; objects in that class will exhibit predetermined behaviors. They will need to do things to meet the demands on the system from the user, to comply with the system requirements. That means that what the classes must do can be extracted from the same sources you used to find classes. In fact, as you think about naming classes, you are also selecting them because of what they do. The only caution here is to be careful not to carry over old implementation prejudices when you look to existing sources for ideas about responsibility. Use them to get started, but only to get started. Once you have a preliminary sense of overall responsibility, move those responsibilities around among classes on the basis of object-oriented values.

In order to maintain a focus on classes rather than procedures, begin to assign responsibility by analyzing a specific class. Write the responsibility down on the CRC card. Don't worry about "duplication of effort." Two classes assigned the same behavior may be an impossible solution in the long run, but they can highlight opportunities for collaboration. They may be a sign of "hot spots" where a nexus of activity must be worked out by trying out different collaboration arrangements.

As you can see, once we have a set of core classes, it becomes very difficult to think in discrete steps about the CRC card technique. Discussion about responsibility merges with discussion about collaboration, and both may lead to modifications in the core classes, renaming classes, and creating new classes. This is why many developers favor moving right to the development of scenarios and role playing.

Responsibility for Knowledge

Although a few classes are limited to responsibilities that are clearly behavior—what they must be able to do, ways in which they will function—many classes also need to be able to supply information about themselves. This is called responsibility for knowledge. If a bank customer wants to withdraw money from her account using the ATM system, some class is going to be responsible for knowing whether the customer has sufficient funds. We had a class, FundsAvailable, in the candidate class list, but decided that this was not a class—that it would have to be the attribute of a core class. Assigning responsibility for knowledge can be understood as the allocation of knowledge of these attributes to the class in which the data is to be encapsulated.

In the ATM system, there is a class named Account. One of the responsibilities of Account may be "know funds available." If any other class needs to know this amount, that class will collaborate with Account. This is how the CRC card technique provides guidelines for the implementation of encapsulation. Note, however, that at this point the knowledge responsibility is still open-ended from the point of view of implementation. Saying "know funds available" implies stored information, but the designers may decide later to make this a calculated value. Conversely, we could call the responsibility "calculate funds available," which would not emphasize or enforce encapsulation of data and might even mean that Account collaborates with another class that knows this information.

The important point here is that responsibilities can be used to flag information and imply encapsulation. They convey an implicit message to the designers at the next stage of the project. When the team goes on to role play the CRC card set, they should respect knowledge behavior and be judicious in decisions to reverse it and introduce collaboration. At the same time, writing down a knowledge responsibility should be based on analysis, not impulse. There should be a reason for assigning knowledge responsibility commensurate with the impact of the capacity for encapsulation on the power and usefulness of object-oriented programming languages.

One caution is not to get sidetracked by listing the values of all of the attributes of a class on the front of the card as knowledge responsibilities. Many classes will have attributes that are not of interest to a particular set of class interactions. List "know" responsibilities that have direct bearing on the domain at hand on the front of the card. If the encapsulation of a particular piece of knowledge is not critical, you can note attributes on the back of the CRC card so that they have been "captured" and do not get forgotten. But these attributes are not key to the CRC card objective. There are no classes that are going to need to access that information, and so there are no implications for collaborations among classes motivated by the knowledge assignment.

Responsibility Detection Pointers

As discussed in the previous section, decisions about assignment of responsibility cannot be made for each class in isolation. Preliminary assignments can be made by distributing classes among team members, but ultimately the whole group has to look at the set of cards and make decisions together. Some teams may find that identifying classes in one meeting, dividing them up among team members, and coming to the next meeting with preliminary responsibilities filled in is a good way to work. In other groups, so many revisions may occur during the group discussion that it is better to set aside more time to work together. We recommend doing as much work as possible in team meetings, unless scheduling constraints make this too difficult.

It is also important to remember that the boundary between assigning responsibility and naming collaborators in this chapter is artificial. We offer some pointers on how to find responsibilities, but they really serve to facilitate the entire mapping process that happens as you use the CRC cards to visualize what is happening in the system. Consider these pointers as work-style guidelines. Use them to improve the utility of the CRC cards, not to introduce rigidity into your analysis practice.

Pointer #1: Brainstorm First, Refine Later

The naming of responsibilities is an extension of the naming of classes. Brainstorming strategies can be as helpful in doing this as they were in coming up with the first class names. The only thing that is different is that the strategy is being applied to a more structured situation. There is already a set of core classes. On the other hand, if work has to be done and there is a responsibility name suggested, it should be included, not excluded, even if a new class is created to accommodate the orphan responsibility. In other words, the byword should again be inclusion and seeking, not exclusion and refinement.

Another side of the brainstorming mood appropriate to naming and assigning responsibilities is that you want to aim for a certain momentum. Do not waste time debating and deliberating the wording of the responsibility. Even if the phrasing feels vague, write it down and use the role play to refine it later. However, do not let creativity become an excuse for cutting off analysis. If there is no clear understanding, it does the project no good to create a mushy set of CRC cards that will fall apart when you try to role play them.

Pointer #2: Think Simple, Factor Out Complexity

If a group has not had a lot of experience with object-oriented projects, the first pass may result in a responsibility allocation that concentrates the bulk of the processing functionality and behavior for the system in one or two classes, leaving other classes largely responsible for knowledge about themselves. If you see this pattern, it is a sign that the analysis is biased by a procedural point of view. The allocation fails to take advantage of polymorphism and encapsulation. In the case of the ATM system, this kind of allocation might result in a bloated Account class that, in essence, coordinates the other classes through a series of collaborations that are really commands masked as responsibilities. The Account CRC card might be written:

Account
Know balance
Verify customer
Authorize transaction
Track activity
Report balance

If this is the case, you may also see classes that are echoes of the Account class responsibilities, rather than classes that define their own behavior. The Withdrawal class, for example, may have the responsibility "Carry Out Cash Withdrawal." When you go on to look at how this affects collaboration, you will see the fanning out of "worker" classes from a "boss." At this point it is difficult to separate the discussion of assigning responsibility from the assigning of collaboration, so you may want to reread this section after reading about collaboration. The point here is that each class should have a distinct role in the system. This ensures a high level of cohesion, a clear sense of mission for that class. To achieve this, you must rethink functionality in the context of a class-driven or class-derived distribution of activity. The goal is to do this in such a way that individual classes have the highest probability of being reused. Their role is clear. They are highly cohesive.

Looking at the Account class with this in mind and turning back to the kind of thinking that produced the core class list, the assignment of so many diverse behaviors to the Account class means that we will have a one-class system. It will be multifaceted, with multiple roles, and it is unlikely that it will be very flexible, should we try to reuse it in the future. To avoid this sort of situation and to take advantage of object-oriented development, the Account class can be simplified by factoring out complexity, reassigning responsibilities to other classes. The Account class has a responsibility "Accept Withdrawal," but the Withdrawal class has the responsibility "Withdraw Funds." The Account class collaborates with Withdrawal, but the Withdrawal itself has a very clear role and might be reused by other classes in the system to "Withdraw Funds."

Factoring out complexity also involves spotting specialized behavior that repeats as you fill out the CRC cards. If the ATM system must be able to capture and respond to user requests whether the user wants to make a deposit or inquire about a balance, that responsibility can be separated out into a class called Form with a responsibility called "ask user for information." In the ATM project in this chapter, the entire user interface has been treated as an interaction with an outside system, so you will not come up against the Form class. However, it provides a good example of how factoring can stimulate new ideas about new classes and simplify or increase the cohesion of classes.

Looking over the CRC cards, you may be surprised by the simplicity of the classes. Responsibilities can be powerful, since collaboration lets others help get things done. So you will find that classes tend to have fewer responsibilities as you get more experience expressing them concisely. One word of caution: If classes turn out to have only one responsibility, reexamine the meaning of the responsibility. Is it really a responsibility that warrants a separate class? Is it something that you want to extract for possible reuse? Or is this an operation that could be assigned to one class, as an operation for which that class is responsible and which no other class is likely to use? In the case of Account, Withdrawal, and Deposit, for example, the decision to assign the actual withdrawal of funds to a separate class allows us to put related responsibilities with the Withdrawal instead of the Account and results in a class that might be used by a number of different types of accounts or to serve as a framework in a future system. The result of this factoring might be:

> Account: know account balance; prompt for source account
> Withdrawal: prompt for amount; accept withdrawals; withdraw funds

You can see already that there has to be some connection between the two classes now. That is how collaboration fits in to complete the picture. When the CRC card for Account is complete, the Withdrawal class will be named as a collaborator on the same line as the responsibility "accept withdrawals." Learning to do object-oriented thinking during the analysis phase means thinking about the opportunities for increasing class cohesion afforded by collaboration. As you move further into this subject, you will see that the CRC cards draw out this kind of thinking by giving the team a visual model with which they can literally see the paths between multiple classes created by decisions made about responsibility assignment for an individual class.

Pointer #3: Use Abstraction to Advantage

As soon as the discussion moves from just naming classes to allocating responsibility, collaboration is not the only trans-class concept that comes into play. You are also going to begin to think about hierarchies of classes. There is a more detailed discussion of hierarchies at the end of this chapter. For now, think of hierarchies as a way to abstract the essence of related classes by seeing where they have common responsibilities, where "common" means that what they do is the same, even if how they do it is slightly different. Or, to put this in object-oriented terminology, look for circumstances in which classes are grouped together because polymorphism makes it possible for them to implement the same responsibility differently. In the abstract, they are the same.

In object-oriented systems, abstract classes can be created for the purpose of factoring common behavior to a single location. This means that there can be an abstract class whose responsibilities are shared by all of the other classes that share those responsibilities. For example, in the ATM system, the similarities between the responsibilities of various transactions could be grouped together and assigned to an abstract class Transaction. The Transaction has a responsibility "execute a financial transaction" which is going to be shared by every subclass of the class transaction. The abstract class Transaction is called a superclass and, as we explained in the chapter on object-oriented terminology, it may never be instantiated. There is no object in the world that is ever of the class Transaction without also being a member of one of the subclasses Withdrawal, Deposit, etc.

Abstract classes are an important part of the effort to make clear and cohesive assignments of responsibility and to take advantage of polymorphism. Look for "kind-of" relationships among the classes on the core class list and consider them candidates for the creation of abstract classes.

Another situation in which abstraction can improve the responsibility load of classes is when there is the opportunity to name a class that is a composite of a number of classes. In this case, the parts are not, strictly speaking, subclasses. There is no inherited behavior, no responsibilities allocated up to the abstract class. However, the signs of the connection will be there, because the composite class will have to know about its parts; it will have knowledge behavior that involves knowing about classes that are "part-of" the composite.

In the banking side of the ATM system, there is no clear example of composites, but if we look at the customer interaction side of things, there is an opportunity to use abstraction of composites to improve class cohesion and allocate common behavior to an abstract class. In the ATM system, the customers interact with the system by using a keypad. There is an abstract class Keypad that is composed of members of the classes NumericInputKey, CancelKey, and SpecialInputKey. The Keypad class is responsible for knowing its own composition—which keys are a part of it—and the Key classes are responsible for knowing that they are part of the keypad. Moreover, the responsibility for knowing which keys have been pressed belongs to the keypad and not to a Key (the abstract class whose subclasses are NumericInputKey, CancelKey, and SpecialKey).

Pointer #4: Don't Marry One Solution, Play the Field First

The most important thing to remember as you fill out the CRC cards is that they are not an end in themselves. CRC cards are part of a technique that facilitates the process of thinking through a system. Filling in the CRC cards helps the team see the system in terms of classes and objects. Assigning is a metaphor, a parallel that lets the user and the analyst work with the designer. They can talk in terms of classes and behavior, when describing systems that may have been documented in procedural language for most of the life of the organization. The CRC technique makes experimentation possible. That is why it is best understood as a tool or technique, and not a methodology or formal notation.

Changing classes and trying out different behavior assignments is what it means to make use of the CRC cards! Even though you are now writing down the responsibilities on cards, you are not making a final commitment. Feel free to experiment with alternative configurations. You can even make multiple versions of a set of CRC cards that can be tested out against scenarios in the role play before you make a final decision. We sometimes use sets of cards in different colors for this purpose. This is not just a gimmick. Taking advantage of the flexibility and gamelike quality of CRC card sets is crucial to their role as a catalyst for better analysis.

Assigning Collaborators

The discussion of responsibility is hard to divorce from the concept of collaboration. Classes do not exist in isolation. They exist as members in a system. The ultimate test of the responsibilities assigned to any single class is how it affects the interaction between classes. This is where the true effectiveness of the system will be tested. This is where the analysis team can use the CRC cards to feel out the impact of thinking about classes on thinking about a system. For every responsibility that you write down, you must ask "Is this a behavior that should be complete unto itself for this class, or must there be some interaction, some collaboration with other classes?" If there is no collaboration, you must ask why, and you must be able to define the responsibility as appropriately and uniquely within the domain of this class.

As you have already learned during the discussion of responsibility, each time you add a responsibility to a CRC card, you make a choice. Is this responsibility carried out by this class alone, or do I need to add a collaborator? If there is a collaborator, write it down opposite the responsibility. However, sometimes these connections will not be immediately evident. You may even be able to see that classes are overloaded and have poor cohesion, but you are not sure where to move which responsibilities in order to sharpen the behavioral focus of the class. In this section, we describe a few strategies that you can use to analyze your CRC cards and make better decisions about collaborations.

Use Scenarios and Role Play

The easiest way to establish paths of collaboration between classes with CRC cards is by setting up scenarios and then using CRC role play to test them. This process is described later in the book in the chapter on role play, "Living the System," so we will not describe it in detail here. Many practitioners move directly to role play and scenarios before even trying to name responsibilities for individual classes out of context. In many cases this is really the best policy. Take the CRC cards for the core classes, make a list of scenarios, and then fill in the cards as you try to role play who does what. For now, however, we offer a few more suggestions on ways to foresee collaboration before working through scenarios and role play.

Collaboration Is a Class Hierarchy Signal

Some developers also find that class hierarchies (described in more detail in the next section of this chapter) are an important signal that there are opportunities for collaboration. We feel that thinking about hierarchies too soon may be confusing. It is better to understand the classes you have first before becoming too involved in abstraction. On the other hand, as you saw already in the case of assigning responsibility, in practice analysts will use whatever concept suggests itself as they examine the system. If, in analyzing the responsibilities of the classes, hierarchies emerge, they cannot be fully understood without tracing the paths of collaboration that follow. Grady Booch sees hierarchies as a basic and early clue to collaboration, so we include a brief summary of his ideas here.

Booch uses hierachy to find collaborators in a few different ways. First, he suggests that you look up and down a hierarchy: down through the subclasses to carry out more specialized responsibilities, or up the hierarchy to classes with more generalized responsibilities. The ATM provides an example of this when you name the superclass Transaction and give it the responsibility "execute financial transaction." It is going to collaborate with the specialized classes Withdrawal, Deposit, etc., to complete its work. Booch also suggests that you look for responsibilities that are shared by peer classes that collaborate with one another (Form, Keypad, DisplayScreen). In the same way, if you have a responsibility that you are trying to analyze, look for ways to break down its structure. Identify subsets of behavior or knowledge that could be factored (distributed) among collaborating classes.

Dependencies Are Collaboration Clues

Collaborations can also be discovered by thinking in terms of dependencies. If a class has to assume responsibility for an action, it often depends upon another class for the knowledge needed to fulfill that responsibility. That knowledge has been appropriately assigned to another class (encapsulated), so the first class depends upon the latter for information. If Account knows about balances, then any other class in the system that needs to know about a balance or change a balance must collaborate with Account. While this may seem cumbersome as you work through the CRC cards, it is a key benefit of object-oriented strategies. Data is hidden, encapsulated, and protected so that, ultimately, only one class can change it.

Clients, Servers, and Contracts Map Collaboration

The concept of collaboration is based on the idea that the groups of classes defined for the system are going to get work done by coordinating with each other so that each class serves as a specialist in its area of knowledge and behavior. To make it easier to visualize these paths of interrelationships, many object-oriented methods use the terms client and server. Wirfs-Brock talks about this in terms of a contract between a client and a server. Booch uses a similar vocabulary, identifying the client as the class that uses the resources and the server as the class that provides resources. In either case, there is a relationship whereby one class is relieved of responsibility for carrying out some portion of behavior necessary to the overall operation because it can request that another class, a collaborator, fulfill that responsibility. It is also possible to see classes as collaborators who negotiate together in order to carry out actions.

At this stage in the analysis, before creating the scenarios and testing them in CRC role play, collaboration possibilities may not be self-evident. Thinking in terms of clients and servers can help get the team started. Look at each card and ask: Are there responsibilities here that could be assigned to another class, a server, so that this class is less complex and more cohesive? Is this class responsible for too many different and diverse behaviors? Is the scope of information implied by the knowledge responsibilities too broad? Can this be improved by collaborating with other classes for which the required behavior or knowledge is more relevant?

We already saw an example of this in the do-everything version of the Account class. If Account is absorbing most of the operational behavior of the system, ask, "What other classes could we create that could do some of this work, that might know some of this information or know how to carry out some of these responsibilities?" If the responsibility is assigned to another class, then Account becomes a client, and that class is the server; the server name is written on the CRC card as the collaborator. (Note that the client name is not written on the server CRC card, because a server does not care who—what class—requires the service.)

At the same time that you are asking which responsibilities of a client could be assigned to a server, think about which responsibilities need to stay with that client because of its knowledge about itself. For instance, the Account has a responsibility to know its balance. We have decided that this is the appropriate class to encapsulate that knowledge. That means that even though we create a WithdrawalTransaction class to know about doing withdrawals, it must collaborate with Account if it needs to know about the balance. In other words, a class may be the client in one collaborative relationship, and the server in another. Client and server describe roles in a particular collaboration, not the role of a class in the overall system.

The idea of contracts can be useful for keeping track of client server collaborations. Even if the connections are written on the CRC cards, they can be hard to recreate once the analysis discussion is over and the team moves on to another path of collaboration between a completely different group of classes. Wirfs-Brock suggests naming each client–server in a contract. Figure 4-3 shows sample contracts for the Account class in an ATM system. During role play, contracts offer a rapid map between classes for the "actors" who are trying to run through scenarios to see if the collaborations on the cards work.

Adding Responsibility and Collaboration to the CRC Card

As the team members come up with responsibilities and spot collaborations, these should be written down on the CRC cards. The responsibilities are written in any order on the left-hand side of the CRC card. The collaborations are recorded by writing the name of the server class next to the responsibility on the client class CRC card. This notation highlights the fact that in order to complete the named responsibility, the client class must enlist the services of the server class. There is no class name listed as a collaborator on the server's CRC card, since the server will carry out the collaboration. If you do not use the client/server approach, you can view collaborations as objects working together through meaningful messaging to negotiate the completion of their responsibilities.

It is easy to see that the rules for recording the responsibilities and collaboration reflect the bias toward reuse. In order to reuse a server, that is, to have an additional client class that collaborates with the server class, no changes need to be made to the existing class or its CRC card. The notation also makes it easier to assess the level of cohesion of a class. If the CRC card is crowded with many responsibilities and few collaborations, there should be a special reason for concentrating so much responsibility in one class. Although the

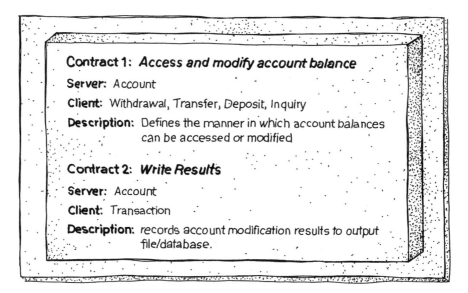

Contract 1: Access and modify account balance

Server: Account

Client: Withdrawal, Transfer, Deposit, Inquiry

Description: Defines the manner in which account balances can be accessed or modified

Contract 2: Write Results

Server: Account

Client: Transaction

Description: records account modification results to output file/database.

Figure 4-3 **Collaboration Contracts in the ATM System**

class may collaborate with a few other classes, it will be very unlikely that any class will name this class as a collaborator. The profusion of behaviors probably will not recur, so this class becomes too idiosyncratic and specialized for reuse. Yes, there should be specialist classes in the system, but they should not specialize in complex packages of diverse behavior.

At the other extreme, remember the warning about narrow-minded specialist classes that have one responsibility. They will occur and are certainly reusable. However, do not use them to mechanically break up a complex class or to accommodate operations that are difficult to assign. Treat one-responsibility classes (often with no collaborators) as a working or draft CRC card. Keep your eyes open for opportunities to assign that behavior to an appropriate home. However, do not be shy about creating working/draft CRC cards in the first round. They may be hard to assign correctly until you have done a role play.

When you have written out the cards, look over the collaborations. At this point, you may know that a particular class needs to turn to a collaborator, but may not be sure which class that will be. Either make a note in the collaboration column or create a draft class and CRC card. You will see that even if two cards end up with the same responsibility written down, the appropriate assignment will be determined during role play. The CRC card set that you have at this point is a rough model of the system. It is a baseline for role play and may have contradictions. In fact, the first version of the CRC cards should be used intentionally to capture contradictions and spotlight areas that need to be cleared up during role play.

Identifying Hierarchies

Now that the classes have been mapped out on a set of CRC cards, the team is ready to test out the relationships they have defined by doing a CRC role play. However, before looking at that process, it may be helpful to spread out the CRC cards on a table and investigate inheritance relationships. The concept of abstract classes discussed earlier can now be used to link up some of the superclasses and subclasses in hierarchies. Hierarchy graphs can be drawn by hand or by using an automated tool.

There are four analysis guidelines that can help you decide when to try to create a hierarchy. Some systems are easy to understand in terms of hierarchies and make good use of abstract classes. Look for these opportunities, but do not feel that you need to force unlike classes into a hierarchy. The point of showing hierarchies is to take early advantage of the polymorphic nature of object-oriented systems. The more that you work with object-oriented development, the more quickly you will see chances to use hierarchies and polymorphism right from the beginning. Just be aware that a false assumption about this relationship will do more damage than good. CRC cards that are not interdependent may be artificially linked and become hard to unravel.

Look for "Kind-of" Relationships

One clear example of a hierarchy in the ATM system includes all of the classes that are a form of transaction, as shown in Figure 4-4. This is a "kind-of" hierarchy in which there

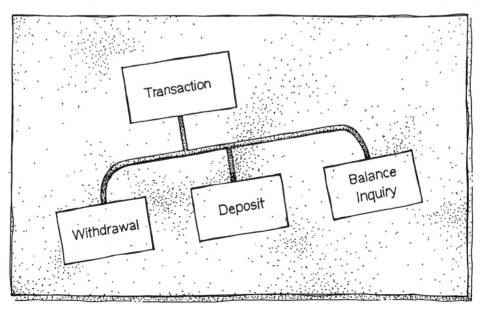

Figure 4-4 A "Kind-of" Hierarchy

is an abstract class that has been assigned a number of responsibilities that are common to all of the subclasses, to all transactions in the system, even if some of those transactions have additional, specialized behaviors.

The class at the top of the hierarchy may be a regular class, that is, a class that will be instantiated in an object that is a member of that class. However, if you look at the Hierarchy graph for Transaction, you may notice that any transaction object in the system is going to be a member of one of the subclasses. There will never be a transaction object that is only a member of the Transaction class. For this reason, Transaction is an abstract class. It will never be instantiated. In a sense it is a holding place for the common responsibilities of its subclasses. It is a notation that illuminates the recognition that we can use polymorphism here to reuse methods for objects of the superclass in objects that are members of the subclass. For this reason, the recognition of "kind of" hierarchies is very important to effective, truly object-oriented analysis.

Do Not Confuse "Kind-of" Hierarchies with "Part-of" Relationships

In many instances there is a class that needs to know about other classes because they are its parts, but it does not share any behavior with those classes. Because there is no shared behavior, there is no inheritance implied. In fact, parts classes may behave very differently even when they do share some of the same collaborators. What a "part-of" relationship can tell us is that the class representing the whole may need to know about its parts, and so will collaborate with them.

Using these criteria, a Withdrawal is not "part of" a Transaction, so we have not made a mistake in this case. At the same time, we can see that when we develop the reporting system for the bank customers, the Withdrawal class may be "part of" a class called Statement. It may also be a "kind of" LineItem. As you can see, all of these relationships are concepts that we use to analyze the system. A class may be a member of a number of hierarchies, and it may be a "part-of" class at the same time.

Name Key Abstractions

When we factored out complexity in order to focus the responsibilities of a class on a clearer, more cohesive task or task combination, we used abstraction to identify common elements of multiple classes. This led to the naming of abstract classes and the drawing of hierarchies. It is another way to find "kind-of" relationships. It is also a good way to identify abstract classes that do not draw on colloquial ways of talking about the system domain in the way that Transaction does. An abstract class generally serves to collect behavior and knowledge which can be shared by classes below it in the hierarchy.

Another situation in which abstract classes can improve the CRC card set is when there is a single class that chooses between behaviors depending upon circumstances. This kind of choice can make maintenance much more difficult. Instead, create an abstract class and distinct subclasses which behave differently. One of the subclasses may simply inherit common behavior and have no responsibilities of its own, while another class inherits the common behavior and also has additional responsibility.

For example, there is a class in the ATM system called Form that captures the user information. If the domain experts indicate that some users want to be able to fill out the form without seeing the information on the screen (to insure privacy), rather than add a behavior for securing input, create a class called SecureForm that has no additional responsibilities, but which will know how to execute any of the behaviors of its superclass, while providing the additional privacy. This hierarchy could then accommodate additional form requirements as they arise by introducing new subclasses of Form.

Look for Frameworks

The analysis of existing frameworks can help us to see new frameworks, collections of classes, among the members of the candidate class list. Existing frameworks can lead you to the identification of collections of classes that can be reused as collections with little modification. One element of the framework that helps in this identification process is what we call a pattern. If you develop a good pattern vocabulary, you can spot these frameworks and see how they apply to your new system. This lets you take advantage of successful patterns, rather than reinventing them. The more you work with object-oriented systems, the larger your vocabulary will be, and the more easily you can use frameworks and patterns to evaluate and group classes for a new system without starting from scratch. Researchers have found that this can substantially lessen the magnitude of the development effort.

In most cases, the classes you develop will fall into previously discovered patterns. Some of the books on patterns and frameworks, especially those by Pree and Coad, will be helpful to the team when you look for your own frameworks.

SUMMARY

Starting with a set of candidate classes based on brainstorming, we showed how to winnow out a set of core classes. The group identified the critical classes, based on a review of the system scope and looking for "hot spots" and patterns. A set of questions were asked of a "good" class, which helped discern responsibilities and collaborations. Finally, we showed that arranging classes into hierarchies and discovering new frameworks and patterns will help. Choosing and defining the core classes are a key element in object-oriented software development.

Chapter 5

A Case Study in Stocks and Bonds

This chapter tells the story of an analysis team as it uses CRC cards to analyze the requirements of an investment portfolio reporting system. Many of the team members have had little or no experience with object-oriented technologies. The choice of a group of novices is meant to emphasize the way in which the process of writing the CRC cards helps them think in terms of classes instead of procedures. We hope that it will also help you warm up to CRC.

In this example, the group follows a rather rigid approach, filling in the CRC cards section by section. The point of the case study is to clarify the use of the elements on the CRC card. To show what kind of analytical problems can be solved using the CRC card technique, the novella moves deliberately. We concentrate on the basic principles for forming a team and getting started with CRC. This includes brainstorming the CRC cards, but stops short of CRC role play. Following the next chapter, which discusses the role play, a second case study jumps in in midstream. That group has already written their CRC cards and wants to use role play to test and refine their choices.

The chapter includes nine important elements: (1) a description of the CTS system case, (2) selection of the project CRC team, (3) warming up the team, (4) brainstorming candidate classes, (5) identifying core classes, (6) assigning responsibilities, (7) assigning collaborators, (8) identifying hierarchies, and (9) looking ahead to the next step. Most sections start with some "Tips" that consolidate the concepts discussed in the previous chapter.

SAVER, SOONE, & EAYRNE'S CYBER-TRADING SYSTEM

Saver, Soone, and Eayrne is a midsized brokerage firm with offices in 10 major U.S. cities. SSE partners have always been proud of their ability to match a traditional, hands-on brokerage with a host of high-technology services. George Eayrne III, 46, who inherited his share of the business from his father and grandfather, provides the eyes and ears for top management on technology issues. His older partners, Thurmon Saver and Thomas Morgan Soone, look after the larger, lifelong clients.

In keeping with the flow of the industry, George has convinced his partners that they must offer on-line access to their customers. As a pilot for a full-blown cyber-trading system (CTS), SSF plans to bring account statements on-line by the close of the fiscal year. However, tradition is a significant force in the firm, and many account representatives are reluctant to see CTS become the major trading channel. They pride themselves on a personal touch for every account. At the same time, being practical men and women, they see the opportunity to increase sales by focusing on bringing new accounts to the firm rather than filling the day with routine trading calls. To ensure the success of the project, John Nyrd, VP for Systems, has insisted that the traders be included in the development process. His Senior Manager, Bill Teckke, suggested they begin analysis with CRC card sessions, a technique he has read about in *Object Magazine.*

Selecting the CRC Team

Tips on Selecting the CRC Team
Pick a team open to change
No more than six people:
    Domain experts (1–2)
    Analysts (1–2)
    Experienced OO designer
    Facilitator and leader

George Eayrne III actually accompanied Bill Tekke to a one-day, high-level executive introduction to object-oriented technology, and he is really worked up about these new ideas. This is good because it gives the CTS project a high profile and top-level support, but Bill would have preferred experimenting on his own before subjecting himself to George's scrutiny. As a buffer, he has assembled his team carefully. They are skilled people with a commitment to the firm and, best of all, high receptivity to change. Let's get to know the team members:

Ben Yu: Ben is Bill's idea of a strong technical person. He will head up the design and, ultimately, write the code for the new system. Ben has five years' experience coding in C++, but he is also new to the firm. Bill plans to team Ben up with Jane for the final design. Bill had planned to bring in a second designer in order to give as many people as possible start-up experience with CRC, but John Nyrd would not let him, arguing the project has to be staffed in proportion to its pilot status.

Rick Getgoe and Tasha Harrison: Bill chose his sharpest analysts to get the project off the ground. Rick will be with the project full-time from start to finish. Rick doesn't know a lot about object-oriented technology, but he has been to a couple of five-day courses and he is an avid reader. He has been tinkering with the concepts and knows something about Smalltalk libraries. Bill still hasn't decided whether to go with Smalltalk or C++, but whichever way he goes, Rick will do fine. Rick also has a good people personality. He can warm up a user like a used car salesman closing on a high-priced Cadillac. He has bedside manner and a good sense of humor, but he never loses sight of the bottom line.

Tasha does not have Rick's charm, but she has a couple of years' experience on customer systems, and she knows which bells and whistles have paid off and which have not. She is a favorite on the user side and has a talent for teaching. Bill regularly has her teach user-training courses, and he counts on her to run the documentation effort. She is new to object-oriented technology, but she is a quick study. Tasha has already read up on CRC and, in her practical manner, has mapped out a meeting schedule with key users.

Lila Wills and Brig Sale: The users on the team are the least comfortable factor for Bill. He has most of his contact with high-level managers, but Tasha was adamant about keeping the work with the traders and account representatives. Rick added his charm, agreeing to do a few managerial-level presentations while they brought in front-line users for the CRC card process. So, based on Rick and Tasha's recommendations, there are two new faces seated at the table. Lila is an old-timer from customer accounts; Brig Sale is a top trader. Bill knows that Lila is skeptical about letting users dabble with accounts on-line, but Brig is hot for bringing the whole process on-line. In the end, this should balance out and result in an accurate but forward-looking system.

Jane Bright: Jane finished a master's degree last year through the employee education program. She has been with the company for six years. For her master's project she completed a small system for tracking trading productivity using Smalltalk. She has also worked in C++ and promises to be the guru for the project. Jane is knowledgeable in OO, bright, and has great people skills. Everyone on the IS staff respects her.

In total, then, there are five team members, plus Jane as the facilitator. The team is an even balance of know-how in technology and know-how in the business. Since CRC is an informal technique, the differences between users and technical people will be leveled by their ability to spot different things about the work to be done.

Warming Up the Team

CRC Warm-up Tips
Give everyone a chance to participate early on
Take time to let the group get comfortable with each other
Avoid technical details; do not jump ahead
Set clear objectives and expectations

Bill Teckke opened the first project meeting with a short overview of the project. "We are going to focus the pilot on the system customers will use to review their portfolio," he explained. "We don't want to bite off more than we can chew. We also want to stick to applications that are information-based. We'll move on to accepting trades and really moving dollars once we have some experience with object-oriented techniques under our belts."

As a warm-up, Bill returned to his project plan and opened the floor for comments. However, before he could begin, senior partner George Eayrne III himself showed up. He gave the team a taste of his enthusiasm and support, slapped Bill on the back, and hauled him off to lunch at the Executive Club.

Jane slipped right into place as the facilitator, leaving Bill to his fate. She started the session with a round-robin of introductions. Even though Bill had presented his version of the team, Jane wanted to set a good tone for CRC analysis by getting everyone talking for themselves right from the start. She followed up the introductions with a brief overview of the way the team meetings would run.

"Just to keep you oriented," Jane explained, pointing to the whiteboard behind her, "I'm going to reserve this space at the top of the board for the current objective. I'll write this down at the opening of every meeting, and if someone wants to modify it, we'll do that before we get into the day's work."

She wrote "Agree on Preliminary View of Pilot" and opened the floor for comments on the Project Plan. She knew that this would be an easy topic for everyone to talk about. It would let the team members get to know each other and give them a feel for her style as a facilitator.

Brig Sale was the most enthusiastic. He jumped in right away with some suggestions for the real-time trading and began to launch into a discussion of problems he felt that they would have to look out for.

Jane was about to cut him off when Rick stepped in and, with his usual charm, steered things back on course, suggesting that before they worried about that, maybe they should just focus on the on-line account review portion. He reminded them of Bill's opening comments and the need to move ahead cautiously: "We can get our feet wet first in that area without running the risk of getting involved in trades. I can see that Brig has spotted some key areas for study. That's why we want to keep the first piece small."

Tasha chimed in to agree, but pointed out that account history could be a pretty big piece. Lila Wills backed Tasha up on that, and Ben Yu jumped in to say that he could see some real risks if they start trying to mess with that data without more knowledge of OO database management. Brig pooh-poohed the data problems, but Lila sided with caution and held up the banner of tradition and personal service.

Jane was pleased. Although the discussion might seem to be laced with controversy, she wanted team members to feel free to express their differences—just so long as the items at issue were relevant to the problem being solved. In this line, she could already see that she would have to curb Brig's tendency to race forward!

"Not only is there a lot of data involved," she pointed out, "but part of the account representatives' feel for the customer comes from talking them through an account review. I am OK with this on-line statement and I know that more automation is coming, but a traditional firm like SSE does not have to be the first one to dive into uncharted water!

"Let's not get caught up prematurely in technical details," she continued. "I'd like to focus on the CRC process. We can begin with the designated piece and, later on, when we have a feel for what classes and responsibilities are all about, we can decide whether we need to broaden our scope. We'll use CRC to get a sense of how complex the on-line statement segment will be."

To bring things back together and include everyone, Jane suggested they take a voice poll on the present project plan and see how the group felt about it. It was important to her that the group meeting end on a point of consensus and with a sense of progress.

"OK," Jane went on, "for the next meeting, everyone collect whatever documentation you can, and we'll begin to brainstorm about classes." Lila got a worried look on her face, so Jane wrote a specific list of items on the flip-chart and asked for volunteers to sign up for each source area. The list they drew up included the following information-gathering assignments:

Rick: Make copies of official system request and collect relevant memos
Tasha: Review current system documentation
Lila: Collect samples of current reports
Brig: Interview Account Reps and collect samples of notes and forms
Ben: Collect database information, file layouts, etc.

Everyone seemed eager to get to work, so Jane let them go. All of the team members now understood the project, and they had concrete assignments for the next meeting. Jane hoped to continue this pattern, balancing the informality of CRC with clear-cut task assignments between meetings.

Brainstorming Candidate Classes

CRC Brainstorming Tips
Have complete requirements resources on hand
Be sure the objective is clear
Don't censor ideas; record them
Don't get sidetracked by details prematurely

Jane began the brainstorming session by polling the team members. She purposely went around the room allowing each person to speak, in order to set the tone for the participatory style she felt would make CRC fun and productive. Briefly, the team members brought the following items with them:

Rick:
Six copies of the Systems Requirement Request
Memos about portfolio reporting needs and on-line trading

Tasha:
Account Report Tracking (ART) current system documentation
Notes from interviews with Account Reps about reporting requests

Lila:
Sample ART customer report
Printout of Trading Screen (ART)

Brig:
Sample folders with Traders' notes developed to "help" them use ART
Interview notes from meetings with Traders

Ben:
File layouts
Database documentation

The team began by reviewing the "Official System Request" shown in Figure 5-1. They read through the document and underlined things that might be classes. Tasha objected that a number of items were not relevant because the pilot would be restricted to phase 1, but Jane suggested that they err on the side of inclusion during the brainstorming part of the meeting.

Jane decided to continue with her team-centered approach. She wrote the day's objective on the board: "Brainstorm Candidate Classes." Next, she explained briefly for the sake of Lila and Brig that a class could be anything that might be part of the tracking system. "Think of classes as things, as nouns. Look through the documents we have so far and find nouns. To get started, let's review the brainstorming basics and get to work." Jane taped a poster with the Brainstorming Steps, and the Brainstorming Principles, on the wall.

Brainstorming Steps
1. Review brainstorming principles
2. State session objectives
3. Round-robin ideas
4. Discuss and select

Brainstorming Principles
1. All ideas are potential good ideas
2. Think fast and furiously first, ponder later
3. Give every voice a turn
4. A little humor can be a powerful force

```
OFFICIAL SYSTEM REQUEST        Saver, Soone & Eayrne Securities
System Name:  Cyber -Trading System    Department:   Customer Account Tracking    Date of Request:    4/1/96
Manager:       Josephine Branch-Barton    Extention:    x4747      email:    xBB@sse.com
new project   X   upgrade _____  maintenance

General Description - Justification for Request:
    The merger with BBQ Bank and Investment Corporation has increased the volume of the account tracking and trading
activity to the point where person to person response to account inquiries and trading requests is placing very heavy
demand on staff.  During the six months from June 1, 1995 to December 1, 1995, system down-time interrupted work
as frequently as 7 to 10 times weekly. This not only angers customers, but increases account representatives' and traders'
productivity due to the burden of callback necessary to fulfill our policy of personal service for our customers.
    A new, automated inquiry and trading system with on-line dial-up privileges for customers with modems could alleviate
many of these staff hours.  While this would change our personal service image, any damage to our traditional image
would be offset by our ability to meet the demand for interactive services.  The proliferation of on-line services at competing
institutions has not only left us behind in productivity; it is placing us at a disadvantage in competing for new accounts
and retaining old ones.
    On this basis of meetings with the Executive Board and a report by Technology Assessment consultants, a new trading
and reporting systems knowm as the Cyber Trading System has been approved.  This system will be introduced in
three phases as specified below:

    Phase 1:  On-line Account Review (available by PC/modem)
         • Display Complete Account Statement      • Allow Inquiries for Individual Holdings
    Phase 2: Trade Review (available by PC/modem & by telephone)
         • Review Pending Trades            • Obtain Pricing Information
    Phase 3: Trading (availaable by PC/modem & by telephone)
         • Submit Orders (Initiate, Cancel)       • Hypothetical trading (Trial Portfolios)
```

Figure 5-1   **"Official System Request" for the Cyber-Trading System**

"What we are going to do is to brainstorm classes. That means we are going to write down the names of as many things that are in the system as we can think of and list them here. We're going to do this by going around the room and looking at what we have in front of us. Start by spotting nouns, anything that could be an object in the system. Give them to me quickly. Don't worry about accuracy. We'll sort them out later. Lila, you can start."

Jane chose Lila as the first person because, as an expert on the system domain, she could get the group rolling and keep the momentum up as items got harder to name. The first couple of rounds went fast. Jane wrote the classes on the board as people called them out.

Within a few minutes the team had identified 15 candidate classes. Although experience told Jane that some of these were not really classes, she said nothing and encouraged the team to keep adding more items.

Even with Jane's encouragement, Rick had to pass. Ben and Tasha also passed, but Lila's trading expertise stood her in good stead. She pointed out that the class "interest" did not apply to all of a customer's holdings.

"Can we have dividends and interest as different classes?" she asked.

"Sure," Jane replied, "as long as we can distinguish between them when we look at their behavior—that is, they are not two words for the same thing, two names for one set of responsibilities. And remember, classes will be instantiated by real objects, so I'm going to write dividend in the singular. A dividend is the candidate."

"In that case," Brig jumped in, "what about 'gain' and 'loss'?" Jane wrote them down. This started the group rolling again as they came up with a string of nouns associated with the determination of gain and loss, including *purchase price, sale price,* and *cost basis.*

Looking over the list again, Tasha frowned and, in her practical way, pointed out that there was no customer information such as name and address.

"Is that really part of this system?" Rick asked. "I mean, we aren't responsible for changing addresses or anything. For all intents and purposes, they are accounts with numbers."

Jane added customer name and address to the list. "We're brainstorming," she said, talking over her shoulder. "No deciding about yes/no yet."

"In that case," Rick jumped in, "what about the screen the user sees?"

Jane added "customer screen" to the list and polled the group. She let them sit for a few minutes. Rick suggested a few more items that he had underlined in the System Request. In the rush of brainstorming, they had forgotten some of these items.

When Rick was done, Jane went around the room once more and everyone passed, so she declared the candidate class list complete. The team's candidate classes included the following:

Account	Interest	DateofPurchase
Customer	Buy	StockPrice
CurrentPrice	Sell	CustomerInquiry
Stocks	StatementPeriod	Dividend
Loss	Gain (Long Term/ Short Term)	
Bonds	DateofMaturity (Bond)	Trader
CustomerName	CustomerAddress	AccountRepresentative
CustomerScreen	TradingRequest	Order
PendingTrade	TrialPortfolio	

This was a big list, and certainly contained items which would not be classes in the final analysis. Jane could see that the group was ready to start picking out the core classes from this list of candidates.

Selecting Core Classes

Core Class Selection Tips
Start with classes for which there is consensus
Evaluate candidates against project scope
Distinguish attributes from classes
Look out for phantoms and ghosts, surrogates and aliases
Get ready to assign responsibilities
Take advantage of frameworks and patterns

"Now," Jane explained, "we are going to review the Candidate Class list and select those classes that are indisputably part of the system. I'll refer to these as critical classes, because without them the system does not make sense. As we select classes, we'll write each of them on a class card. I'll pass out these index cards, and then we'll just go around the table writing down the class names."

Before beginning to discuss the list, Jane saw an opportunity to teach a little bit more about object-oriented systems. She pointed to the list and said, "Looking at the list, I see some not-so-subtle differences between the candidate classes we have named. For example, look at the class Account. It is going to have to have responsibilities like reporting its balance. A class like Stock may have to calculate dividends. This means that classes are not selected just because they are nouns, but because they are nouns that refer to things that do something, that can be described by their behavior."

Jane passed out the cards and showed the group a sample CRC card to remind them where to write things down. She returned to the concept of encapsulation and suggested that responsibilities that did not "fit" any of the candidate classes might indicate missing classes. "Brainstorming is meant to produce an exhaustive list, but it is still only a start," she explained. "As we work through the analysis using the CRC cards, we will think of new classes. We may even create classes that make sense in terms of the CRC cards, but which are not obvious to us because we are influenced by ART, by the old system."

The team chose several critical classes from the candidate class list. They were all items that showed up in the old ART reports that could not be eliminated in any new system. These classes included:

Account	Stock	Bond
Customer		Cash
Interest		
Dividend	Buy	Sell
Gain	Loss	AccountRepresentative

The next thing that Jane suggested was that they review the scope of the system. She placed an overhead on the projector that showed the three phases of the CTS development. These phases were (1) on-line account review, (2) on-line trading, and (3) trading projections. Looking over the phases and comparing them to the candidate classes, the team eliminated several classes that were outside of the scope of the first phase: PendingTrade, TrialPortfolio, TradingRequest, and Order.

"I hate to count myself out of the picture, but if we are just reporting on accounts," Brig asked, "do we really need the Trader and the AccountRepresentative?"

Lila pointed out that each Account "belongs" to an Account Representative and that each "Buy" and "Sell" needs to be credited to a Trader in order to calculate commissions. Ben agreed, but pointed out that this would be done by a different system. The idea of different systems was confusing Lila, so Ben sketched out the diagram shown in Figure 5-2. He pointed out that any class name associated with a box was a part of the domain of another system.

This brought them right up against the issue of the Customer and the problem of access. Tasha could feel the auditors breathing down her neck. If they were going to put these account reports on-line with modem access, there had to be very tight security. Rick pointed out that each account is tied to a customer, so they could control things by including access information with the Account class. "We don't really care about the customer in

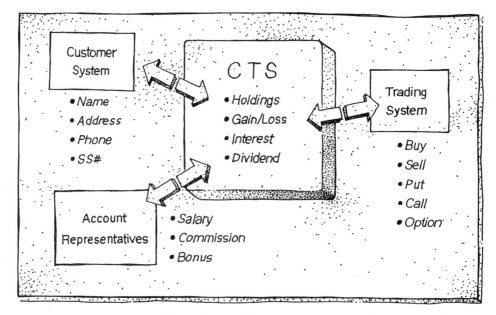

Figure 5-2 *System Scope of the Cyber-Trading System*

that way," he argued. "All we care about is that there is a limit on who can view an account. It doesn't matter if they are a customer or an Account Representative from the point of view of this system."

Jane suggested that they name a class to deal with account access and to remind them to resolve this when they analyzed responsibilities. Ben wrote out a card for a class called AccountAccess. He didn't like making up what might prove to be red-herring classes, but Jane was right. Including a Customer and an Account Representative would be even more misleading. On the basis of the inclusion of the new class, the team agreed to eliminate Customer, CustomerName, and CustomerAddress from consideration as core classes.

Brig was beginning to pick up on the idea of scope, so he suggested that they drop a lot of the details about Stocks and Bonds from the list. Lila disagreed and pointed out that there are certain things a Portfolio Report needs to include, like the Stock Price, Dividend, Interest, Gain, and Loss. Jane seized the opportunity to remind the team about the difference between attributes and legitimate classes.

The group was divided on what to do with the candidates that fell into this category. Lila liked the idea of listing attributes on the back of the cards, but Rick had read that this could be a waste of time, and could also lead to a premature dismissal of items that looked like attributes now, but which turned out to have behavior that would be important to the system—that is, legitimate classes.

"I'd put Customer as an attribute of Account," Lila suggested with a laugh. "Around here, the customer is really just something we know about an account. That's personal service!"

"I think that we're getting sidetracked," Jane said, interrupting a round of jokes that followed Lila's comment. "We have that AccountAccess class. Let's see what happens later when we sort out responsibilities and collaboration. For the moment our mission is to evaluate the rest of the candidate classes."

The team was now comfortable enough to tackle some of the more ambiguous class selection issues, so Jane asked if anyone had any comments on Buy and Sell. Tasha was in favor of including them as classes because she felt that the customer reports included a section that listed "buy" and "sell" items. "This is a report on trading activity, so we have to have Buy and Sell," she concluded.

Lila agreed that these were classes from the point of view of trades, but pointed out that from the point of view of account reporting, they were things that were done to stocks or bonds. "I'm getting confused," she said. "I am not sure how to separate the classes from the things they do. This is really a different way of thinking!"

"You're right," Jane said, seeing a chance to do a little mentoring on OO for the domain experts Lila and Brig. "We have to decide what is going to be the subject of our system. What is going to determine the point of view. Do I want to say that a 'buy' is a class that can 'acquire some type of holding,' or do I want to say that a 'stock' is a class and it can be bought and sold? What makes sense in this system?"

"Here's another way of seeing it," Brig interjected. "I think in terms of an account that buys or sells, not a stock that gets bought or sold. If I were a company issuing the stock, then it would be different."

Ben went along and noted that the database tracked buys and sells for an account, not for a stock. "I don't think we ever look at things from the stock's point of view. We don't have queries like 'for a given stock, who bought and sold it?' That might be useful for trading analysis, but it is not relevant to this system."

"What it means," Rick added, "is that we have a thing called an Account, a class. That class can record the addition (buy) and deletion (sell) of stocks, bonds, whatever. The stock is a class too, but it does not buy and sell itself—at least, not until we get to the system that permits on-line trading."

"In that case," Tasha suggested, seeing it differently now, "I want to keep Account as a class, but let's take 'buy' and 'sell' off the class list. They might be responsibilities, but they are not core classes."

Jane could see that the discussion was not going to clear up until they moved on to responsibilities. Jane pointed out that whatever they decided, it was one solution to a problem, not an absolute.

The session had been going for almost two hours, so Jane followed an old premise for teamwork by cutting things off while they were going well. She didn't want the group to get too tired, and she knew that putting together chains of collaboration and determining responsibility would be harder than just naming classes. She also wanted each of them to think about the system on their own before working on the problem as a group, so that the pressure to get something done did not lead team members to go along with things they didn't really like.

In keeping with her policy of setting clear goals, Jane announced, "Before the next meeting, I would like everyone to write down as many responsibilities as you can on the CRC cards that you're holding. Write them down on the lines below the class name, skipping one line under the name. We'll use that space to identify superclass and subclass relationships at a future meeting. The next meeting will focus on making sure we have the right classes doing the right things so the system really fulfills its objectives."

Assigning Responsibilities

Responsibility Allocation Tips
Focus on "what," not "how"
Don't overload; factor out new classes instead
Take advantage of polymorphism: the same name for the same
    behavior
Take advantage of inheritance: hierarchies show class
    relationships
Take advantage of abstract classes: generalize common behavior

Responsibility Detection Pointers
1. Brainstorm first, refine later
2. Think simple, factor out complexity
3. Use abstraction to advantage
4. Don't marry one solution, play the field first

By the next meeting, everyone had their CRC cards filled out. To make things easier, since this was a first project, Jane had asked each person to prepare an overhead foil as well. Another alternative would have been to enter them into the automated system and use the projector, but Bill Tekke had indicated that he wanted to stick with the paper cards for this first pilot.

Jane reminded Bill that starting too soon with standards that required diagrams and formal methods had not worked well before. Jane opened the meeting by suggesting that Tasha lead the run-through of the cards, since she would be leading CRC training sessions in the future. Tasha put the Account class card on the overhead viewer first.

Account (preliminary)	
Verify customer access	
Record stock and bond buys	
Record stock and bond sales	
Determine interest	
Determine dividends	
Calculate gain/loss	

"Wait a minute," Lila said, "I have 'calculate gain/loss' as a responsibility of the Stock class!"

Tasha laughed. She was beginning to see that Jane had set them up by starting with Account. If they put everything that the system does in order to report the contents of the portfolio in the Account class, using classes was not going to be much of a help in analyzing the system. The Account class responsibilities looked a lot like the functional bubbles on the high-level data flow diagrams for the old ART system.

"This is where it gets interesting," Jane explained. "Let's think in terms of the connections that let one class do something and another class use that information through a request. Rather than discussing Account, let's go to a less expansive class. Lila, put up your CRC card for the Stock class on one viewer and the CRC card for Bond on the second viewer, and I'll show you how this works."

Stock (preliminary)	
Know current price	
Know dividend rate	
Know purchase price	
Know date of purchase	
Calculate current value	
Calculate gain/loss	
Calculate dividends	

Bond (preliminary)	
Know current price	
Know interest rate	
Know purchase price	
Know date of purchase	
Calculate current value	
Calculate gain/loss	
Calculate interest	

"Wow," Rick exclaimed, "those classes look really overloaded too! Do we need to set a limit on the number of responsibilities?"

"You can't just dump these things," Lila protested. "They are basics. The list is not really very long."

"How long is long?" Jane asked rhetorically. She could see Ben smiling to himself. Did it all boil down to the old discussion of how many lines of code to a module and how long should a program be?

"The idea is not to set a number right now. We'll leave that to the metrics people and the designers. However, we may be able to use the idea of inheritance to get us away from this trend toward overloaded classes. We can take advantage of polymorphism to make a better allocation, but before we do that, what happened to Buy and Sell?"

Rick had those class cards. He showed them to the group:

Buy (preliminary)	
Know stock/bond name	
Know purchase price	
Know date of purchase	
Calculate closing date	
Calculate commission	

Sell (preliminary)	
Know stock/bond name	
Know sale price	
Know date of sale	
Calculate closing date	
Calculate commission	
Determine gain/loss	

Ben suggested, "The things that a Sell and Buy do, their behavior, are not relevant to the business of Portfolio Reporting. I suspect that as classes, they are not relevant to our system. They are the work of the trading system. All we need for reporting is the after-the-fact information. I vote for Buy and Sell as Stock and Bond class *attributes*, things they know. Besides, you shouldn't have a separate class which has only data and no responsibility."

"For now," Jane concluded, "why don't we stick with purchase and sale knowledge as part of the responsibility of the Stock and Bond classes. We may go back on this later, but let's just see if we can identify superclasses that do things common to a number of subclasses. Let's try to see how responsibilities can be passed down through a line of inheritance."

"What about grouping all of the types of holdings together?" Brig asked. "Seems to me we can say, at some level, that the items in the portfolio are all holdings and they have to have some behavior in common."

"Great," Jane encouraged him, handing Brig an index card and a blank overhead foil. "Let's create the Holding class. And under that we have StockHolding, BondHolding and so on."

"Is a StockHolding the same as a Stock?" Lila wondered aloud. Her original class card seemed to be losing potency fast.

"Well," Brig said, "you could say that a stock, the Stock class, is really just the stock itself, regardless of whether it has been bought by a particular account. Holding is the superclass, and StockHolding is the subclass. Whenever a Stock is added to an Account, a new instance of the Holding superclass is created because a new instance of the subclass StockHolding now exists. StockHolding and its superclass Holding are distinct from Stock, the class that is instantiated in a particular stock regardless of whether it is held in any given Account."

"Right," Jane chimed in seeing another chance to teach the team some basic concepts. "The way it works is that we can have a StockHolding class that knows, for example, how many shares are held in an account and when they were purchased. The Stock class knows the price and the dividend, and it can calculate the annual yield. That way, the fluctuation in day-to-day price and dividend is kept separate, encapsulated, in the Stock class. When StockHolding needs to calculate income, it can ask the Stock to report its yield information. For the same reason, you may want to list a responsibility 'report yield' rather than 'know'."

Tasha put up two new foils and named them Stock and StockHolding. As the team settled on responsibilities for each, she wrote them down.

StockHolding (preliminary) Superclass: Holding	
Know purchase price	
Know number of shares	
Know purchase date	
Calculate current value	
Calculate income	
Calculate gain/loss	
Display attributes	

Stock (preliminary)	
Know current price	
Know description	
Know dividend	
Report yield	

"Let's see if we can do the same for Bond," Ben suggested. "My Bond class looks a lot like the first version of Lila's Stock. Let's redo that one and create BondHolding." The team then wrote the new class cards.

"We still haven't settled the issue of whether gain/loss is calculated here or by Account," Rick pointed out.

BondHolding (preliminary) Superclass: Holding	
Know purchase price	
Know commission	
Know purchase date	
Calculate income	
Calculate gain/loss	
Calculate current value	
Display attributes	

Bond (preliminary)	
Know current price	
Know description	
Know interest rate	
Report yield	

"You're right," Jane conceded. "Let's think about polymorphism for a minute. That is the capability of having two classes with two responsibilities that have the same name, but which require different implementations in each case. For instance, in the case of both StockHolding and BondHolding we have a responsibility 'calculate current value.' It is the same in essence, but the exact way that it gets implemented for a StockHolding and a BondHolding will be different. To put it in programming terms, which really only matter to Ben right now, that means that we can send the same message to two objects. They will each know what to do, how to implement that message."

"I'm almost beginning to see a little of what happens in the programming side," Lila exclaimed, a bit amazed. "We're looking for common behavior even if it is not carried out in exactly the same way. If that's the case, I think that 'calculate gain/loss' is another case of polymorphism."

"Right direction," Jane encouraged, "but we can be even more general in that situation. Is there even a difference in implementation of that responsibility? Couldn't we say that both BondHolding and StockHolding can inherit that responsibility from Holding?"

Tasha put the Holding overhead on the viewer and began to write.

"That is sort of strange," Brig mused. "You are never going to have a Holding as such. Isn't it always going to be a BondHolding or a StockHolding? I see that you can generalize these responsibilities, but why?"

"This is called an abstract class," Jane explained. "In this case, you are right. The class Holding will never exist, never be instantiated. Every Holding must be a BondHolding or StockHolding; the abstract class Holding will never be instantiated. Abstract classes do not always generalize to this degree, but sometimes it is useful to create an abstract class as a way of identifying these common responsibilities. We can do this because all of the sub-classes share common behaviors, even though they may be implemented differently. This is an example of polymorphism. In this way, the CRC cards can send very clear information to the design team. In the system there are objects that belong to classes which are exactly the same, which are similar, and which are completely different."

"OK, now back to Account," Brig said. "What is left for that poor class to do anymore?"

"What about the roll-up information?" Lila asked, holding up her copy of the ART report. "I see that there has to be somewhere that we calculate out net figures for these accounts. That would include all of the individual instances of StockHolding and Bond-Holding."

Rick began the discussion, "It may be that we have to have some class that buys and sells holdings when we do the trading system, but for now, we just get that information from the old system. That part will be Ben's worry. We just read the results and display the current status of the account."

Ben rolled his eyes. "You're right. We are going to have to get the data from the existing trading system so it is definitely not something the Account class in this system has to do. I'm going to have to meet that requirement for now with an interface to the trades database."

"I think that we can use the Holding CRC card to guide us," Lila said. "We can create an Account responsibility for Net calculations that is parallel to the pattern we have for Holding, BondHolding, and StockHolding. Of course, no matter *how* Ben decides to do it, Account will have to know *what* holdings it has."

Lila dictated, and Tasha wrote the new Account responsibilities on the overhead. When everyone agreed that it looked right, Brig created a new index card for Account.

Account (revised)	
Identify all holdings	
Calculate value	
Calculate gain/loss	
Calculate earnings	

Lila frowned. "I'm still worried about that access issue. How do we know who is looking at the account? Can we get back to that?"

"I've been working on this," Ben offered. "I think I have an idea for the Account-AccessTransaction class. My idea is that it is very similar to the Transaction class pattern I read about in a book on object frameworks. The class will have the responsibility to check user authorization for the reporting system. We can let this class send messages to Account for the reporting work to be done. It will interface with the existing security software to check if the user 'isAuthorized' for this account, and also to report attempted security breaches to the auditors. When we get to the design, the security experts and I will figure out how to do this. All we need now is a class that tells us that before information is viewed, the access has been verified." Ben gave Tasha an overhead foil with his version of Account-AccessTransaction.

AccountAccessTransaction	
isAuthorized	(outside security system)
accountReports	Account
auditCall	(outside security system)

"We did a good job today," Jane complimented the team. "We are at the point where we need to coordinate the interdependencies between classes to be sure that we have assigned responsibility in a way that makes sense. Let's call it a day and come back with fresh minds. But before we break up, I'd like to poll the group and see how this is going for each of you." Jane let each member of the team comment briefly on the day's work. She summarized their ideas on a flip chart, identifying a few questions to get to in the next session on collaboration. The work was hard, and she wanted to be sure that everyone left feeling progress had been made.

Assigning Collaborators

Collaboration Tips
Hierarchy signals collaborations
Identify clients and servers
Collaborations complement responsibilities
Add collaboration as you see connections between classes
Collaborators are pathways tested through scenarios

Jane began the session by reminding the team that, in most situations, CRC cards would include discussion about collaborators in the same session in which they assign responsibilities.

"I purposely postponed writing down the collaborators," Jane explained, "because this is our first project, but once you see how it works, the two steps will be heavily intertwined. For example, when we analyzed the Stock class, we ended up thinking about classes that would have to collaborate with Stock. If you think of a class that is important, identify it on a card, even if you are not ready to work out all of the details at this stage of the project.

"You can see how collaboration can help us determine what interface classes we need. In this case, we know we have to add a class for security, which we've called Account-AccessTransaction. At this point, we do not need to work out all the logistics of handling security. But let's get back to the Stock and StockHolding classes and see if we know what their responsibilities are!"

Jane put the overheads for the CRC cards Stock and StockHolding on the viewers. She wrote Stock in the right-hand column of the StockHolding card across from the responsibility "Calculate current value."

"Remember that we placed responsibility for knowing price with Stock. That means StockHolding will have to send a request to Stock for the price on the day that the current value is calculated."

"Won't the same thing be true for income?" Lila asked. "The yield information has also been assigned to Stock?"

Jane added Stock to the right of "Calculate income" in the collaboration column of the CRC card for the StockHolding class.

StockHolding (preliminary) Superclass: Holding	
Know purchase price	
Know number of shares	
Know purchase date	
Calculate current value	Stock
Calculate income	Stock
Calculate gain/loss	
Display attributes	

She placed the Bond and BondHolding CRC cards on the viewer, and the team filled in the same collaboration pattern: "Calculate current value" and "Calculate income" both show Bond as a collaborator.

"Now what about Holding?" she asked.

BondHolding (preliminary) Superclass: Holding	
Know purchase price	
Know commission	
Know purchase date	
Calculate income	Bond
Calculate gain/loss	
Calculate current value	Bond
Display attributes	

At first Rick thought that Holding should collaborate with both Stock (for price information needed to determine gain/loss) and StockHolding. Ben pointed out that you don't need to collaborate with Stock if you can get the current value from StockHolding. "When we look at gain and loss, we go to StockHolding for current value, and then StockHolding goes to Stock for price."

Ben looked pleased. He could see that they had a good sense of the chains of collaboration involved. Although users would never fully appreciate the intricacies of his job, at least these CRC cards let them all talk about the same classes and told him what he needed to know to make his database more airtight and error-proof!

Now the group looked over the set of CRC cards again.

"We still haven't done collaborations for the Account class," Brig pointed out, lifting the third version of this CRC card from the table. "We show that Account is responsible for calculating the totals, the value of the Account. Where does it go for the information?"

Tasha suggested Account should ask Stock and Bond, but Rick reminded her of the pattern that they established with the Holding class. The team decided that Account should follow the pattern, by asking the Holding class to report back. Holding would be able to collaborate with specific StockHoldings and BondHoldings, and so on to Stocks and Bonds, as necessary. This is, after all, the whole idea of a collaboration path through different classes. Each class knows how to do its own work, and how to collect its own data.

Account (revised)	
Identify all holdings	Holding
Calculate value	Holding
Calculate gain/loss	Holding
Calculate earnings	Holding

Jane again reminded them how polymorphism would support these collaborations. "We can have a responsibility called 'Calculate value' which will be implemented differently for Account and for Holding. This clarifies our view of the system and allows us to call attention to similarities. In the long run, this also increases the opportunities for creating reusable classes. Use difference to identify subclasses, but don't make false distinctions. Let names and inherited responsibilities convey what's being done."

Identifying Hierarchies

CRC Hierarchy Tips
Explore "kind-of" relationships
Name key abstractions
Separate mixed classes where necessary
Place super/subclass sets in hierarchies
Look for reusable behavior (frameworks and patterns)

In the context of discussing sameness and difference, Jane seized the opportunity to go over the idea of hierarchies. She described the way in which CRC cards can be arranged in hierarchies that help the team visualize inheritance relationships.

"In the case of our pilot project for CTS," she explained, "things are fairly simple and we only have one hierarchy, but as you expand the project, you may want to use hierarchy graphs to keep track of these relationships."

The team picked out the members of the hierarchy immediately. They placed the CRC cards for Holding, the superclass, and StockHolding and BondHolding, the subclasses, on the table in the tree shape shown in Figure 5-3.

Brig wanted to put Stock and Bond farther down the tree, but Ben objected. "Remember," he pointed out, "we purposely made those two independent classes that encapsulate data used by members of the hierarchy, but that do not inherit any responsibilities."

Brig conceded that this was true, and, looking over the cards, he saw that Stock and Bond were not subclasses from the point of view of this part of the system. Everyone agreed that when they got to the trading side of the project, they were going to see all sorts of hierarchies among the types of holdings bought and sold for accounts. Fortunately, all of that complexity could be tackled later, after they had seen the pilot account report project through.

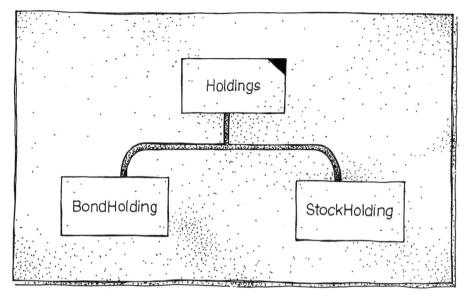

Figure 5-3 **A Class Hierarchy for Holdings**

Account (final)	
Identify all holdings	Holding
Calculate value	Holding
Calculate gain/loss	Holding
Calculate earnings	Holding

AccountAccessTransaction	
isAuthorized	(outside security system)
accountReports	Account
auditCall	(outside security system)

Holding (final)	
Calculate value	StockHolding, BondHolding
Calculate income	StockHolding, BondHolding
Determine gain/loss	StockHolding, BondHolding
Display attributes	

StockHolding (final)	
Know purchase price	
Know number of shares	
Know purchase date	
Calculate current value	Stock
Calculate income	Stock
Display attributes	

BondHolding Superclass: Holding	
Know purchase price	
Know commission	
Know purchase date	
Calculate income	Bond
Calculate current value	Bond
Display attributes	

Stock (final)	
Know current price	
Know description	
Know dividend	
Report yield	

Bond (final)	
Know current price	
Know description	
Know interest rate	
Report yield	

SUMMARY

The Cyber-Trading System is now ready for role play. The next chapter maps out the process by which a group comes up with scenarios and uses them to try out the classes and collaboration patterns written on the CRC cards. Role play is really the heart of the CRC technique. During role play, many of the questions that have come up while the team is writing the card can be answered by trying out alternative solutions.

We have purposely kept the Cyber-Trading System case study small to demonstrate how much can be learned from a tightly focused pilot project. The role play for the team should proceed smoothly. Instead of following the Cyber-Trading System through to the final stages of CRC card analysis, we are going to discuss the basics of the role play in the next chapter and then, in the following chapter, introduce you to another, more complicated project.

Chapter 6

CRC Role Play: Living the System

Filling in spaces on CRC cards does not guarantee that the model the team has selected will address all of the demands that will be placed on the system in day-to-day operations. An interactive, dynamic modeling strategy that mimics the interaction between classes when work is being done can ensure accuracy. CRC role play extends the CRC technique by using the CRC cards as the basis for acting out the system. Scenarios give us the advantages of prototyping without writing any code.

In many projects, CRC role play is actually used to develop the CRC cards, as well as to test them. For the sake of teaching the technique, we introduce role play after the first version of the CRC cards has been written. In other words, in terms of project sequence, you could follow the strategies already discussed for brainstorming classes when developing CRC cards, and then test them using a role play. Alternatively, you may choose to jump right in, develop a list of scenarios, and write the CRC cards as you begin to role play those scenarios. In either case (or in any combination of the two approaches), the reasons behind the role play, and the teamwork process involved, are the same.

We again offer guidelines that summarize the key points in each section of the chapter. In the case of role play, which depends on group dynamics and which must, therefore, adapt to each particular set of people and each organizational culture, these guidelines should be used to strengthen group spirit, not to inhibit group energy.

Successful role play depends upon an understanding of and respect for interactive learning theory and strategies. For this reason, we have divided the chapter into sections, some focused on that theory and others on practice, to show you both why you're doing things and how to do them. In each case, we encourage you to enhance our suggestions and improvise your own as your team gains role-playing experience.

THE THEORY BEHIND THE PRACTICE

Before undertaking a role play in your organization, it is important to understand why and how this technique works. We have seen some unfortunate projects try to do a role play without this foundation. Inevitably, these groups abandon key elements of the technique because neither the facilitator nor the participants really understand why they are crucial to success. For example, warming up the group may seem silly when "everybody already knows each other." Similarly, mechanical parts of the technique, such as holding your CRC card up in the air if it is your turn to act, are tempting to abandon because they often make people feel self-conscious.

To make it easier for teams to do role play, we recommend that everyone read over this chapter and talk about how role play works. Even in groups that are used to working with CRC cards and role play, it may be worthwhile for the facilitator to remind the group about guidelines and principles at the beginning of role play for a new project. In work, particularly in the context of computers and program languages, it is easy to fall into mechanical behavior, and from there it is a long and difficult journey to the kind of active and energetic thinking that produces good systems. Take a few minutes out from project plans, charts, and timelines before you role play, to jump start the energy with some creative thinking and even a little philosophical discussion.

The Problem of Shared Meaning

One of the key qualities of good communication is shared understanding. The objective of any analysis technique is to help the analyst and the user communicate. To the extent that the user and the analyst are both able to interpret the meaning of the system in the same way, the system will be constructed on a common foundation. Often, problems encountered at the time of system delivery can be traced back to poor communication early in the analysis stage.

One way we try to avoid miscommunication is by reviewing system requirements documents. However, sometimes the miscommunication is based on misinterpretation of the written word, that is, two readers review the same document and see different things. Data dictionaries are critical to structured methods because they guard against misreading, but nonetheless, whether we write paragraphs or label diagrams or fill in CRC cards, the ambiguity of language plays a part. We need some way to test meaning and create common interpretations.

As a case in point, we can turn to Lewis Carroll, who uses this conundrum as the key to his wonderful story *Through the Looking Glass*. Early in her adventures, Alice encounters a character named Humpty Dumpty who engages her in a discussion of his view of the world. Alice becomes frustrated by the way that he uses words because his labels (his classes) seem to have a completely different meaning (or behavior) from hers. Exasperated, she tries to argue with one of his words. "Glory," Alice objects, "does not mean 'a nice knock-down argument' . . . ."

Her point is sound—if you think that words somehow have intrinsic definitions that are obvious to everyone. However, the lesson that Alice is in Wonderland to learn is that meaning is not stable. Humpty Dumpty reinforces this lesson telling the bewildered Alice, "When *I* use a word . . . it means just what I choose it to mean—neither more nor less."

Anyone who has tried to work on a large system knows that things quickly conform to the Humpty Dumpty model. Teams that choose the CRC card technique are no exception to the rule. Before a set of CRC cards can be used as a reliable backbone for design, the terms that have been used to record ideas need to be tested out and cleaned up. The team needs to be sure that all its members—users, analysts, and technical people—are reading the same meaning into the names of classes, the scope of responsibilities, and the chain of collaborations.

CRC card role play is one of the best weapons a team can use to avoid the Humpty Dumpty miscommunication tar pits. Using the CRC cards as a script, the team "dramatizes" a series of scenarios. If there are not enough classes (missing actors), more may be added. If classes need to do more or less (add/delete responsibilities), these changes can be made and the role play can be repeated until it runs smoothly. If patterns of collaboration seem awkward or just plain wrong, they can be corrected. When the role play is complete, everyone on the team agrees that the cards mean what they say and say what they mean.

The effectiveness of role play as a guarantor of meaning is so strong that many organizations choose to begin to role play as soon as they have developed enough candidate classes to initiate a scenario. For example, as soon as we know that an ATM system involves

Figure 6-1 **Humpty Dumpty's View of the System**

an Account and a Withdrawal (a key framework), we can try to play out the scenario "customer makes a withdrawal" and fill in the CRC cards as we go.

Beware the Limits of Working Alone

All good magazine editors know that even the best intentions cannot protect us from the tendency of the human mind to fill in what it expects to see. Reading over written text or looking over diagrams to check for errors is a tedious and seemingly impossible task. Even with spell-check, grammar-check, and elaborate CASE tools, small mistakes and even major oversights often elude detection. That's why even the *New York Times* runs a small box of corrections in every issue! That's why no matter how many times you look over the system requirements specification, no matter how much money you invest in CASE tools, and no matter how skilled your staff, the final system might come up short.

We can learn something that will help us here from those magazine editors. They have some time-tested tricks of the trade for copy editing. For example, in many proofreading situations, one person reads the text aloud while a partner reads the printed page silently. As the silent reader hears the spoken word, he can spot places where the mind of the first reader has filled in a phrase or corrected a word that is not in the written text. By working together in an interactive situation, the two editors are able to catch more mistakes than either one could spot working alone.

The same principle applies to the review of the CRC cards. If you want them to be accurate, you will be wise to involve multiple people and to use a system that gets them all involved interactively. Just reading over a set of CRC cards does not fill the bill. Each member of the team must *actively* make use of the same information at the same time, if the verification method is going to work.

Active Learning: The Rationale for Interactive Review

The respect for the value of active learning began with Socrates, who rejected the traditional didactic methods of imparting knowledge. Instead of telling his disciples what to think, he provoked them with questions that led them to discover the ideas he wanted them to learn in their effort to respond to his questions. Zen masters use a related practice by teaching in the form of paradoxical stories. Listening to the story and pondering the paradox leads the student to a flash of insight that conveys meaning in a way that moralizing and lecturing cannot.

Figure 6-2 shows a continuum of learning styles common to many analysis practices. On the continuum you can see that there is a reverse relationship between the degree of involvement and the ability of people to understand the system (comprehension), come up with ideas (innovation), and catch errors (verification).

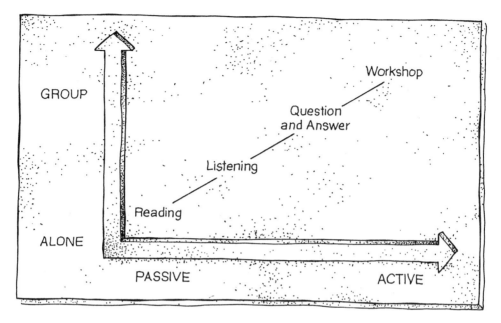

Figure 6-2 ***The Learning Continuum***

Figure 6-3 shows the analysis/learning continuum with specific CRC card styles added to the diagram. The CRC role play has all of the strengths attributed to active learning patterns. It is an effective reading-aloud technique. Every member of the group must do something (perform the role of a class), which forces them to think more about the meaning of the words on the card. In addition, because all team members are working simultaneously, misinterpretations will surface quickly. This is what makes the CRC role play a kind of prototype. During the role play the team members actually get a feel for what is going to happen when the information on the CRC cards "goes live."

You can see from this quick look at learning styles that simply reading over a set of CRC cards is not a good way to evaluate them unless you have a very small system. Role playing the CRC cards is the best way to honestly test the meaning behind the cards. Role play is the core of the CRC card technique, the part of the process that makes this simple idea so effective that even many proponents of complex formal methods agree: CRC cards work!

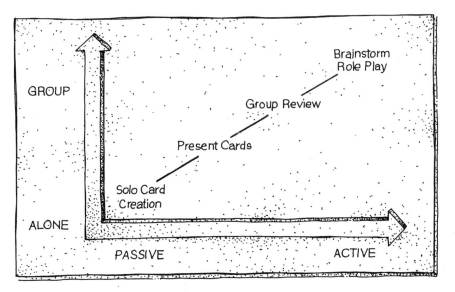

Figure 6-3 **Passive Versus Active CRC Analysis**

How CRC Role Play Works

The Basic Steps of CRC Role Play
Step 1: Create list of scenarios
Step 2: Assign roles
Step 3: Rehearse scenarios
Step 4: Correct CRC cards and revise scenarios
Step 5: Repeat steps 3 and 4
Step 6: Perform final scenarios

CRC card role play involves six major steps. First, the team draws up a list of scenarios that will provide them with a line of action. The initial list does not need to be comprehensive, especially if the role play is being used to fill out preliminary CRC cards. However, before the analysis process is over, you should develop a complete list to confirm that the CRC cards allow the system to meet all of the demands or routine operations and major exception handling.

After the scenarios have been listed, each team member is assigned the role of one or more classes. The CRC cards for those classes are given to the actor (step 2). Next, using the scenario as a script, the team acts out the behavior and collaborations written on the cards (step 3). Performing the part of their classes, team members make requests when there needs to be a collaboration, or announce what they are doing themselves. If a behavior or piece of information is missing from the card, the action is interrupted and the CRC card or cards involved are corrected. This cycle (steps 4 and 5) is repeated until the action flows smoothly. When basic scenarios run without interruption, the CRC cards are used to role play scenarios for the less common scenarios and major exceptions (step 6).

The CRC role play is very different from a structured walk-through. Instead of listening to the presentation of a scenario by one team member, everybody gets involved. Often the roles assigned involve cards that the actor did not write. As a result, the review process is distributed among all of the members of the team, and taps into the knowledge of everyone in the group.

Above all, the objective of the CRC role play is to make the class interactions accurate by making the process of discovery more interesting! Based on what we know about human learning styles, in almost any situation people will pay better attention if they are participating. Just for fun, let's return to Alice again and see what happens to her when she is asked to role play in the Queen of Hearts' croquet game.

When Alice arrives on the grounds of the royal palace, she is assigned the scenario "play croquet." Her behaviors are defined by the possession of a flamingo mallet. Presumably she can now fulfill the responsibility of scoring points. However, when she tries to play her role she finds that the responsibility of scoring involves hitting a hedgehog (the ball in this game) with her flamingo mallet. This proves to be all but impossible. Even worse, her collaborations do not follow any useful pattern. She is never sure when it is her turn, or why it is her turn, or who is talking to her. When the Queen sends the message "Off with their heads!" Alice has no way of knowing if this message is meant for her or for some other unlucky player!

In sum, whether we are Alice or analyst, acting out a scenario is an excellent way to test validity. During a role play, team members will find that, like Alice, they see places where the action is muddled and confusing. When "looking over" the cards is supplanted by "acting out" the system, faulty logic inevitably surfaces. Of course, there are always a number of alternative solutions to follow. CRC cards do not provide absolute answers, but they do force the team to try out (and really see) the repercussions of alternatives. If, in fact, the optimum mallet available is a flamingo, at least we know exactly what we are up against. At best, by putting all our heads together, we can come up with a better solution.

DEVELOPING THE ROLE-PLAY SCENARIOS

> **Role-Play Scenario Basics**
> Concentrate on "must do" first
> Develop "can do if" to handle contingencies
> Record "might do" to test flexibility
> Explore exceptions last
> Frequently assess

A scenario is like the script of a play. Scenarios are a way to work out the dynamics of the system by scripting what has to be done, and the order of events. Scenarios are an orderly sequence of class interactions which meet a specific need in the problem space. They define the way classes work together to accomplish goals. It's not necessary, and sometimes not even possible, to have every possible scenario written in advance. Often, as we go through the role-play process, new scenarios jump out when one member of the group says "Wait! What if . . . ."

The development of a complete set of scenarios is key to getting results from CRC role playing. Creating scenarios draws on the same exploratory thinking we used when naming classes. Approach the development of scenarios in the same way. For instance, purposely configure your work space so that it encourages brainstorming and open thinking. Set up flip charts, and be sure there is ample space on a whiteboard. As a group, list routine scenarios. Use this as a warm-up, then select those scenarios that touch central frameworks and label them "must do."

Once the obvious "must do" scenarios are recorded, the team will inevitably come up with borderline cases, scenarios where the routine activity will go on only if certain conditions can be met. These nests of conditional scenarios should be separated out from the straightforward scenarios and written on a second chart or board as "can do if" items. For emphasis, it helps to use a second color for the list. Some of the items on this list will be routine activity circumscribed by efforts to ward off exceptions; other items will tend to be exceptional activity that occurs very infrequently. As the team starts thinking in this direction, place a star by items that are rare and discuss whether or not they belong on the third list.

The third list is the "might do" list. The scenarios on this list are combinations of situations that may be so complex and/or unusual that they are not necessarily going to fall within the boundaries of this project. Others may be scenarios that are not yet necessary, but which you can expect to see down the road. These scenarios may not even be part of the initial CRC role play, but as the CRC cards stabilize, they spur the group to identify new scenarios. These new activities may look as if they are outside of the scope of the project. Don't worry. List the scenarios. The team may not use them right away, but they are important. Once the basics of the system are in place, role play of those scenarios with the existing classes can give the team a sense of the flexibility of the system design and its adaptability to change (i.e., reuse and enhancement). You don't have to spend a great deal of time detailing these cases. In fact, you shouldn't!

Ward Cunningham has proposed "abuse cases" as useful in uncovering scenarios which provide useful insight into the system's interactions. By "abuse," he means the construction of scenarios which are unusual, difficult to handle, or otherwise potentially bothersome. Abuse cases have the potential to uncover poor collaborations you've built, as well as showing the need for interactions the team didn't yet discover. This is a potentially innovative approach which is worth trying.

You'll never be able to act out every possible scenario, so your group will have to pay attention to those that are most important. These are the scenarios which involve key classes, so that they will be helpful in gaining insight into the system (what we call the "Aha!" moment). How many? On a large system, up to two baker's dozens; proportionally less for smaller systems. Ivar Jacobson has done the most work on scenarios and what he calls use-cases, and his book is worthwhile reading for at least the facilitator. Although we use many of his strategies for organizing the scenarios, CRC is more of a discovery technique than would be permitted by a strict application of use-cases.

When brainstorming does not yield any more use-cases, go to the "must do" list and, if it is longer than six items, identify six key scenarios for the CRC role play. Remember the work that was done in naming classes (especially if you are using role play for the discovery of responsibilities and collaborations). For example, the project team for the ATM system would do best to focus first on a standard withdrawal scenario, already identified as a framework, because any CRC card solution must meet the requirements of this scenario. Once the team knows that the CRC cards work for a standard withdrawal, they can move on to other sorts of inquiries and, eventually, to exceptions such as withdrawals where there are insufficient funds.

Drawing up the list of scenarios is another checkpoint for scale. If the lists of "must do" scenarios and "can do if" scenarios are very long, the project may need to be subdivided. CRC can be and is used for large systems, but in smaller chunks. Also, role-play sessions will bog down if you attempt too many scenarios in one sitting. Probably, the team will already have a sense of this in the number of classes, but if role play is used to explore classes, you may not realize that your scope is too broad until you begin to list scenarios. A large number of classes in a limited set of scenarios may be doable, but if the number of scenarios is also large, then inevitably, as you work through the role play, the number of classes will mushroom exponentially and the analysis effort will be undermined. The process of the role play will help the team see what is going on between classes, but if there are too many classes, the ability of the group to comprehend and evaluate patterns will diminish and the technique will not be as effective. (For more on this issue, see the upcoming chapter on managing CRC projects.)

THE THEORY OF "AHA!"

Role-Play Session Pointers
Clarify goals and objectives
Make sure team members are comfortable
Promote new ideas, encourage discovery
Confusion is rarely permanent

Once the team has a list of scenarios, they are ready for role playing. The CRC cards will be actively edited. Each scenario is initiated by an actor (a team member) who plays the role of a class and sends requests to other classes in an effort to meet the requirements of the scenario. Before explaining the specifics of carrying out the role play, we are going to review the basic premises of the technique. Acting, even in this limited context, is difficult for many people. A savvy facilitator will review the rationale and goals of the role play with each new group. This ensures that everyone is comfortable with the process and understands the expectations. If a member of the team is still anxious about using the method, assign them a role that is less active (minor classes), or to classes which do not come into play until the second or third scenario.

The Psychological Model

Role playing is a strategy borrowed from interpersonal psychology for conflict resolution. During the 1980s, with the increased emphasis on diversity in the workplace, human resources experts started looking for ways to prompt people to learn more about themselves. They developed a self-discovery approach based on the educational values derived from the Socratic method of teaching through questions. However, in a role play the idea of making the students learn by doing is taken further. There are no leading questions. Instead, the members of the group act out hypothetical situations playing any of a number of roles: themselves, their co-workers, their managers, or their customers. Group members gain an understanding of how people feel and behave in different situations. This leads to self-correction based on self-knowledge, a much stronger, long-lasting route to insight than passively receiving criticism from someone else.

In systems development, our mission is less ambitious, or at least less psychological. Unlike counselors, we do not seek hidden fears or deep emotions. The part role playing has adapted is the idea of interaction, the idea that we can achieve better understanding of a situation by acting it out. In the case of CRC cards, we are looking for ways to expose assumptions about how the domain is organized so that we can come up with more effective allocations of behavior, find ways to make a group of classes work more efficiently, and use patterns that are flexible and responsive to change.

Some team members may have had experiences, positive and negative, with role play in human resources workshops. Be sure that they understand that role play in CRC uses the process as a way to clarify the interaction of classes, and to discover collaborations. It is not, in any way, a test of the participants. The role play should be fun, a game that converts the tedium of review into entertainment and that, by the way, yields insight.

Confusion Is Rarely Permanent

The enthusiasm for role play in all sorts of situations is based on studies which show that when people work on a problem, they tend to repeat old habits even if they think that they are trying something new. For instance, a person may find that the kind of reactions that are problematic at work are the same ones that get him into trouble at home. The same thing holds true for role play of systems. We may find that no matter how new the domain, we cling to old ways of organizing things. This is the very opposite of the intelligent reuse of frameworks or patterns. In psychology, they say that someone is "stuck in a rut"; in systems, we might say the same thing. Role play is one strategy that psychologists have found for helping people see habitually repeated behaviors and for motivating them to search for new solutions.

The spirit of experimentation in CRC role play is crucial. At the heart of the discovery process is that valuable phenomenon role-play experts call the "Aha!" experience. When a person sits outside of a situation or reads about it, they can compartmentalize and rationalize or ignore chunks of experience. When a person acts out a scenario, the actor becomes caught up in the action. It's not quite the same thing as the adrenaline rush that allows a small boy to lift a timber off of an adult in a burning building, but the acting-out side of the role play stimulates the brain. Solutions that might otherwise go unnoticed surface. Unexpected connections occur. People say "Aha! This is how we can do it!" or "Aha! Here's the mistake in our thinking!"

In this way, role playing brings the power of active learning to the analysis experience. Instead of listening to each team member "report" on a slice of the domain (passive), the team tries out the script, and everyone gets involved (active) in thinking about the whole system. This is particularly effective in object-oriented systems because classes are not very meaningful if they don't collaborate. When the group follows through a scenario, preconceptions about how a class might be configured, what its responsibilities "should be,"may be jarred loose, and unexpected possibilities for paths of collaboration may emerge. The "Aha!" moment may occur!

The power of this phenomenon increases with the complexity and novelty of the application. In their discussion of the Buy and Sell classes in the case study for portfolio reporting, the team had some trouble discovering their key classes. One way of handling this kind of confusion in a CRC card analysis session would be to move into a role play. If the team had tried to role play the Buy and Sell class, they might have found that (1) it was difficult to name scenarios for these two classes that fell within the scope of the Reporting System, and that (2) scenarios for critical frameworks such as determining loss and gain needed to know if a Holding had been bought or sold, but did not involve the Buy or Sell class at all. Aha!

Figure 6-4 **The "Aha!" Moment**

As you read the more complex case studies, you will see that naming classes and filling in class cards often leads to false assumptions that are not corrected until they are spotted during role play. This is what makes the CRC card technique fun. Whether you fill cards in and then role play, or use the role play earlier, you will see that role play generates insight and rewards the players. Over time, this assurance creates confidence in the technique itself. Team members eagerly dive into role play no matter how fuzzy their idea of the system, assured that acting out the classes will reduce confusion and lead them to at least one solution, and possibly to multiple alternatives.

ROLE PLAY: PERFORMING THE SYSTEM SIMULATION

> **Running an Effective Role Play**
> Stick to the scenario
> Limit the time
> Always warm up
> Separate acting from analysis
> Assess the results

Three activities borrowed from psychological role plays are helpful during CRC role-play sessions. Each session begins with a warm-up, moves into enactment (the actual role play), and concludes with an assessment. The enactment-assessment activities may be repeated several times when a number of scenarios are used. Stick to these activities all the time. Including all three activities in all role play sessions is valuable because it forces a deliberate style on the CRC review process. In the analysis phase of a project, systems review has a tendency to be haphazard. Unlike the testing of code, the testing of tools such as CRC cards is rarely systematized. As a result, many parts of the system are treated as self-evident. The requirements documentation is scanned, and obvious problems are discussed, but the entire package is never really verified. The result is that the final system exhibits inexplicable errors in the most unexpected places.

For this reason, although it is tempting to run through the CRC role play without consciously including all three activities, we do not recommend such a casual approach. We encourage teams to learn CRC role play in a deliberate, self-conscious, and systematic manner that maximizes the power of the technique. The point of doing the role play is to avoid sliding over problems without noticing them, making assumptions that later lead to misconceptions in design and delivery, and short-circuiting the editing and verification process. Even if it feels awkward and forced at first, there will be big payoffs to the team that utilizes all three activities in their role play sessions.

Timing the CRC Role-Play Session

Before describing the role-play session, let's look briefly at the time involved. Since the objective of the meeting is to review material and work out problems in the conception of the system for a given set of CRC cards, the ability of the members of the team to be alert is critical to the success of the technique. Don't hold off on the role play until you have completed all of the CRC cards for your project. If you do, you will end up with a role play session that is a marathon, involves too many issues at once, and will probably force you to rewrite almost all the CRC cards! Start early and use the CRC role play on small segments of the system as you get them done, so that the adjustments you make can carry over to the next set of classes you define.

At best, the CRC role play session should be kept under two hours. Spend a few minutes in the warm-up without feeling pressured to skip over it. If each scenario takes about 10 minutes for the enactment and about 15 minutes for more rethinking during the assessment, the team can handle about four scenarios in a session. As the system becomes clearer, role plays that are repeated to confirm decisions already tried out in an earlier enactment will move even more quickly, and more role plays can fit in each session. Just remember, the insights and new ideas that are critical to the assessment phase are not going to happen if the team is exhausted. Frequent one-hour role-play meetings will be much more effective than a single all-day meeting.

The Warm-Up

> **Warm-Up Tips**
> Warm-up time is never wasted
> Warm up for every session
> Inspire confidence
> Don't get too serious too fast

Technical projects tend to have a rushed, "let's get to it" feel. Time spent in transition from one work mode to another can look like coddling. Good professional people are expected to adjust rapidly to changes in focus. This is an excellent ideal, but it overlooks some basics of human nature. People are sharper and work better together if they have some time to shift gears. This is why seemingly trivial conversations about the weather occur so often. It is a way of testing the water, getting used to interacting with the other person, and making the transition from outside issues to the subject at hand.

Warm-up does not need to take up a lot of time, but it does need to happen. Initially, a group may want to be very deliberate about using a warm-up that gets people ready to do the CRC role play. This might mean choosing ice-breaker exercises that allow people to drop their armor and inhibitions. This can be as simple as a mock brainstorm on a subject that has nothing to do with the system. Let everyone name their favorite movie hero. Make a list of all of the TV shows one should not have watched in the last year. Choose frivolous topics that relax the group, so that the brainstorm happens easily and everyone has a chance to open up. One of our favorites is asking everyone what they would do if they won a million-dollar lottery. Parts of people's personalities may be invisible when they are working. Uncover unexpected common ground—and enhance interest and commitment.

The following list of warm-up options can help, but don't be afraid to try out new ideas. Let team members bring in warm-up exercises. Use every aspect of the process to build group identity, to focus group energy, and to increase participation. In CRC card role play, the work of the group is distributed to everyone because everyone has to play the role of some number of classes. The silence of even one person during the role play can leave essential issues unturned.

Facilitating the Warm-Up

The following techniques can get groups warmed up rapidly in diverse situations: introductions, games, interactive exercises, light-hearted brainstorms, and more formal go-arounds.

Introductions: This is especially good with new groups. Have everyone tell his or her name and role in the project, and three things about themselves the others might not know. Encourage participants to talk about hobbies, family, things from outside the project.

Games: The more light-hearted, the better. Put group members in pairs and have them ask each other questions that can only be answered by "yes." Or use a game of twenty questions: one partner may choose to be an animal; the other partner has twenty questions to find out which.

Interactive Exercises: Any exercises used to get a group working together will be a good warm-up. Physical activities are especially good because they make it clear that everyone must be involved. You can't bring a ropes course into a conference room, but sometimes you can move tables and chairs to create a puzzle for the group to solve. Mental exercises work well, too. Collect brainteasers and puzzles. Bring them to the session. Let everyone contribute, so that looking for warm-up material becomes a group activity between meetings.

Light-Hearted Brainstorm: This is always a good fallback in any group. Thinking up lists can be done as a group or in small teams. Small interteam competitions can help people get to know each other. People who may be quiet and reluctant to talk about official topics often open up when a warm-up brainstorm hits on a personal interest. As long as the topic is light-hearted, no one is threatened and the group dynamics can be improved.

"Go-around" Review: Sometimes organizational culture makes it preferable to choose a more serious warm-up style. You still shouldn't just jump right into the work at hand, skipping the warm-up. Begin with a round-robin review of what everyone has done since the last meeting. Or build an agenda by polling to find out what each person hopes to accomplish at this meeting. Give everyone a chance to talk before the facilitator or project leader "takes charge." Even if you stick to business, use this process to make sure that everyone feels he or she has a voice. This is critical to the success of the role play.

Sometimes new people will be brought in for a role play because of their expertise in either the user domain or the technical domain. Their introduction should also be part of the warm-up. Rather than just announcing, "This is Mary. She is here from the Orders Department," take advantage of the new person to let everyone give a brief self-introduction, including the new person. This will make the new member more comfortable, and it will warm up the group by letting everyone speak.

Do not drop the warm-up just because team members know each other well. Even a repertory troupe of actors who work together day after day for years, will begin every rehearsal with a warm-up. Although role play is not theater, it is rooted in the same energy for engagement. Get the group going with a warm-up, draw their focus to group, and establish a common energy. Don't assume that just because everyone has been on the same project, they are all in the same mood with the same focus on any given day. Even a word game or a puzzle that revolves around concepts completely irrelevant to the project can set the mood for cooperation and raise the energy of the group. Name all of the states and their capitals. Bring in brainteasers. Borrow puzzles from books and put people in teams working against the clock. In as little as five minutes, you can draw the group together, flush out extraneous moods, and have everyone ready to work.

Include the final setup of the agenda as a part of the warm-up before every meeting. List the scenarios the group will run through and assign an approximate amount of time to each one. This gives the team a sense of how long the meeting will last, allows them to pace themselves (or get an extra cup of coffee), and sets the tone for a forward momentum. It will also help to keep the enactment phase of the role play on track and minimize digressions. You may even want to appoint a timekeeper for each role-play session. Rotate this role, because it puts someone in the unhappy position of having to interrupt and cut discussion short.

The idea of the warm-up is to combine setting an organizational tone ("what we will do today") with establishing a precedent for participation by everyone ("what I will do today"). It may seem like a silly device to people who are comfortable in groups and who like to dive into conversation, argument, etc., but for many people, taking part in a group involves sparking motivation and feeling somehow critical to the process. If the CRC role play is going to be effective, it needs to take place in an open atmosphere where everyone is ready, focused, and committed. Time spent on the warm-up is never time wasted.

Enactment

> **Enactment Guidelines**
> Identify and summarize scenarios (use agenda)
> Assign roles to actors (distribute CRC cards)
> Initiate scenario
> Correct minor errors
> Take assessment notes
> Act out multiple scenarios

Enactment is the heart of the CRC role play. Once the group has a list of scenarios, they are ready to "act out" the system. The first step is to identify the scenarios the group will work on first. In the first role play, the team is looking for a scenario that touches a central framework. Several scenarios can be covered in one role-play session, especially after the kinks have been worked out of the cards. The order of the role play can be decided as a part of the warm-up or, where they may be scheduled in a systematic way, working from "must-do" scenarios to "can-do-if," and finally to "might-do" scripts.

Distribute the CRC cards to the team members. At first the distribution may be somewhat random, but cards should be allocated so that collaborating classes are assigned to different actors. Wilkinson suggests that the classes be assigned to the domain experts for those classes. Do this if possible, but don't make it a hard and fast rule. When the system is large and there are a number of role-play sessions, it may be more productive to rotate class assignments. Often a new actor will have new insights into a role, which can help the team improve the system.

The enactment begins when one of the classes initiates a scenario by holding up their class card and stating what they need to accomplish. During the first round of a role play, the team may have trouble figuring out which class starts the action. You may even find that a class which was eliminated as "outside" the scope of the development effort may be useful to get things going. For example, in the ATM, it may be easier to initiate the role play if the Customer acts in the role play until the team clears up the relationship of the Customer to its surrogate and feels comfortable using BankCard to initiate the process.

During the role play each actor reads the responsibility written on her CRC card and asks for help from a collaborator if necessary. The collaborator then responds, lifting that CRC card to indicate that he is "in play." The actor reads her behavior and either continues holding up her card, calling another collaborator, or lowers it, having completed her part. Although participants may feel silly holding up their cards, once you get used to the utility of seeing what classes are in play, the practice will become a habit. For this reason, even if members of the group "keep forgetting," the facilitator should be assertive about encouraging this practice.

Some groups like to work with the actors "in play" standing, so that everyone can see which classes are involved in a scenario. This is good because it reinforces the use of the visual dimension to analyze what is going on. However, it can prove tiresome and awkward. We suggest raising the cards as a regular practice and then using standing if it helps to clarify what is going on in a complex scenario with a number of classes. Whichever your team prefers, the effect is the same!

As the enactment progresses, the whole team can visually follow the collaborations and see how allocation of responsibilities for information and behavior (encapsulation) affects the action. Are certain classes called on frequently by the same class? Are they really separate classes? Does the allocation of behavior and information between classes allow them to collaborate more easily with other classes (to be reused in different scenarios with different classes)? Have necessary classes been left out?

Watching the action of the role play should make the impact of allocation decisions clear. If the wrong class holds the wrong information (poor choice for encapsulation), it will show up during the role play. If the client–server relationships do not make sense, the team will see how difficult it is to get the work done. Class actors will realize, based on their cards, that they are missing information or that they are being asked to carry out responsibilities they don't have. It may be that they need to collaborate with a class not yet listed on the card. Actors can also keep track of the effect of multiple scenarios on their parts. Do they have responsibilities listed that never come into play? That duplicate the work of others?

Do not try to resolve all of the problems while role-playing the scenarios! Have a scribe take notes about the points at which problems occur and where a scenario gets stuck. If there is an obvious change, make the change on the CRC card and run through the scenario again. If the analysis really needs to be thought through, record this and move on to the next scenario. Poll the group, scan the remaining scenarios, and decide whether to continue to role play. If the problems are complex and don't permit the completion of the scenarios, go immediately to the Assessment phase. Follow the time estimates on the agenda and postpone long digressions and discussion until the Assessment.

As the system evolves, the role-play enactment will move more and more smoothly. Once the team can role play the "must-do" scenarios without interruption, go on to the "can-do-if" scenarios. Once those are in place, take on a selection of "might-do" scenarios. In the last case, since you may be crossing outside the current system's scope, don't lose the details or make unnecessary changes to the CRC cards. Do a run-through of the role play and then move to an assessment. Don't make changes which cause problems for the "must-do" scenarios at the core of the system.

Assessment

Assessment/Revision/Enactment Cycle Guidelines
"Go-around" comments
Identify problem points
Create problem-solving priority list
Change or confirm CRC cards
Identify scenarios to repeat or classify as completed

The Assessment phase is the time in which the group can really delve into any problems encountered in the role play. This may be a straightforward discussion and approval process, or it may involve a repetition of the Enactment (repeat of the role play) and Assessment (discussion) cycles. Establish focus and make the transition out of the acting mode. As a group, create a list of scenarios for review and their problem areas. Use a "go-around" to confirm that the list is complete. To avoid discussion before the list is in place, limit comments to a minute or two.

When you have a list of items to address, prioritize the items by impact. Early in the project it may be hard to spot a high-priority problem because the team does not have a clear idea of how the classes are going to fit together, but as soon as you have been through a couple of scenarios, focal points will emerge. Complex changes to the classes need to be discussed first.

Once the assessment begins, keep the team focused on the objective: confirming CRC card behaviors and collaborations. Use the goal of articulating the system by writing CRC cards to drive the discussion. This will help curb a tendency to get lost in functional details instead of concentrating on classes. If the discussion starts to sound like hammering out procedures, it is a sign that the people are getting tired and losing focus. Stop the action. Take a break. You may even want to transform the Assessment Agenda into a tentative agenda for another meeting.

Often the Assessment phase is straightforward and, with a couple of changes, the group is ready to reverify cards with another role-play enactment. If you have a number of scenarios to discuss, it helps maintain group momentum to go back to enactment before working on the next scenario. However, be careful never to become wedded to the "completion" of the CRC cards while scenarios are pending. Use the cards and the discussion to work toward those "Aha!" moments. The goal is insight now that will save effort later, no matter how many cards you have to change, and no matter how many times you have to change them.

Although you are rotating between enactment and assessment, try to keep the team aware of where it stands in the process (are we role-playing now, or is this assessment?). Avoid the kind of intermingling of phases that can lead to frustration. This can create a sense that the role play is generating a lot of random discussion, speculations about classes, and disagreements about collaboration that get nowhere. Stick to a pattern of Enactment as role play and run-through, and Assessment as review and revision.

How do you know when you're done and the CRC cards are correct? The first answer is that the cards must work to fulfill the goals of the users, as scripted in the scenarios you've defined. Take advantage of the brainstorming techniques discussed earlier. Even when it is obvious that the CRC cards don't "work right," how to fix them may require some creative solutions. Don't let yourself become wedded to the CRC cards that the group wrote the first time through. Feel free to radically reorganize class responsibilities and collaborations. Take advantage of the flexibility of object orientation and give free rein to revisions. The more open you are to revising the CRC cards, the more they will help you to maximize the benefits of encapsulation, polymorphism, and inheritance on the distribution of work and data. Again, how do you know when you're done? The classes will be able to work together to fulfill the scenarios. This is a creative process, so there will always be more than one possible solution! You'll see in a later chapter some quantitative guidelines which can help evaluate the cards, but you'll never know just by the numbers. You'll know because the system can do its job.

SUMMARY

The biggest advantage of using the CRC card technique is that it gives a team the means to prototype the system before writing even the most preliminary code. By using the CRC cards as a guide, the analysis team can see the impact of responsibility allocation and collaboration networks. CRC cards that are used as a documentation system without role plays offer few advantages over any other analysis method. The most important and unique contribution of CRC cards is the role play, because it forces the team to step through all of the classes so that they see how they really work together. We've seen many of the ways in which this creative activity can be structured so that these benefits come to pass.

In the next chapter, you will see how this works for a team that already has a set of CRC cards to use. We will show you one possible way to do the CRC role play. However, keep in mind that the process will be slightly different in every case. The important thing to keep in mind is to include all of the phases (warm-up, enactment, and assessment). Make CRC card role-playing a chance to learn, and an opportunity to have fun!

Chapter 7

Fashion Pro: Role-Playing Core Classes

In the previous chapter, we discussed the theory behind the practice of CRC card role-playing. This chapter's case study novella demonstrates the CRC role play, as an analysis team figures out the collaborations necessary for a new system to automate fashion design at De Mode Fashions. The discussion picks up at the point where the team has finished brainstorming classes. They have already selected the core classes and are about to role play. In contrast to the earlier case study, where the team filled in responsibilities and collaboration *before* role play, the team at De Mode Fashions has decided to use the role play to visualize what is happening before filling in the CRC cards.

The chapter includes 7 sections: (1) an introduction to the Fashion Pro Project, (2) a description of the project team, (3) a review of the core classes and the technical terms that apply to the domain, (4) sketching scenarios and considering frameworks, (5) role-play enactment, (6) assessment, and (7) a summary of the chapter and a look forward to the rest of the development process. In all of this discussion the focus is on the team's efforts to develop scenarios and the use of the role-play enactment to construct, assess, and revise the CRC card set.

FASHION PRO: A NEW IDEA IN GARMENT CREATION

The world of high fashion was once the exclusive domain of hand-cut, one-of-a-kind garments, but today's economics have pressed many high-profile fashion houses into the world of ready-to-wear. De Mode Fashions is no exception. While trying to sustain a distinctive custom line, the house has opened up to younger designers who feel equally challenged by the demand for upscale fashion in the mass market. They are also a lot less conservative than their predecessors and, having been trained in schools side by side with architectural designers using responsive CADware, they are open and eager to find computer-assisted design systems they can use.

Michele Theriot, the daughter of founder and senior designer François, is only 25, but she has already broken ground by bringing in a crowd of "Generation X" designers. She has convinced François to let her work with Brad Stone, a college classmate at Pratt Institute, who runs a small software house he's called Software Tools. His experience with interior design systems will be helpful as they create a tool for Michele and her Gen-X crew. They want to design on-line, automate the generation of the pattern, and produce a layout for fabric cutting. The system will also permit designers to reuse and redesign pattern pieces so that new garments can be based on existing garments, making the conversion from designs to patterns faster and easier.

The ultimate goal of the project is to be able to do everything from initial design worksheet to pattern layout with Fashion Pro. For now, Brad has convinced Michele to pilot only the creation of styles. When the software for this part of the process is satisfactory, they can go on to solve the problems involved in pattern generation, laying the pattern out on different fabrics, and producing a mock-up of the final garment hang. The phases of the project are going to be:

Phase 1: Pilot Project: Design Worksheet
  – design garment using on-line worksheet
  – create style
   (a) use (and modify) existing design elements
   (b) generate new design elements
Phase 2: Generate Patterns
  – style uses existing pattern pieces
  – style requires generation of new pieces
Phase 3: Layout Patterns
  Mark Pattern
   – simulate garment hang for different fabrics
   – generate cutting layout for selected fabrics

The heavy graphic interface made this look like a good candidate for object-oriented technology, so Brad plans to use an object-oriented language. When he told Michele, she said, "Great," in the same tone of voice she uses with her auto mechanic.

M. Theriot is skeptical about the place of computers in the creative process, but he sports a hidden pride in his daughter. He is only ten years from retirement and knows that the business of exclusive and hand-drawn fashion work may not outlive him. (He also harbors secret hopes for a match between Brad and Michele!)

THE FASHION PRO ANALYSIS TEAM

As domain experts, Michele has placed her top young designer, Susie Li, on the team along with Matt Goldberg, her father's top layout person. Susie understands the kind of vision Michele has for Fashion Pro. Matt knows the history of every garment that has left De Mode for more than thirty years. Both of them have had considerable experience with CADware. In preparation for the project, Michele sent them to a short course on the basics of object-oriented development, including an introduction to CRC cards.

Brad selected one of his top developers, Joan Walsh, to handle the Fashion Pro project. Joan has used object-oriented technology extensively, and she is also a bit less of a "techie" than Mark Green, the guy Brad usually sends out on pilot technology projects. He also knows that Joan, who knows how to dress, will be a lot better fit than Mark, who can barely choose his socks, much less spot high style if it were offered to him for free.

Brad is also using Julie, his younger sister and a whiz with database design, as the second technical person on the project. He wants her there from the beginning even though her main role will be design and coding. She is fluent in object-oriented languages, but she also knows how to put a dress together on a sewing machine. She has never seen the industrial version of this process, but she does know about patterns, fabric, and cutting.

Joan will act as facilitator for the CRC card sessions and function as project leader for the whole project. Although there is an MIS staff of three at De Mode, they work only with the accounting systems and have no experience with object-oriented development. Joan knows up front that the technical people from Software Tools and the fashion designers will each have a lot to learn. That's why she has chosen the CRC technique. It should help her keep the analysis moving forward while everyone is learning about the domain.

RECAPPING THE CORE CLASSES

Just as Joan expected, even though she and Julie can cut and sew from a pattern, there were a lot of things to learn about doing this professionally on a large scale. The first few CRC card sessions were like a language immersion class at Berlitz, but they did yield a comprehensive candidate class list. The team got a bit frustrated with the slowness of the learning curve, but Joan could see that all of this time would pay off in a system that matched the way things are done at De Mode. Too many projects end up the other way—with clients painfully revising their work to accommodate the technology.

The number of new concepts on the candidate class list gave Joan the idea of making groups of classes for different steps in the clothing design process. Susie mapped out the life cycle for a garment design (shown in Figure 7-1). This helped the group connect the class names with things from the real world. It also gave Joan a chance to clear up the difference between classes and attributes, and to explain why some candidate classes might end up in either camp.

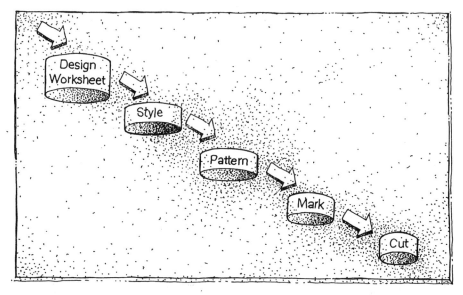

Figure 7-1 **The Garment Design Cycle**

On the basis of the life cycle, the team created a candidate class list organized to shadow each phase. Figure 7-2 shows how the candidate classes fit in these categories. Joan pointed out that this division would probably mirror the progress of the project, allowing them to concentrate on understanding classes as they moved through the life cycle of the system. They used this as a basis for evaluating candidate classes, at least temporarily eliminating items on the list that did not fit into any phase from consideration as core classes. Candidates such as measurement, drape, length, fabric surface, seam allowance, and yardage were set aside as attributes of classes.

To make sure the team members all understood and agreed with this approach, Susie reviewed the process for creating a garment while the others looked for omitted classes. Because you, the reader, may not be familiar with clothing design, we've included Susie's explanation and a few illustrations. Otherwise, you'll have trouble following the upcoming scenarios and their role plays.

"First," Susie began, "a new design is drawn on a *design worksheet*. It is based on a *croquis* or basic body type (shown in Figure 7-3). Then a *silhouette* of the garment shape is laid over the croquis (see Figure 7-4). This is important because the shape of the body will influence whether or not a certain silhouette looks flattering. Of course, what we consider 'flattering' changes from year to year. Remember the chemise from the Twenties; it's back again.

"Once we have chosen the shape of the garment, we add *components* (see Figure 7-5). That's things like the sleeve and neckline. These are often standardized. You may also draw

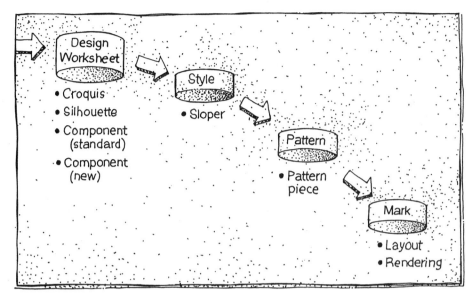

Figure 7-2 **Clothing Design Phases and Core Classes**

Figure 7-3 **The Croquis**

Figure 7-4 **The Design Silhouette**

some completely new components. And, I should mention, the designer may change the *length* of the silhouette or of a component to get a new look. If we do design a new component, we want to be able to save those for future reuse."

Susie continued, "Once the designer is satisfied with the work, she or he will save it as a style and we give it a number. It is now ready to be converted into a *sloper*. That's the shape that will be used for the pattern piece without determining where the seams will be, or, to simplify the idea for Joan and Julie, it's the pattern without seam allowances. The next step is to determine where to add seams and generate a *pattern*. The last steps in the process involve laying out the pattern on the fabric, marking it, and creating a rendering of the garment. But the last part is not going to be part of the pilot, so we don't need to know all the details now."

At this point, the team was ready to draw up scenarios as the basis for role play of the CRC cards. Joan decided that the role play should move them through the system slowly so that they could create an effective CRC card set with fewer passes.

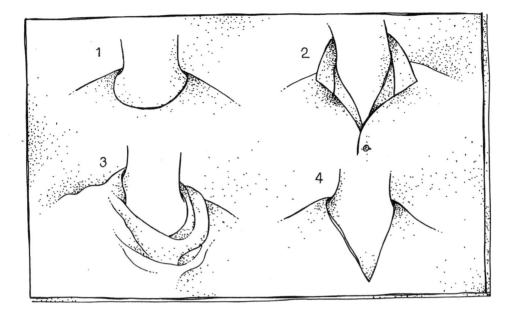

Figure 7-5 **Clothing Components: Necklines**

SKETCHING SCENARIOS

Joan began the development of scenarios by asking Susie and Matt to translate Susie's explanation of the system into some situations that could serve as scripts for role play. They began by mapping out the "must-do" scenarios. For the first phase of the project they suggested four general scenarios: creating a design on a Worksheet; accepting the design and assigning it a Style Number; converting the style into a Sloper; and generating a Pattern.

The list looked simple, but when the team began to discuss each scenario, complications emerged. Matt pointed out that things can run very smoothly if the designer is using existing components, but this is not always the case. Susie supported his position, adding that one of the objectives in automating design was to cut time and costs for altering components, so they could create a new look without a high price tag.

"The point," she explained, "is to make it so that the baseline (standardization) that works for the cost people does not cut into the creative side. We would like to be able to respond to a style that is catching on and adapt it to various body types. The trend-setters work with a slim, tall croquis, but as you know, not all of our market fits that body type. Responsiveness is key."

As a result of Matt and Susie's comments, Julie suggested that they divide the first scenario into subsets. "We can begin with a design that does not involve any changes to existing components, one for which we have already created pattern pieces either as part of the stock components or during a prior style creation. The next scenario can be for a design that modifies existing components, and, in the third, we'll see what is involved in creating a new component."

Reusing Analysis Frameworks

As the team continued reviewing their preliminary class cards, Joan suggested that they look through Peter Coad's book, *Object Models,* to see if any classes fit preexisting software patterns. Perhaps they could get a better idea of the Fashion Pro class responsibilities and design a better OO approach. The Fashion Pro class cards for Style and for Pattern reminded them that the end point of the system would be the generation of pattern pieces that are going to be sewn together in a garment. That garment would look like, that is, recreate, the clothing design put together from parts on the DesignWorksheet and accepted as a Style. It was a familiar relationship where one class, Style, "is composed of" instances of other classes.

Julie looked up aggregate software patterns and found six types: "container-content," "container-content line item," "group-member," "assembly-part," "compound part-part," and "packet-packet component." She explained each to Matt and Susie. They quickly ruled out "container-content," which Susie had compared to a warehouse or folder because the system was building up a Style and translating it into a Pattern, not storing Styles in a Pattern.

"Container-content line item" was dropped for the same reason. "Group-member" clearly did not apply, because there was nothing in Fashion Pro that was analogous to a team or collection, a set such as employers and employees. "Packet-packet component" also seemed too far afield. However, both "assembly-part" and "compound part-part" looked useful, because the suggested applications for these frameworks included hardware assembly–hardware part. On the other hand, the pattern implied that a major behavioral concern was knowing how many of a part was included. In garments, the number of Components (say, sleeves or pant legs or necklines) does not vary, so the "compound part-part" pattern was still not a close enough match to be useful.

The best match was the "assembly-part" pattern, which included behavior for monitoring the parts needed for a given assembly. This software pattern could be used to model classes such as engines and engine parts, which wasn't too far off from a garment and its parts! "What we really need to know," Joan pointed out, "is which parts we are assembling and any changes to that assembly. The focus of our Fashion Pro system is putting together instances of parts into a whole, which is comparable to putting together pattern pieces into a pattern or design elements into a style. Each whole differs by the variations in parts assembled."

The team agreed to list the "assembly-part" pattern as a possible reusable pattern. The pattern is shown in Figure 7-6. Joan pointed out that this would be important to them in the future when they expanded the project to include computer mock-ups of garments on different fabrics.

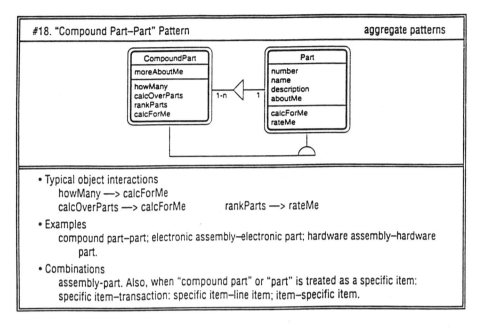

Figure 7-6   **The "Assembly-Part" Object Pattern**

Source: OBJECT MODELS- by COAD & NORTH, © 1995. Reprinted by permission of Prentice-Hall, Inc., Upper Saddle River, NJ.

Continuing the Scenario List

Julie, thinking in terms of her eventual object libraries, asked what happened to the in-progress designs that were not officially accepted. "Oh yes," Susie exclaimed, "we keep all that because you might have made the wrong choice and then you remember you had something awesome that looked wrong the day before (or the year before). We have to keep all of that preliminary work!"

Julie suggested they add two subscenarios. "We need one scenario that just follows through and assigns the Style number, that results in a Style, and another where we store the Design Worksheet. Do the designers go back to these worksheets?"

"Sometimes," Matt responded, "but isn't that going to be the same whether they save it because they are going to lunch or they save it because they are not getting anywhere with the design?"

The group agreed that this was the case, so they decided to run the "no problem" scenario as a worksheet-to-style script, and to make the decision not to create a style the second variation. Joan wrote the new scenario list on a flipchart sheet and asked for any additions, objections, or other comments:

1. Create a design on a worksheet using existing components and accept it as a style.
2. Create a design on a worksheet using existing components and save it without approval as a style.
3. Create a design on a worksheet using a modified component and accept it as a style.
4. Create a design on a worksheet using modified components and save it without approval as a style.
5. Reopen a worksheet and complete the style.
6. Convert the style into a sloper.
7. Generate a pattern.

Matt was concerned about some of the intermediary steps. He pointed out that the designer might change the length of a silhouette or a component, extend an A-line to the floor, or shorten sleeves. Joan felt that all of this fit under the modification of existing components. The team decided to keep track of possible problems like this—Julie began a list—and make sure that they were covered by the end of the role play.

"Are the croquis and silhouettes set forever, too?" Julie asked. The fashion designers who use the system are expected to work with the croquis and silhouettes offered, and these would have to be updated periodically.

Joan pointed out that the tickler list could be used for the "might-do" scenarios. The team discussed it and decided that in this particular system all of the scenarios seemed to fall into two categories: "must-do" and "might-do," with no "can-do-if" situations in between. They took a few minutes and drew up two "might-do" scenarios to test the flexibility of the CRC cards after the "must-do" scenarios. The "might-do" included:

1. Design using your own, newly created components.
2. Add new stock croquis and silhouettes to the system.

"OK," Joan concluded. "We are ready to test fly our classes. We can add more scenarios later to be sure that the CRC card set covers everything required of the system, even some of the major exceptions to routine work. The important thing is that we have included the core of the system, the 'hot spots,' in our list. Come in tomorrow and we'll play out the script."

Scenario Reminders
Look for reusable frameworks
Try out "no-problem," "must-do" scripts first
Separate out conditional scenarios from "must-do" scenarios
Develop "might-do" scenarios that test for flexibility

ROLE-PLAY ENACTMENT

Joan decided to pass around a few brainteasers to get everyone going. There was hot coffee in the room, but there had also been a weekend and a couple of days of work since the team last met. Since she started facilitating role plays, Joan had built up a file of these puzzles. At first she felt foolish bringing "games" into a professional setting, but their success convinced her that self-consciousness had no payoff. The brainteasers she selected for De Mode are shown in Figures 7-7 and 7-8.

When the jokes died down, Joan asked Julie to pass out a sample set of CRC cards so that the group could warm up with a real role play using completed CRC cards for a familiar application domain. She chose a document preparation system based on the software used at De Mode. The CRC cards included the classes DocumentWorkspace, Document, Text, Graphic, and Object. The team played out the scenario for adding text, a bar chart, and a piece of clip art to a document.

As Joan had anticipated, they quickly discovered that they would need a GUI class, a class that could be a stand-in for the subsystem that communicated the user's selections to the classes in the document system. Once they had the GUI, Matt began as a document and, following the information on the card, displayed himself. Susie, as text, Julie, as clip art, and Joan, as text, all responded to GUI requests that they display themselves. This led to the idea that all three classes were subclasses of a DocumentElement class.

Joan coached them, reminding people to hold up their cards when they were "on stage" or "in play." Matt was stubborn about this and stated up front that he thought it was stupid, but after a few minutes he was less sure of himself and saw how quickly the team

---

A hunter arose early, at breakfast, and headed south. Half a mile from camp he tripped and skinned his nose. He picked himself up, cursing, and continued south. Half a mile farther along, he spotted a bear. Drawing a bead, he pulled the trigger, but the safety was on. The bear saw him and headed east at top speed. Half a mile later the hunter caught up, fired, but only wounded the beast, which limped on toward the east. The hunter followed and half a mile later caught and killed the bear. Pleased, the hunter walked the mile north back to his camp to find it had been ransacked by a second bear.

What color was the bear that tore up his camp?

The clues are all there.

Answer: White. It is a polar bear, for the North Pole is one of the places where you can go one mile south, one mile east, and one mile north, and still end up at your starting point. (The others are near the south pole.)

Figure 7-7 **Verbal Brainteaser**

Source: From Games for the Super-Intelligent by James F. Fixx. Copyright © 1972 by James F. Fixx. Used by permission of Doubleday, a division of Bantam Doubleday Dell Publishing Group, Inc.

In Your Cups

Take a long piece of string and thread it through the handle of a teacup, exactly as shown, and tie the free ends to something. Can the cup be removed from the string without cutting it or undoing the knot?

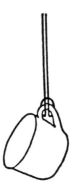

Answer: Although it may look impossible, it is in fact very simple to get the handle of the teacup off the string. Take the loop where it passes behind the two strings on which the cup hangs and pull it until you have a loop large enough to pass around the cup, from the back forward, and the cup will be released from the string.

Figure 7-8 **Visual Brainteaser**

Source: From *Games for the Super-Intelligent* by James F. Fixx. Copyright © 1972 by James F. Fixx. Used by permission of Doubleday, a division of Bantam Doubleday Dell Publishing Group, Inc.

could lose track of which classes were involved in a chain of collaborations. At this point, Joan cut off the warm-up because the team was beginning to get sidetracked by the specifics of document preparation. In a brief assessment, she emphasized the idea of assembling parts into a whole and asked everyone to remember this during the Fashion Pro role play.

The "official" role play began with the addition of a GUI class based on what had been learned during the warm-up. The team then began a role play for the first scenario: Create a design on a worksheet using existing components and accept it as a style. Matt, as the GUI class, held up his card and requested that DesignWorksheet, Susie, initiate a new instance of herself. He selected a Croquis, so Julie raised her card and announced she would display herself. Then GUI requested a Silhouette and Joan displayed herself, but there was some confusion because the Silhouette had to be associated with the Croquis, conforming to its shape. This reminded Joan that she, as Croquis, had never been added to the DesignWorksheet. General confusion took over as everyone speculated at once.

Seeing that she herself had contributed to the interruption, Joan called the team to attention and cut the role play short. Because the CRC cards had not been filled in before the team tried to role play, it was difficult to finish even one scenario without discussion. To insure that enactment and assessment were not blurred, a situation that could lead to long-drawn-out sessions later on with constant interruptions in the flow of the enactment, Joan decided to move to assessment now and then rerun the role play. She gave everyone a few minutes to fill in some responsibilities on the CRC cards based on what they had seen so far.

Next, Joan let the group discuss the issue of timing on the association of croquis, silhouette, and components with a DesignWorksheet. The group decided that, for now, the clearest case should be a responsibility that lets the DesignWorksheet know what croquis and silhouette are displayed. They repeated the role play with the following sequence of action:

GUI: I request that DesignWorksheet display itself.
DESIGNWORKSHEET: I have displayed myself.
GUI: I request that Croquis display itself on the open
    DesignWorksheet.
CROQUIS: I have displayed myself.
DESIGNWORKSHEET: I have recorded Croquis.
GUI: I request that Silhouette display itself on Croquis.
SILHOUETTE: I display myself.
CROQUIS: I am adding Silhouette at snap points.
DESIGNWORKSHEET: I'm updating my list of elements displayed.
GUI: I want to add a Component (which could be neckline).
COMPONENT: I am displaying myself.
SILHOUETTE: I am attaching Component.
DESIGNWORKSHEET: I am updating my list of elements.
GUI: I want to save this design and make a pattern of it.
DESIGNWORKSHEET: I am assigning myself a style number.

The team ended the scenario pleased with the way that it went. They could see that the same roles could be repeated for as many elements as necessary. They also decided that it might be useful to create a DesignElement superclass with Croquis, Silhouette, and Component as subclasses. Julie liked the idea because it opened up room to add DesignElements later. Susie agreed, thinking that even though the pattern generation would only use components that needed to be marked, there might be future uses for a system that allowed them to add decorative DesignElements that behaved the same way, but which would never be used as the basis for a pattern. They would have all the same behaviors as the current subclasses of DesignElement, even though they would not be involved in pattern generation scenarios.

> **Role Play Reminders**
> Always start with a warm-up
> Enact and assess one scenario at a time
> Add and revise but do not digress; hold discussion until
>   assessment
> Identify active classes by raising cards
> It's OK to have fun

ASSESSMENT

In reviewing the newly annotated classes, it was apparent that the team needed to consider the responsibilities that come into play as a clothing designer is adjusting the garment, changing length of sleeves, trying it on different body silhouettes, and the like. The team role played out the third scenario: "Create a design on a worksheet using a modified component and accept it as a style." They also decided that the second scenario would be the same as the first, except that the scenario ended before the GUI requested that the DesignWorksheet assign itself a Style number, requesting that the DesignWorksheet simply close and save itself as a design in progress.

The third scenario turned out to be the same as the first until the designer/GUI requested a change in the length of the Silhouette, when the following took place:

GUI: Silhouette, I want to raise the hem.
SILHOUETTE: I don't know how to do that. I had better add a responsibility to the CRC card, "Change Length" and, since I am snapped to Croquis, Croquis must make necessary changes in snap-points.
CROQUIS: OK, done. I'll add that to my responsibilities.
GUI: Now, Sleeve. (Component) I want to change the flare at the wrist.
SLEEVE (COMPONENT): I have made that adjustment.
GUI: I'm satisfied. This is the design that I want for the garment. DesignWorksheet, assign yourself a Style number.

Joan opened the floor for discussion. The team now agreed that the CRC cards addressed the routine scenarios. Joan suggested a quick run-through of the fourth and fifth scenarios (create a design on a worksheet using modified components and save it without approval as a style, and reopen a worksheet and complete the style), which went well. The team moved on to role play the creation of the sloper and pattern generation. They filled in the rest of the CRC card information. The final set of CRC cards set looks like this:

DesignWorksheet	
Display itself	
Save itself	
Assign style number	Style
Know its name	
Know its design elements	Design Element
Open/initialize	

GUI	

DesignElement Subclass: Croquis, Silhouette, Component	
Display itself	
Modify dimensions	
Copy itself	DesignWorksheet
Create a pattern	Pattern

Croquis Superclass: DesignElement	
Display itself	
Associate DesignElement (snap-points)	
Know its name	

Silhouette Superclass: DesignElement	
Display itself	Croquis
Modify dimensions	Croquis
Know its name	

Component Superclass: DesignElement Subclass: Sleeve, Neckline, PantLeg	
Display itself	Croquis
Modify dimensions	Croquis
Know its name	

Pattern	
Create itself	Style
Produce a sloper	
Determine seam allowance	
Estimate yardage	
Size itself	

Style	
Display itself	
Know its design elements	DesignWorksheet
Know its pattern pieces	Pattern

The team was then ready to try one of the "might-do" scenarios to test for flexibility. After doing the final role plays listed earlier, they assessed the final set of cards and confirmed that none of the changes made to the CRC cards prevented role play of the original scenarios. With all of these role plays completed, the analysis team had a good feel for interdependencies in the system and collaboration between classes. The CRC cards were stable enough to be used as the basis for design.

SUMMARY

The folks at De Mode Designs have some great ideas for their new Fashion Pro system, and it looks as if object-oriented analysis gave them the means to bring together software techies and flashy dressers. They were able to take their core classes out of the brainstorming stage, and into scenario creation and enactment. As they created scenarios, the technical people showed how a previously defined object model, the "assembly-part pattern," could help them figure out the Style class. And during the scenario enactment and assessment, the creators of high fashion showed what actually takes place when they work, and thus how the classes really have to interact. The CRC cards that came out of the brainstorming and role plays look like a good base definition of the classes in the Fashion Pro world.

At this point, however, the CRC cards are not a design. They map out the frontiers of the classes, the behavior that must be incorporated in the design. The group has an analysis package and even a recommendation for reusing a pattern that will make the system design easier. The balance of the chapters in this book explore how this deliverable fits into the larger picture of project management, and the rest of object-oriented programming. We'll see how to manage an object-oriented development project in order to insure success. And then we'll transition to design and coding, so that you get a feel for the potential, and the limitations, of CRC card analysis for direct use in OO software creation.

Chapter 8

Managing Object Analysis

We've come quite a ways in seeing how teams can use CRC cards productively to analyze systems. Up until now, our point of view was that of the team actually doing the work. We mentioned only in passing how the team fits into the development organization. In this chapter, we will talk more specifically to managers and their project team members about the differences between the object-oriented project life cycle and the life cycle in more traditional development. This is particularly important if you want to be able to establish benchmarks and standards for future projects or to measure your progress against benchmarks borrowed from other organizations. You cannot do this if you do not understand how the progress of object-oriented projects is different and adapt your tracking mechanisms appropriately.

We describe the SDLC (system development life cycle) of object-oriented development projects as Incremental and Iterative. It is a user-centric perspective and places emphasis on the role of evaluation and checkpoints characteristic of object-oriented projects. Along with describing this life cycle model, we offer a number of guidelines for making it work. Our emphasis continues to be the CRC card technique and the analysis process, so we confine our discussion of metrics to this portion of the SDLC.

The chapter is presented in eight sections. (1) We begin the chapter with a description of the changes in the SDLC when you work with object-oriented techniques. (2) We propose a new SDLC, one that is incremental and iterative, and explain how this is used to manage object-oriented development. (3) We examine criteria for a good pilot project, (4) discuss the initiation of the project (when to start) and how to use training to maximize success in your first project, and then (5) look at the role of SWAT Teams and Gurus. (6) We address the issue of how legacy systems fit into the picture and (7) offer some metrics for assessing your use of CRC. (8) Finally, we offer some brief comments on using CRC cards as a bridge to methodologies, a topic we explore in more detail in the last chapter of the book.

OBJECT-ORIENTED DEVELOPMENT CHANGES THE SDLC

Managers depend upon an SDLC model to provide a map that indicates what needs to be done, when to do it, and how the work of one part of a project affects other parts of the project. They detail development inputs, activities, and milestones. Milestones are especially important because they establish the rate of progress and help managers anticipate the quality of the delivered system based on an assessment of its current stage. For example, if there is a major problem during the analysis phase, such as a missed requirement, faulty mapping of users' needs, or a mushrooming of scope, using comparison to standards means that it can be addressed at an early checkpoint, before more work based on a false premise is undertaken. SDLCs also enable management to do cost estimation and to track estimate-to-actual at defined checkpoints.

There is a close connection between SDLCs and standards. The use of formal checkpoints not only keeps the development team conscious of targets; it provides a mechanism for measuring progress that can be used by management to evaluate what is going on, to commit more resources to a project, or, if projects cannot keep up with targets, to consider canceling them. Early projects map progress to the SDLC and collect information that will become benchmarks for future work. In moving to a new development approach, it is therefore necessary to move to a new SDLC and to establish new milestones, new checkpoints, and a new vocabulary for standards.

Managing object-oriented projects can be problematic, especially at the beginning. The design and programming techniques are complex and involve mastering large libraries of classes, studies of frameworks and patterns, and other very specific experientially-derived knowledge. Many managers will be less than expert. However, no matter how formal or casual their knowledge is, they need to manage according to a plan and apply standards. To do this they will need to understand the affect of object orientation on the SDLC they choose as the basis for evaluating progress and planning projects.

In our consulting, we have found that most organizations currently depend on an SDLC that is some modification of the waterfall model. In some cases, these have been adjusted to accommodate a spiral model. The problem is that neither of these SDLCs is going to work if you want to use object-oriented technologies. To understand why, let's first review the waterfall and spiral models; then let's look at the reasons they fail to match what is going on in an object-oriented project, and see what needs to be done to the SDCL to make it a useful model with valid checkpoints.

The Waterfall SDLC

The model used by most corporations today is a variant on the waterfall standard. This model, shown in Figure 8-1, is so common it is enshrined as an IEEE standard. In the real world there is a lot of disagreement about specific details, such as how many phases should be included in a project or the exact nature of activities within the phases, but, on the

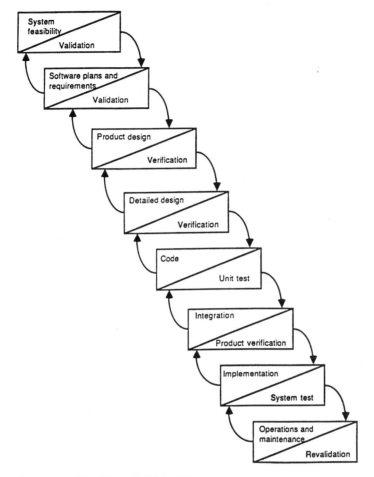

Figure 8-1 ***The Waterfall Model***

Source: Boehm, B.: *A Spiral Model of Software Development and Enhancement,* IEEE Computer, May 1988. © 1988 IEEE.

whole, the idea that a project progresses with the momentum of water falling down in a series of cascades dominates the way that management approaches the assessment, budgeting, timing, and staffing of software development projects.

Before dismissing the waterfall model, we do want to say that despite the wealth of popular magazine chat about alternatives to and weaknesses of the waterfall model, there are some valid reasons why so many organizations cling to this model and its variants. Perhaps the most valid is that it supports the management of software development by imposing a common standard with clearly defined milestones on a wide variety of projects. This is a welcome tool in a world where a lot of the activity involved in completing a project is creative and, consequently, often unpredictable. Any analyst or programmer has a wealth of stories about projects that looked impossible and miraculously fell into place, and an equally abundant supply of horror stories about the system that got away. The only way to tread a middle road through these two extremes, from the point of view of organizational planning and control, is to adopt a model that provides you with some specific checkpoints and measures for success.

The waterfall model, with its clear stepping stones, suggests various ways of measuring progress. If there are definite steps that need to be completed, standards can be set and progress reported in terms of deliverables associated with milestones. Common grounds for approval can be established. The order of development processes can be mapped to set phases. Specific staffing assignments can be made by coordinating a project management tracking system with the SDLC model. Internal organizational standards, audit requirements, and other corporate checks can be integrated into the model. Design metrics can be applied to assess quality. Although staff may grumble about the gap between standards and reality, progress along a waterfall-type SDLC provides a baseline of comfort and control for management.

On the down side, the waterfall model is often and justifiably criticized as mechanical and rigid. When applied literally, the checkpoints can take over and drive the project. This often leads to a "meet the deliverable" attitude that puts pressure on the technical staff to push ahead, shortchanging interaction with users, for example, because it involves unpredictable and time-consuming meetings. Analysis and design as a whole are often cut short because of the drive to arrive at coding checkpoints and produce measurable results. In an effort to meet management goals, projects veer away from reality. In the end, the system delivered to the user may meet project standards and conform to targets, but it does not fulfill the users' needs. Sometimes, a project fails on both counts, disappointing users and running over budget and behind schedule.

The Spiral SDLC

In an effort to maintain the baseline of forward progress marked by definite checkpoints provided by the waterfall model and, at the same time, bring the model more in line with the reality of doing projects, Barry Boehm introduced an SDLC he called the spiral model. This model, shown in Figure 8-2, preserves the implicit forward motion of falling water, but suggests that phases move in spirals. Boehm emphasizes the inevitable need to repeat aspects of a prior phase based on new information or new insights that result from a later phase.

The image of a spiral captures the way in which a project spirals back on itself. Although there is always a forward motion, it is not linear. Work phases that had contributed to the current phase may be revisited later on. However, the return is not the same as the first pass through the phase because the products of the first pass are not abandoned; they are revised. Thus, a team progresses by completing certain kinds of work, but then reviews the products when elements of early phases repeat in the context of the work in a subsequent phase. For instance, in structured techniques, the first product of the project is a context diagram. Later on, an initial set of data flow diagrams is created, the context

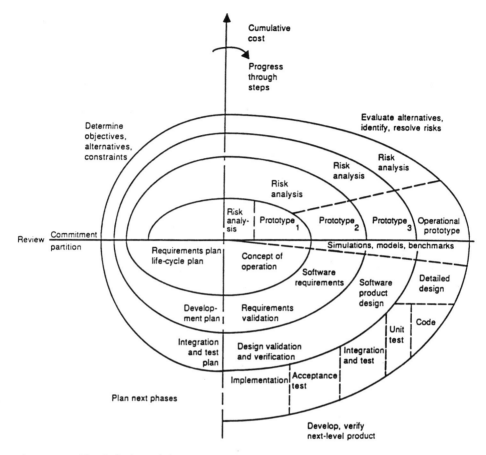

Figure 8-2 **The Spiral Model**
Source: Boehm, B.: *A Spiral Model of Software Development and Enhancement,*
IEEE Computer, May 1988. © 1988 IEEE.

diagram is reexamined, and, if necessary, revised. In fact, even after a system has been delivered, enhancements are introduced by repeating phases and revising the products of the modeling process.

The key to the spiral SDLC is the emphasis on iteration and the development of prototypes. The first pass through a checkpoint indicates that the work produced during that phase is adequate, but not final. It is sufficient for an effort to complete the next level of activities; however, as those new items are tackled, shortcomings in the previous phase will probably surface, and the project will have to go back, again carrying out activities formally relegated to the prior phase. For example, instead of seeing the end of the design phase as the complete closure of design activity, preliminary coding begins with the idea that it may well lead to questions that send the team back to design (or redesign) of some modules.

The spiral model, therefore, gives up the few, large deliverables of the waterfall model in order to accommodate iteration, but it preserves the basic pattern of checkpoints that can be used to track a project. In the spiral model, the SDLC phases are linear, but the actual work involves a circular pattern. Looking again at structured methods using a spiral SDLC, we can say that analysis "produces" a set of data flow diagrams, for example, but the process of translating those diagrams into structure charts may uncover missing pieces that send the project back to redrawing and rethinking the data flow diagrams. This idea of spiraling is particularly appropriate to the use of the interlinked models characteristic of structured methods and the verification capacity of CASE tools.

One of the obvious drawbacks of the spiral model is that the ability to double back makes cost estimates and risk–benefit analysis more difficult than in the linear context of the waterfall model. For this reason, although projects may involve doubling back, management continues to favor a waterfall SDLC or to treat the deliverables in the spiral model as the final product. This puts pressure on teams to place standards first and theory second. The contradictions between a waterfall SDLC used by management and the practice of structured techniques is often at the root of organizational disappointment with the promises of both structured methods and CASE tools.

In order to avoid repeating this experience in the migration to object-oriented projects, we need to look closely at the impact of iteration on the SDLC. Even more than structured methods, object-oriented projects are going to move in overlapping waves of understanding, where progress forward often means understanding what to change about what we did before. Naming classes, for example, may be step one in the analysis phase of the SDLC, but it is also an activity that continues to be done and redone throughout the project. It moves us one more step away from the waterfall model.

This is not all bad news. A significant strength of object-oriented development is that it encourages a coming together of design and deployment that makes the spiral even tighter. This means that, as soon as there is sufficient understanding to "try out" the system, rapid prototypes can be sketched out (a design activity) and implemented. At the same time, this prototyping is not equivalent to delivery activity in the spiral model. It is a probe that is meant to lead to discoveries and knowledge that sends the project back to amend and improve the understanding and requirements for classes, a deliverable associated with analysis. For this reason, neither the waterfall SDLC nor the spiral SDLC provides a management model that can accommodate the realities of working with object-oriented technology.

THE INCREMENTAL AND ITERATIVE SDLC

At the core of object-oriented methods is a shift from system-centered approaches to a user-centric context for development. The connection between the language of objects and the language of the user domain has been tightened even further than it is in structured methods. The way in which the user works can become the way in which the system models itself, and ultimately the way in which it processes information. The opportunity for user involvement, both during analysis and in design and implementation, not only promises higher satisfaction but makes user input more valuable at all phases. This means that the SDLC must accommodate the give and take involved in collecting information from users, creating rough cuts of portions of the system, testing them, and redoing them. The system is developed incrementally, by iterating through the processes of discovery, analysis, design, and coding many times. Thus, we call this an Incremental and Iterative SDLC, which maps phases of the project in terms of units that build, rather than in terms of phases that are completed one at a time. In this sense it is modular, but always remember that revision has a critical impact on the quality of the final system.

The Incremental and Iterative SDLC takes the old models and applies them to a series of repeating mini-cycles that overlap. This overlap echoes the iterative pattern captured by the spiral model. In the short term, this means that the SDLC is repeated for each subset of the system. However, because of the capacity of classes for reuse, the result is in an incremental building up of a single, large system. When a phase is repeated, the project is working at a higher level of understanding. Moreover, as an organization moves forward and continues to use object-oriented methods, future projects can be seen as beginning somewhere farther along in the SDLC because they build on the classes already implemented.

This overlap can be designated by phases that are made up of and that interleaf analysis, prototyping, and revision activities, as shown in SDLC in Figure 8-3. Overall, the model holds onto the analysis and design activities, but within each SDLC phase, there are mini-cycles of analysis–prototype–revision–implementation. For example, in the overall analysis phase, CRC cards are treated as an analysis activity that yields a kind of prototype in the role play. In the design phase this pattern is echoed, but the prototype takes the form of a live system. The test phase is also different in the Incremental and Iterative SDLC because testing activities may be interlaced with more analysis and design. Each prototype activity, whether it is the CRC role play or a version of the live system, is a form of system testing and establishes testing patterns that are used throughout the project. In other words, the discrete steps of the waterfall model have been abandoned, and the iterative aspect of development is dominant.

The Incremental and Iterative model is also different from the spiral model because, as the project team becomes more familiar with the system under development, reusable classes and polymorphism tighten the iterations. Each iteration in this SDLC is based on definite information collected from the testing of the prototype. This is more useful in assessment than the elastic concept of revision in the spiral model. When, for example, a CRC role play can be acted out without dead ends, that corner, that block of the system, is essentially ready for the hard prototype of the design cycle. At the same time, analysis will be repeated for related blocks of the system that reuse classes or sets of classes that have already been set, and will augment classes.

The progression from one point in the cycle to the next cycle is seamless from start to deployment. The system builds steadily and, as parts are completed to satisfaction, those

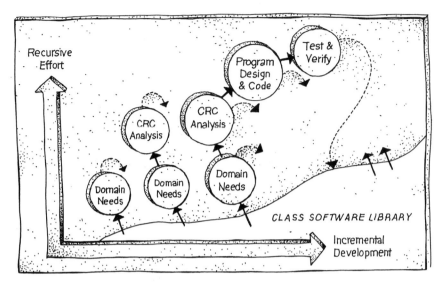

Figure 8-3 **The Incremental and Iterative Model**

classes become the basis for early releases. These releases are often, in essence, reusable classes. In this way, smaller parts of the whole can form and then gel with what has already been done. The system develops rapidly from smaller to larger entities. This means that standards and measurements must address the elements of the incremental build, rather than working through specific checkpoints in one large project with one path of linear phases.

Using the OO SDLC to Manage Projects

OO Development Tips
Develop large systems in small steps
Manage iteration and maintain focus
Measure your progress
Update estimates and plans fast and frequently
Remember reuse
Teams should focus on work; work should focus on teams
Management commitment must be strong

All of this iterative development makes the life of the analyst and programmer more exciting, less rigid, less predictable, and, we hope, more successful. Unfortunately, this also means that managing software development can suffer the impact of these same qualities. Without definitive steps, how do we determine progress? How do we know whether we are on schedule or over budget? How do we accommodate reassessment and revision, and still maintain control? Here are some suggestions for project management in an object-oriented context that will help you answer these questions.

Develop Large Systems in Small Steps

The first thing you are going to have to do is to incorporate the builds of the Incremental and Iterative SDLC in project planning. Incremental building applies a system that maps a series of repeating mini-cycles which overlap. This means that a large project must be partitioned into chunks which can be analyzed, designed, and realized in code in one turn or cycle. This may even be subdivided further in mini-iterations, with analysis deliverables such as the CRC card set and successful role play treated as one cycle repeated for different parts of the system. Hot spots and scope diagrams can help you visualize partitioning that can be substituted for waterfall steps in an SDLC project evaluation plan.

Above all, what is important is to be sure you do not attempt too much during each increment of the development cycle. Keep analyzing, designing, and building small pieces which can be extended during the next build. Each iteration should have a schedule attached to it, along with a list of the specific items intended to be completed. There is no general rule for all situations, so you will have to experiment to find what works for you. However, we have found that this iterative approach works best when each cycle is defined on a scale that can be completed within a week.

Manage Iteration and Maintain Focus

We mentioned earlier that the Incremental and Iterative SDLC also draws users into the heart of development activity more intensively and more frequently. Instead of making an initial request and then waiting until a full-blown project is delivered, the users are providing frequent input and being asked to respond (to accept) smaller, more frequent delivery of system mini-products that range from CRC role play to various levels of sophistication in prototypes and test versions.

The danger here is that the users get caught up in the revision side of the process and produce a steady flow of ideas for new features and functional enhancements! There is no easy solution to this, because we need the users in the development process and we need their enthusiasm as a motivation for participation. The flexibility of classes can look like a chance to try anything. The best way to hold demands in check, but keep users involved is to institute a method for recording and postponing ideas that are outside of the scope of the current cycle. Maintain focus on the task at hand. As you saw in the facilitation of CRC card sessions, clear statements of objectives for each cycle can be a strong support and drive a project forward.

Measure Your Progress

As each build is completed, record the results in a format that can be standardized. This information might include a list of the functions developed, the time spent on each activity (e.g., writing CRC cards, formulating scenarios, role play, assessment). For each cycle, how much time was spent in analysis? In coding? What is the performance of the code (efficiency, speed, memory)? Is the product reliable, tested, and able to be reused? Most important, did the results match the expectations of the users? Did the result actually perform as required by your client? This is the most important measure of success.

The key to this management strategy is that you must develop common points of comparison as you build parts of the system. Make elements of object-oriented methods elements of measurement. At first you may not know how many classes or how many collaborations to set as a standard, but if you record the evolution of the system and use consistent measures for user acceptance, you will gradually develop measures that you can use to chart progress and completion.

Update Estimates and Plans Fast and Frequently

The other side of making measurements is that you need to apply them to what is happening and use the input to revise your estimates and plans frequently. Don't wait until a project is bogged down and participants become discouraged. This will only lead to a search for scapegoats, and the most likely victim is going to be whatever is new. Take advantage of the incremental build of a system to make changes so that as soon as one cycle is over, you replan the next. Especially if you are new to object-oriented methods, or even to a technique such as CRC, let the process of using the technique teach you what to expect.

The exact number of times you move through the iterations depends on the nature of the application domain. We have found that a small to medium-sized system will increment through four to eight cycles of development. In any given cycle, the team may develop ten to twenty CRC card sets that each include a baker's dozen of classes. The total development time for such a system might be a year, but each cycle may last somewhere between one and two months. Track each cycle and evaluate them carefully. Learn to assess the impact of hot spots on succeeding cycles. Adjust the project schedule to allow ample time for initial and complicated analysis, and shorten expectations for cycles that are able to build on prior knowledge. In other words, do not try to micromanage each team meeting, but keep a close eye on the effect of each build on the next increment.

Remember Reuse

There are two sides to remembering to reuse. First, you should try to reuse existing classes wherever you can. Second, you must develop new classes so that later projects will be able to integrate them in new systems. If classes are going to be reused, they must be carefully thought out. This should be a critical element in your management style. Rushing a team to finish up, pressuring them to get done without fully analyzing the impact of their decisions on reusability, can mean adding time to the next cycle when, instead of reusing classes, the team must invent new classes. The biggest payoffs in object-oriented development are going to be increased reuse, reduced maintenance, and ease of enhancement. Do not make artificial deadlines the cause of rushed thinking and gangly classes that can only be used in one set of circumstances.

Beyond thinking about individual classes, for many parts of a system, there are going to be existing patterns or frameworks which can be reused. Encourage project teams to integrate this in their practice. Once the team has identified a "hot spot," they can review the library of patterns to see if they have a generalized template to guide them in their understanding of the classes involved. In some cases, an existing pattern can be reused fully. In other cases, the team may have to modify the reused pattern. Any existing pattern will make the addition of responsibilities and collaborations to the CRC card much easier.

Finally, for organizations that are just beginning their object-oriented efforts, reuse is going to pay off in the future; it is not an immediate benefit. There is no getting around the fact that this is a disadvantage. It is one of the many reasons why early adopters of object-oriented technologies have a competitive advantage, paying back their work as pioneers. Fortunately, many authors and software developers are now distributing models of object strategies which offer blueprints that give you class patterns which may be reused in your system, passing on some of the advantages of reuse to newcomers. Looking at such patterns, you can apply them to the CRC cards you are writing and speed up the process of analysis.

Teams Should Focus on Work; Work Should Focus on Teams

In this book, we have placed a strong emphasis on teamwork. Although object-oriented development can be useful in small projects, most of the time groups of people are going to be working together on a larger system. This means that it is not business as usual for an organization, where the old way of working is based on the idea of a lone programmer battling it out with her application. Classes and reuse mean that applications do not get developed in solo flight. For managers, this also means that some time and thought must be dedicated to team dynamics and making sure the team can work well together.

In the chapters on brainstorming and role playing, we have talked a lot about the role of the facilitator and the value of choosing team members carefully. For the manager, looking at the Incremental and Iterative SDLC, this can mean careful attention to an evolving team. Do not roll over the composition of teams too rapidly, because each group that has gone through a cycle now knows something about the system and something about working together. In role play, for example, learning how to use active playing out of CRC cards can be as important to a new area of investigation as specialized expertise. Bring visitor-experts in and out of the project when necessary, but aim for a consistent and increasingly experienced team.

That means that the measures of the development process should also include measures that reward team effort. Plan progress reviews with an eye to the accomplishment of the whole group. Deemphasize individual roles by rotating presenters during management reviews. Do not scapegoat individual team members. As a manager it is your responsibility to address problems, but leave implementation of solutions to the facilitator and the group.

It is also important to be sure that you do not overlook seemingly trivial things such as a clean meeting room, some refreshments, and an atmosphere that is truly free from interruptions. Respect your team and do not pull individual members in and out for fire-fighting. Give them both the privacy and the tools they need. Make sure that in addition to peace and quiet, they have adequate supplies, whiteboards, markers, desks, computers, and Net connections (if necessary) right at hand.

Management Commitment Must Be Strong

Little things such as supplies and big things such as planning are all part of the confirmation of management's commitment to a project. In offering advice on managing object-oriented development, we are assuming that managers want to take on the challenge of trying something new. Choosing a pilot project wisely, picking the right team, giving them the tools they need, and providing a backdrop of confidence are all actions that depend on a positive attitude. Lest we seem too naive, we also acknowledge that this kind of commitment is not always easy to make. Programmers, especially the sharpest people in an organization, may be frustrated with the limitations of current methods and push for change. Are they headed in the right direction? If you are not sure, you may undermine your own success. Take a little time now to assess your own level of commitment and its effect on the projects under you.

Interest in object-oriented development often emerges at the technical level. Programming staff, eager to keep their skills moving with the technology, read up on new languages, talk to friends in the field, and take advantage of courses offered by internal and external training programs. This interest is reinforced by a flood of articles in popular computing magazines, academic journals, and other professional publications. All of them promise (once again!) a new age in computing. Is this true? Should you, as a manager, rush ahead on the basis of promise? After so many "silver bullets" turned to lead, maybe you would feel better if you were to stand tight?

The answer to these kinds of questions is never cut and dried. If you wait too long, you may fall far behind. As we said earlier, pioneering groups are now receiving the payoff for their work in the form of experience, benchmarks, and confidence. Nobody really knows yet whether OO will "make money," but there is certainly great potential. The *potential* for rapid development, ease of maintenance, and increased reuse is really there. On the other hand, nobody will deny that the learning curve for object-oriented design and coding has turned out to be much steeper than the early promotions suggested. It can take even a skilled programmer twelve to eighteen months to become proficient. This means that the risk–benefit equation is going to be affected by time. To manage the kind of change involved, managers must be ready to manage change in the organization, to allow time for change, and to provide commitment to change.

There are some aspects of object-oriented projects that can help you manage change. Using the kind of quick and frequent evaluation and planning cycles we have described is one tool. Another is to take advantage of user involvement and user-centric practices such as CRC cards and role play to increase user commitment. These analysis techniques are easy to learn and easy to use. In addition to providing designers with more accurate requirements, they buffer the organization from the more difficult side of the changeover to object-oriented development. They provide a force that works against tendencies to lean on a few individuals—to invest a small number of gurus with too much power and too much responsibility.

Summing Up Our Advice

Managing object-oriented development is going to mean managing organizational change. You cannot succeed at this unless you are ready. You must be willing to spend time developing new project plans, new evaluation techniques, and new standards. You are also going to have to back up this work with a touch of public relations. If you are managing from within the systems area, you are going to have to be able to explain your targets and your ways for determining whether you have met them to general management in the organization. You are going to have to decide how the changed SDLC is going to affect your budget, your schedule, your hiring, and your work assignments. You are going to have to convert the guidelines just described into plans and standards.

An external consultant who has the advantage of prior experience can be a valuable resource if you are serious about change, but beware of trying to replace the time involved in learning with a short-term investment in services. Look for a person or group who want to power up your people. Look for a proposal that addresses the character of your organization. Beware of offers to do too much for you, and welcome offers to teach strategies such as CRC card analysis that leave behind more skills than reports. Don't mistake your lack of familiarity with object-oriented technology for ignorance about management.

Of course, what this all boils down to is a management style that is grounded in commitment. Hesitation and hedging will only get you in trouble here. If you are still too unsure to make some clear choices about pilot projects and to look for the support of higher management, you may not yet be ready to manage the changeover to object-oriented development. This does not mean that you cannot begin to explore it. Review the suggestions we are going to make for choosing a pilot project. Apply them to your situation. Is there a "hot spot," a starting point, a test case, that you can identify? If you must narrow down the scale of your effort to ensure a full-scale commitment to the effort, do so. Remember, reuse and incremental builds mean that none of this initial work will be wasted. If you decide that you like the new way of doing things, you can go on, moving up from a small pilot to a wider cycle.

THE PILOT PROJECT

Pilot Project Guidelines

Nurture a cohesive team
Provide abundant support
Make early completion a priority
Work with a reasonable scale
Take advantage of opportunities for user interface

Whether you are on your first object-oriented project, or are starting a subsequent object-oriented effort, the capacity of the technology to allow development of subsets of work makes the notion of a pilot project a wonderful way to leverage for success. Rather than getting lost in the entire world of a new system, carve out a cornerstone and use that as the context for learning about the domain and establishing user terminology. If this is not the first object-oriented project, look for areas in an earlier project you can reuse and base the pilot on an area that will build on the previous one.

For the first object-oriented project, it is very important to select the domain and scope of the pilot carefully. We have tried to emphasize this by describing the rationale for selection in the case studies in this book. Choose a pilot that lends itself to utilizing the strengths of object-oriented technology. For example, application areas that involve a heavily graphical user interface component lend themselves readily to object-oriented design and implementation. This does not mean that there must be a graphical interface for object-oriented methods to be used; it means that the strengths of the approach in comparison to other methods are often easily apparent in this kind of project. In any case, for a pilot, select an application that makes good use of the key benefits of classes: information hiding, encapsulation of responsibility with knowledge, abstraction, and polymorphism.

As a manager you want a pilot project that can be measured against existing development strategies. Don't let a flashy new application distract you from that basic management responsibility. The pilot should let team members who are involved in a significant learning curve, especially during design, see what they have earned for their investment. This can be difficult, because a good deal of the benefit of object orientation will come down the road in the ability to reuse earlier classes and to make rapid responses to requests for enhancement, as well as in reduced maintenance effort. This is one more reason for looking at an application with a user interface that shows off the ability of object-oriented methods to shorten previously time-consuming efforts.

In sum, the goal of the pilot is to emphasize those characteristics of object-oriented methods that offer the greatest and most visible advantage over existing system development methods. A successful pilot can be the key that opens the door to readiness for change on a large scale throughout the organization.

Nurture a Cohesive Team

Any CRC analysis team must include a blend of technical staff and users, who are "domain experts." The technical staff should be skilled in object-oriented development, with at least one person who can act as a leader and a teacher. The users on the team should know a lot about the real-world needs which the system is intended to support, whether or not they have participated in an object-oriented project before. Keep the teams to a reasonable size so that everyone can get to know each other. Bonds form even during the hard work of analysis. Brainstorming and role playing can reinforce this, compensating for any underlying friction or doubts about the value of switching to a new technology. If your organization has been using object-oriented methods for a while, these same activities can help break down barriers between the novices and the initiated.

Whether this is a new development strategy or just a new team of people working together, also be aware of differences in learning styles and problem solving habits. We have tried to emphasize these intangibles in the case studies. No rule or guideline should be enforced without exception at the expense of dividing team members over issues that are not truly germane to the work that is being done. On the other hand, do not be afraid of differences. CRC cards and the informal work style they entail allow all sorts of people to work together. As long as the goals and subjects of discussion are clear, differences can actually improve the results of brainstorming and role play.

Provide Abundant Support

Good workers rarely succeed without support from management for the tools and environment necessary for success. This is all the more important for a team of people embarking on a pilot project. Recognize that people are working with new ideas and that they need to put in an extra effort. As we said earlier, make sure that the workplace facilitates learning by providing tools and time. Sometimes this means addressing needs on an individual basis. For example, building knowledge and enthusiasm might involve keeping up with what other people in other organizations are doing. If reading *Object Magazine* is important, don't depend on people to scrounge up their own copies. Make a subscription for each team member a part of the budget.

Training needs are also important even when they seem costly as an up-front investment. We suggest starting with training before the pilot begins. Send key staff to seminars and courses. Include both novices and current gurus. Although a few may come back with some doubts about what they have seen, you will find that responses to early training efforts produce a core of personnel who will then be key to the momentum of the project.

Finally, do not forget the type of support which is hard to quantify: the visible political support which management should give to the pilot project. Clear statements should be made about the reasons for the decision to proceed down the path of object-oriented technology. Far from feeling as though their careers are in jeopardy if they get involved in something new and indeterminate, team members should see the pilot project as an exciting assignment, sure to lead to advancement even if the system itself is not completely successful the first time around.

Make Early Completion a Priority

In the same spirit, the pilot project should be short enough to allow for timely assessment—that is, six to nine months, or less than one fiscal year. Using our approach, that will mean roughly three to six iterations. If the pilot goes well, other teams and managers will be interested in getting on board. If the pilot takes too long, it may become an extended learning experience for the team, but to the rest of the organization it may look like an assignment to purgatory.

Another reason to look for a project that can be completed in a short time is that you may have to redo early efforts later as your people become more skilled. This can easily develop into a sense that pilot projects are somehow phony. Make the possibility of revision a part of the time frame, keeping the first run moving forward, allowing enough time to learn, but not dragging out the pilot effort. Remember that we do learn from mistakes. The first implementation will be a window to better approaches in the next round.

In the pilot project, all of the phases of the development cycle will be compressed. You can expect to hold productive review and approval sessions as frequently as every three weeks and to complete a project in about six months. For a larger project, there may be a frequent review pattern for subsystem increments and a pattern of more widely spaced reviews, perhaps every third month, of the system as a whole. Also, remember that although we are going to map out some metrics, numbers do not need to do the work of the system. Include demonstrations of prototypes (even a run-through of a final format role play) as part of the management review of project progress. Plan project presentations that build management sophistication about object-oriented development.

Work with a Reasonable Scale

In order to control the scope of the project, a rule of thumb for a pilot might be an application that involves less than a dozen interacting classes. The metrics for CRC cards discussed later in this chapter will give some idea of the exponential complexity involved in larger groups of classes. Since object-oriented systems lend themselves to clearly defined interfaces between subsystems, features added later can fully utilize the original pilot application classes. That means that including a wider domain and more classes in the initial pilot effort may not be the most productive approach, and it is certainly not necessary.

The pilot's scale should also demonstrate the value of reusability by seeing its impact on related areas of development. When you break down a project into segments and choose both a pilot and a follow-up to it, anticipate related classes by examining hot spots. If the scale is small, a team can plan to work through two small projects before considering their work "complete." They can take advantage of reusable classes, as well as reworking classes when they see that the first effort is not as flexible as it might be. If the scale is small, you can do this; if the scale is too large, too much may be "lost" by going back. Don't be seduced by longings for the discrete steps of the waterfall model. They will only get you in trouble when it comes to your pilot project.

Take Advantage of Opportunities for User Interface

All object-oriented languages provide excellent GUI components which can be reused, making it relatively easy to demonstrate platform capabilities quickly. This kind of feedback in the pilot project can complement users' involvement in analysis strategies such as CRC by giving them tangible results that respond to their input. The user interface is an easy way to communicate with users about the design of the system in response to their analysis of the problem domain. Moreover, once the GUI is used to improve understanding of the user domain and collect feedback, it can be rapidly improved.

The object-oriented SDLC has a big advantage in the area of user interface. Going back while building up and moving ahead becomes very tangible when the development of the user interface is reused later on. Users may not understand how classes are used in programming, but they can see the way in which sameness affects ease of use for an interface.

If you usually do real-time systems or embedded software, it may be hard to find a pilot with a user-interface component. In such a situation, we would suggest considering the use of a simulation assignment as the pilot project, and implementing a GUI interface even if your company usually uses text I/O for its simulations. Management is always impressed with new graphics! The heavy graphical interface will show off the strengths of object-oriented technology, while the team will learn about the gains ahead as they explore and add to the existing vendor-supplied class libraries.

Choosing a Pilot from Our Case Studies

Let's apply these criteria to the two cases you have seen so far in this book: the stock portfolio and the fabric cutting system. Which one of these would make the better pilot project? At first glance, the stock portfolio looks like a good candidate. It is a clearly delineated application with a limited charter. The information handled by the system seems straightforward and, as we saw, it lent itself easily to the CRC card approach. The team was able to learn a lot about defining classes, and they saw some of the snags involved in allocating responsibilities. The report that the system produces not only gave the team a jump on finding classes, but it looks like a deliverable that would impress the user.

The problem here is that whatever method you use to do a pilot project for the stock portfolio report, the result is going to look and feel the same. It is essentially a transaction-oriented system, which means that you might even lose points because the time it takes to learn the existing class libraries, and to get used to role play, appears to drag out a trivial application. Although the user may be pleased with the improved communication of domain issues to the development team, the manager may not care if the only thing you have to show is a report that isn't even linked to an OO database management system. If you are already moving ahead on an OO project for the entire Portfolio system, the Portfolio Report would make a nice pilot segment, but as a first-time project, it is a weak performer.

Instead, you should look for an application more like the design and pattern system (Design Pro) or the traffic intersection we describe in the next chapter. These are good candidates for showing off the talents of OO for handling a graphical user interface. The manipulation of information on-screen lends itself to rapid prototyping as well as CRC role play. Each application presents graphical representations of objects which managers, as people with real world experience, can readily relate to: cars and clothing!

On the other hand, one potential problem with any first project is the one we already saw in the role plays: the number of classes tends to mushroom rapidly. This is a serious problem, especially for new CRC analysts. However, just as our team decided to fence off sections of the domain, we can follow through on that decision in the scope of the pilot. Instead of trying to map out the entire system right away, use an incremental and iterative approach. In the design and pattern system, for example, we used CRC cards to role play just the style assembly. Choose a discrete domain segment, then rapidly prototype it. Present this to users and management for assessment. Then, with their approval and new timing estimates, go back to the CRC cards to link up to the next segment and work forward from there.

GETTING STARTED IN YOUR ORGANIZATION

Start-up Guidelines

Start now, but start small
Collect data right from the beginning
Make the training investment up front
Plan a coherent training ladder
Develop a core of experts
Use your experts to spread knowledge

When you begin your own project, there are going to be some priority areas of concern. The first is going to be deciding how long the pilot project will take and mapping out a project plan. Next, you are going to have to prepare your people to work on the project. This will mean a considerable investment in training, an investment that should be part of the plan and timing for your first project. Many organizations run into trouble because they try to hold down costs by using a plan that attempts to test object-oriented methods before fully investing in training. This is a deal with the devil that will never give you an honest measure of success or failure. We are going to argue strongly in favor of a realistic, face-the-facts approach to object-oriented projects. Even if you have already started and have made some mistakes, bringing in these management practices now can make a big difference in the yield of your investment.

Timing

Now that you have made the commitment to move to object-oriented development and you have selected a project, how do you actually get started? Timing the project has two aspects: First, how do you order the life cycle (process) activities? Second, how long do you spend on each activity once you start? Timing in object-oriented projects is especially problematic because of the paucity of quantified data on previous projects for organizations that are just starting. Even where object-oriented development has been in use for a while, few organizations take the time to collect data on the development processes. This means that searching for precedents and guidelines may be impossible because even outside of your organization the benchmark data just does not exist. So, the first maxim for the next project is: Monitor your process, whatever it is, so that you can improve in the future. The common-sense subsequent maxim is: Get started anyway!

Earlier in this chapter, we looked at an overview of the incremental and iterative SDLC. To recap, we talked about the crucial importance of frequent and early prototypes, along with iterative development and incremental building of a working system. It is a given that if you are starting with prototypes as a basic development tool for defining and confirming user requirements, it will not be possible to set out a detailed, full-term project plan from the start. However, as the application space is partitioned into subsystems which can be integrated incrementally after partial builds, management's ability to plan accurately will increase.

When the project timeline is mapped to the life-cycle phases, as shown in Figure 8-4, you can see that there are several checkpoints where project estimates are set and reviewed. These are the intervals between the evaluation of a cycle and the initiation of the next incremental cycle. Initially, the timeline projections you make may only be accurate for the next cycle. However, if you are collecting data and monitoring progress, the later phases of the pilot project will become more predictable, and by the time a second project is underway, the collected metrics will enable you to make closer and closer estimates. This is one of the advantages of this SDLC pattern—the combination of iterative patterns and incremental interlocking elements of the same system makes timing easier and easier to establish as the project progresses.

The fact that the iterative approach brings the team back to old ground does create a paradoxical situation. On the surface, it may look like a potential infinite loop. If each step forward means a step back to redo what was set before, how does the project ever move ahead? Initially, a team that is new to object-oriented techniques may find progress is very slow and that the more they learn, the more they have to rework and revise previous decisions. However, at some point the classes and their relationships do gel. Then the loops make definite spirals up and away from each other with only minor revision to previous work. On a project with experienced team members, a reasonably large system might be subdivided in such a way that there are, on the average, three to five incremental iterations. For a team new to OO, there may be this many iterations for even a small pilot project. The important thing to remember is that even though the iteration may take you back to the same parts of the system, the level of sophistication that you bring to the review is always increasing and, because of the testing facet of the prototype approach, each cycle is based on an increment in the level of confidence that the system is a match to the users' requirements.

Training

Object technology is today's most promising technology. It offers great hope for overcoming some of the worst Achilles heels of the software development community. The promise of substantial savings in development and maintenance costs seems near, but before these savings can be realized, a substantial training effort must be undertaken. Although the techniques for user involvement, such as the CRC cards, can bring untrained domain experts into the process, the systems team itself must have a solid grounding in object-oriented techniques. This costs time, effort, and money.

A Fortune 500 training manager told us that "object-oriented techniques have proven to be the most expensive and most difficult training project we have ever undertaken. It's costing us much more than we expected." Experienced programmers uniformly agree that the transition to a fully object-oriented approach was the most difficult learning task of their careers. They estimate that it takes a minimum of six months of practice for an experienced structured programmer to become somewhat proficient in a pure object-oriented language. Up to a year is necessary for true proficiency. Clearly, this learning curve is a great

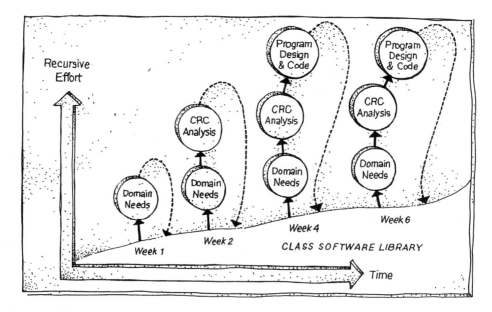

Figure 8-4 ***Timing of the OO SDLC***

deal longer than it was for structured techniques and CASE tools. Why this is so may be open to debate and discussion. Whatever the reason, it is clear to all who have adopted object technologies that programmers need lots of training. The payoff on OO is not in short-term gains; this is a long-term investment.

Another important thing to consider is that, if the training is going to be effective, it must be approached systematically. Many of the programmers we have talked to found the transition even more difficult because training was offered in an ad-hoc, exploratory style that did not give them systematic and timely preparation for an actual project. Obviously, this is not only a source of personal frustration; it also aggravates the planning process. If team members are training up as they go, planning each increment in the cycles of the project will continue to be difficult. The sooner and more methodical your training program, the sooner you will reap the results in predictable time frames for project phases.

The most successful training programs combine formal and informal methods. We have found that rather than sending programmers to a formal course right away, it is better to initiate the process by providing time, manuals, and software for them to "play" with for several weeks. Once they have a sense of the elements and strategies used in the software, they are really ready to absorb and remember the information they will get in a formal seminar. If they have a basic vocabulary going into the course, they will be able to understand everything that is said. If they do not, many things mentioned by the instructor will go by unnoticed, and the programmers' ability to ask constructive questions pertaining to their own work will be limited.

One way that an organization can try to shorten the gap between learning and undertaking a real-life project is by bringing in an outside consultant who is already an expert to lead the team and guide the selection and implementation of a pilot project. This is a good place to start. As Nancy Wilkinson points out in her map for CRC card sessions, a group facilitator who has a lot of object-oriented development experience can help the group see the connection between problems in the role play and possibilities for revising the CRC cards.

On the other hand, although consultants offer a short-term solution that can accelerate the learning process, adapting object-oriented technology is a long-term investment. In the long run, outside experts cannot make your organization successful. You have to learn how to do things yourself! Therefore, another important training decision you have to make is how to breed knowledge in your own organization.

SWAT TEAMS OR GURUS?

There are many approaches to developing in-house staff. The one we favor involves the development of a leadership group. This concept is similar to the elite police "SWAT" teams, whose training and personal standards are going to provide an example and an inspiration to the rest of the force. A significant training decision involves careful thinking about the members of this "SWAT team." The team should consist of a core group of programmers, between four and six (a number consistent with the scope recommended for the pilot project), who are trained and then designated to work on the pilot project. This allows them time to become conversant in object-oriented technologies. This team then becomes the core within the organization, the in-house "gurus" who will facilitate for new teams.

You do have to be careful with the SWAT team approach. It is inherently problematic because it leaves the organization dependent on a few individuals. This exposes you to some of the same risks you face with outside consultants. Once they know their stuff, your in-house experts will have to be well compensated or they may jump ship, leaving you no better off than you would have been hiring from outside. So, don't shy away from this expense. Use it to your advantage and utilize these experts as teachers. Do not leave them to themselves, but develop a plan for consistently bringing in more people and growing more in-house expertise.

Another problem you must face is one that is inherent to the idea of being a guru: the experts come to consider themselves indispensable and altogether perfect. This happens because these gurus do know their stuff, and they get gratification out of disseminating their ideas to others. Turn this to your advantage! Emphasize the fact that the SWAT team is a group. Select members of the team not only for technical aptitude, but because they have the interpersonal skills to take on a teaching role. Choose people who will be able to lead subsequent teams as a group, looking for ways to bring everyone into the process rather than looking for other individuals to single out and initiate one at a time. Choose people who are motivated by motivating others, not by intimidating them.

Finally, although there is a clear connection to team practice and organizational objectives, in order to be successful on their first assignment, the SWAT team must be given some privileges. They are going to need extra resources, higher funding levels, and twice the time they think they need. If possible, this group should have the authority to take part in the object-oriented platform selection. All team members should have equal access to documentation and computer equipment. These support items should be of the highest caliber available.

ACCOMMODATING LEGACY SYSTEMS

Legacy Integration Guidelines

> Do not throw out working software
> Create dynamic links to call non-OO code
> Reuse responsibilities and the code that supports them
> Parts wrappers can protect legacy code

Management rarely likes to throw away expensive tools which are still used to run the business, and old software is no exception. Fortunately, there is no reason why you can't incorporate existing procedurally based code into object-oriented systems. The two systems can coexist well. In fact, if you draw clear lines between existing systems and object code, the old software can ease the entry of many programmers into object thinking.

Don't feel as if you have to start over from scratch. Instead, aim to reuse every part of the existing system you can. If the code works, and it meets current needs, it makes economic sense to keep it in production. The old maxim of "if it ain't broke, don't fix it" applies: What we are trying to fix is the ease of reuse, the productivity of development, and the effort of maintenance. We are not trying to reinvent the entire body of code that now exists in the world, variously estimated at some 40 billion lines of code!

Integrating old systems is going to mean that some front-end analytical work must be done. Review the old system and develop a definition of that system in terms of classes, responsibilities, and collaborations. This is a difficult task, since the old system was not designed to be thought of as interacting classes. However, it is a crucial task if you want to keep as much of the old code in use as possible.

CRC cards can be a big help here. Even if you have to "force" the design into some of the frameworks or patterns you find in other systems, writing the CRC cards and role-playing them will help you to translate the old system into an object-like version. This may not be adequate for the parts of the system that are going to be replaced, but it will help you see what can be reused and how to relate the reused portion of the system to the new portions.

To help you think about old systems in new terms, we have identified three patterns of legacy reuse: communication by executables, direct reuse in responsibilities, and parts wrappers. Although some idiosyncrasies of the old system will persist, working with them in terms of these patterns may be a wiser approach than throwing out years of work and retiring still-useful systems before their time.

Communication by Executables

This is the easiest form of reuse, since it leaves the existing code base alone. The new object-oriented software calls legacy code, most commonly through the use of a dynamic link library (DLL) function. When non-OO code is called, the message usually has to be configured as a typical procedure call (sets of characters, numbers, and perhaps delimiters), and any returned data will be, in a way, "reclassed" at the boundary of the DLL by the receiving class.

What is nice is that this also works in the reverse, so that legacy functions and subsystems can communicate with new object-oriented software the same way! Neither side needs to know anything about how the other does its business, so it is often called the "black box" approach (as is the case with the testing strategy of the same name). This approach is well liked by maintenance programmers, who can continue to work on legacy systems even though new functions are added in a purely class-responsibility-collaboration object-oriented environment. In this way, rather than choosing between old systems and new technology, you get both!

Direct Reuse in Responsibilities

Most classes have to do things, and objects in that class will exhibit predetermined behavior. They need to perform actions to meet the demands on the system from users, to comply with the system requirements. This means that what the classes must do can be extracted from the same sources you used to find the classes. In fact, as you think about naming classes, you are also selecting them because of what they do. Be careful not to carry over old implementation prejudices when you look for ideas about responsibility. By the way, you'll find that although it is common to directly reuse responsibilities for behavior, this is not the case for knowledge responsibility.

Once specific action responsibility has been assigned to a class, you may find the action has already been coded in a legacy system. Good examples of this type of responsibility are complex interest rate calculation, or a specific sorting algorithm. These algorithms can be directly incorporated into the responsibilities of newly designed classes. They become the documentation of the action, and can usually be directly translated into the new object programming language with little change.

Parts Wrappers

We have a different type of problem when the basic core of a system being designed is class based, but important parts of the implementation must rely on existing production software. We're creating a new class-based system and have to reach out to existing code still in the function-oriented world. One way to accommodate this is to create a sort of a virtual DLL: you make up a class which exists only to interface to the outside code. This is becoming common as new graphical user interface tools allow us to drag and drop objects on the screen, along with connections between their icons. What this means is that you'll have an object which is primarily a screen interface (an icon, a list box, etc.).

This GUI "part" is often referred to as a "wrapper" around the legacy code. The wrapper takes care of the interface between procedural software and the object world of classes and collaborations. In this case, legacy code is placed in an object-oriented "wrapper" so that it appears to be a class. What's happened is that a new GUI has been created to mediate between legacy and object code. This is the approach taken in several new visual programming environments, such as the IBM VisualAge family and the Digitalk/ParcPlace Parts system.

METRICS FOR CRC ANALYSIS

Now that we have an idea of training needs, and a clear idea of the project life cycle, it is time to talk about assessment. How do we evaluate the development effort? How do we know if we are on the right track? One way to do this is through a set of metrics. Since the focus of this book is on CRC, we will concentrate on metrics that apply to the early analysis

IFPUG: International Function Point User's Group members are working on extentions into the OO arena. They may be reached in Ohio, USA at 614-895-7130.

MIT: At the Massachusetts Institute of Technology look for articles by S. Chidamber and C. Kemerer, such as *A Metrics Suite for Object Oriented Design* IEEE Transactions on Software Engineering 26(6) 1994, 476-493.

NC A&T: *SMARTS*, the Smalltalk Metrics Analysis Reality Tracking Software, is a project at North Carolina A&T State University, funded by IBM Software Solutions. Copies of the software, related documentation and articles can be obtained from dbellin@ncat.edu.

UTS: The University of Technology in Sidney Australia is doing useful metrics studies and comparisons. Of particular interest is the work of Professor Brian Henderson-Sellers: *Object-Oriented Metrics*: Measures of Complexity (1996: Prentice Hall).

Figure 8-5 **Metrics Resource Pointers**

phase of each life cycle. There is a great deal of current research in the areas of object-oriented metrics for quality, reuse, testing, and development. We cannot cover the full topic here, but Figure 8-5 includes some pointers to key citations.

Metrics means counting: We want to collect numbers which might be indicators of poor (or great!) CRC designs. Although object orientation is new, we can establish some guidelines based on data that has already been collected. This data can be found in articles and university research, but one of the most effective ways to benchmark is going to be to keep track of your own metrics as you work. Using the metrics we discuss, you can measure your designs and then, by mapping problem areas to metrics, identify and guard against any poor practices that habitually show up in your group. Metrics are particularly necessary when adopting a new technology, since the only way to know if effective practices have been put in place is to measure them for quality.

In a project that uses an iterative and incremental SDLC, each small incremental cycle can be associated with specific progressions through a project plan. Measuring these might include evaluation of the budget, criteria for successful teamwork, and mileposts for meeting requirements. Once you set up the criteria for evaluation, they should be reapplied each time you iterate through development. This will give you a baseline for deciding what you should expect to accomplish. By the end of the pilot (and several cycles), you will have the numbers that you need to make your next plan, schedule, and budget more accurate and your team composition more effective.

You may be a believer in the saying, "Measuring the wrong thing serves no purpose." There is some truth to this, but it should not be used as an excuse not to measure at all.

We've found that the very act of taking some measurements will help you discover what is beneficial to measure, and what serves no purpose. Remember, object-oriented development is still a new experience that demands a higher tolerance for exploration. Some measurement is going to be better than none at all, even if some of the data that you collect proves irrelevant.

Analysis is always an area where it is hard to define concise and easily measured units of activity, so we tend to concentrate on looking at the time elapsed. Working with classes gives us an opportunity to add one concrete element to the picture. Some key measures we use to evaluate the analysis portion of the SDLC are these:

Person-days per class
Classes per person
Person-days per incre-cycle
Incre-cycles per project
Percent classes reused
Percent frameworks/patterns developed

Note that the discovery and definition of classes gives us a way to use measuring to get an idea of the relationship of effort to results. Just keep in mind that classes themselves vary. You will have to look at the analysis metrics in the context of the CRC metrics discussed next.

Let us point out a few things about these measurement start points. First of all, if they are going to be useful, you should be able to create estimates for the project as a whole, and also at the start of each incremental cycle of development. Even if your initial estimates are way off, they are a basis for comparison and provide a clear picture of what you *thought* you needed, even if you had no experiential basis for projection. Unless you begin with a firm statement of those expectations, you cannot learn to use metrics to adjust expectations based on reality.

As you gain experience, you can make adjustments to the estimate. Each cycle should yield slightly more accurate estimates. In this way, the "actuals versus estimates" can be kept as a historical record of the project. In the next project they become benchmarks. Over time, both the quality of projects and the quality of benchmarks will steadily improve, and you will have a clear record of that progress.

The percentage of classes reused, and the percentage of frameworks/patterns developed, are difficult to measure, but over the long haul they may be the best indicators of success. Percentage of classes reused is the count of classes from previous projects which the team was able to use in the new one. This measures the amount of the software which was not designed from scratch this time around.

As with many measures, *class reuse* cannot be quantified perfectly. We've found that although design groups eventually reuse classes, they rarely reuse them without change! It is difficult, however, to obtain a useful measure of how they are changed. Our feeling is that the benefit offered by the opportunity to start with an already developed and tested class is so great that it outweighs the problems we have measuring the amount of change. In the end, it may not even be important to measure the changes, since they do not serve as deterrents to reuse or make it any less valuable.

The measurement of the extent to which frameworks and patterns have been developed in the system is another important way to evaluate the development effort. This is the converse of the percentage of classes reused, because it looks forward to the next project instead of measuring the current project against existing systems. *Percentage of frameworks/patterns developed* speaks to the ability of the next projects to potentially reuse this system's classes. To the extent that the classes can be conceptually packaged as frameworks during analysis, the potential for reuse, at a greater payoff, is increased. Again, however, this is only an imperfect measure. We really have no way to know if the frameworks developed for this project will really be reused in the future. All we can say is that this process produced a greater *potential* future benefit if this measure is higher than before.

Measuring the CRC Analysis

Because the focus of this book is the CRC card technique, let's look more closely at a few metrics that can help us evaluate our use of that technique. Given the role of CRC as an early "first cut" in the software life cycle, there are only a small number of relatively simple metrics that are appropriate, but as we said before, combined with the measurement of other project planning factors, they can help you develop a sense of how well your team is working. Three specific metrics apply to the development of the CRC card set: *maximum depth of inheritance*, the *number of responsibilities* assigned to each class, and the *number of collaborators* for a class. You will notice that they are all based on elements of the CRC cards that can be counted as the group is working. These are high-level indicators of the potential of the CRC allocations for ease of object-oriented design and coding. In other words, they can be used directly to evaluate the CRC cards themselves looking forward to design and code.

Each of the metrics recommended for use in the CRC phase of the project has been chosen because it can be counted without special tools or an enormous investment of time. Let's look at a description of how you count each one and a brief explanation of why we feel that metric is an important indicator of quality.

The *maximum depth of inheritance* metric counts the class hierarchy. It reflects how many times you have created "kind-of" subtypes of objects. This subtyping is the kind in which an investment class is divided into stocks, bonds, and cash. Each shares the overall responsibilities defined in the investment class. For short hierarchies, this is a positive benefit of OO. If the string of subclasses becomes too long, it becomes difficult to trace the flow of responsibilities, resulting in overly complex systems that are difficult to test and to reuse. If there are more than six layers of subclasses in a CRC card set, careful review is needed.

As we saw in the earlier case studies, it is important that a class have a clearly defined set of duties. This can be measured by counting the *number of responsibilities* assigned to each class. One class should not have a huge set of responsibilities covering the whole system. This situation in a CRC card set would indicate an imbalance in design. Refine the overly complex class into a series of simpler objects. This will make the system easier to understand, easier to implement, and easier to reuse. The value for this measure varies greatly with the type of application. For most commercial transaction oriented systems, we have found that values between approximately eight and eighteen are common. Any more than around a dozen responsibilities for a class card in a CRC analysis should be cause for a careful analysis review.

The converse of the responsibility measure is the count of the *number of collaborators* for a class. In an effort to have a small set of responsibilities for a class, the analysts may create several new collaborators. However, beginning analysts have a tendency to do this where it is not appropriate. In other words, collaborator classes are created where subclassing is more suitable. This will create a situation where a class card lists many collaborators, but has few children. There is a tension between subclassing and interclass collaboration. You want to take advantage of inheritance and encapsulation to minimize collaboration, but you do not want to overload a class and lower the cohesion of the class, so you are going to be looking for collaborators. We've found that a value of more than around eight collaborators for any class card in a CRC card set should be cause for careful review.

THE NEXT STEP

We've seen how object-oriented analysis changes the traditional software life cycle into a series of user-centered iterative repetitions. These changes need a new management style, openly committed to object technology and emphasizing pilot projects, early checkpoints, and heavy training. Fortunately, legacy systems can be accommodated within the object-oriented approach, so the existing software inventory is by no means obsolete. Good management practice includes some objective measurements, and we saw that there are some which can be used as you get started using the CRC card techniques.

CRC cards create a first-cut analysis for complex systems, and let analysts and users examine the operation of discrete subsystems. It has been both our experience and that of many others that CRC cards are invaluable input into more formal methods, as well as being a great way to build teamwork and common understanding. CRC cards and CRC role plays remain invaluable to anyone using the more complex methods.

To see how this works, in the next chapter we look at one last case study, a traffic control system. This time we will concentrate on the results as much as the process so that you can see the kind of picture of the system the CRC cards create. We will also look at how the CRC card set created for the traffic control system can even be used as the basis for design and implementation. The chapters following the case study show how programmers use this information to design and code a first simulation of the system. Finally, we will also use the traffic control system CRC card set to talk about the bridge between analysis (CRC card technique) and the introduction of a formal methodology.

Chapter 9

Case Study 3: Traffic Control

The objective of this chapter is to see how a more experienced team works with an outside consultant to refine their CRC card set. The case study begins with a first-cut CRC card set. The chapter also includes some initial exposition on the application to bring you up to speed. By the end of the chapter, you should understand the final CRC card set and the application well, since they will serve as the context for the discussion of design and coding in the rest of the book.

Although many readers of this book may be novices in traffic control, we expect that most of you have had considerable experience waiting at intersections and trying to anticipate the traffic light changes. This experience, combined with the inherent teaching qualities of the CRC card technique, should let us prove to you that CRC cards are an excellent way to break down an application in a team that brings together domain experts and technical people.

The chapter includes an introduction to the problem faced by the town of Chapel Hollow, the project team, and a summary of the project plan; a review of traffic management vocabulary and basic intersections; the enactment of the first-cut set of CRC cards; the assessment with a professional facilitator; the enactment of the revised set of cards; and finally, a discussion of how the system can be extended to include zones.

TRAFFIC PROBLEMS IN CHAPEL HOLLOW

Chapel Hollow used to be a quiet college community with simple traffic patterns. The main street through town passes in front of the university campus, and most homes are in quiet neighborhoods. However, the relaxed atmosphere of the community has begun to draw a host of retirees along with a commuter population working in the nearby industrial park. The price of this popularity is a rising volume of traffic, as well as heavy traffic periods in the morning, at lunchtime, and in the late afternoon.

Before the problem becomes any worse—which it will, as new developments spring up in the outlying farm areas and new businesses flock to the burgeoning office complexes along the entry corridor to the town—the City Council has decided to invest in an automated traffic control system that will govern individual intersections. Eventually it may coordinate the flow of traffic through multiple intersections along the main traffic corridors. A bond for $1.5 million has already been approved, and Frank Desoto has been hired as Traffic and Safety Manager. The full project is expected to take about two years to implement.

A key characteristic of the system is flexibility. The increasing population density will require frequent adjustments to any traffic control system. To meet the pressure for adaptability, Frank has decided to take an object-oriented approach. He used object-oriented techniques in a highway capacity system a couple of years ago, and he felt good about the way the project turned out. In the case of the Chapel Hollow Traffic Control System, Frank is not sure whether he will go with C++ or Smalltalk, but he plans to submit the results of the CRC card analysis to two consultants who will bid on the job. He has decided that the system will be implemented on a network of PCs, since employees in the Public Works Department are already comfortable with this technology.

The project is now a month into the analysis phase. After collecting information and conducting interviews, the project team created a set of CRC cards for the basic entity in the system, an intersection. Code-Lite, a consulting firm with expertise in object-oriented project facilitation, has been asked to come in and help with the refinement of the model.

THE CRC CARD TEAM

Frank has put together a small but experienced team. He has also included Joe O'Donnell from the Public Works Department because he is responsible for the physical maintenance of the system, as well as monitoring the traffic control side of things.

On the technical side, Frank chose Ellen Reine. She has been handling technical support for computer systems in Chapel Hollow for over ten years. This means that she is known and trusted by almost every department in town. That may be very important to user acceptance and to the ongoing expansion of the system as the town grows. Ellen has had some experience with object-oriented languages, but this will be her first soup-to-nuts project. Frank himself will serve as one of the domain experts, as well as managing the technical team that will implement the project.

Obviously, Frank had to pull in some hard-core expertise to back up the team. Neither he nor Ellen has the experience to maximize the benefits of object-oriented technology. To make up for the shortfall in in-house skills, Frank has set up a contract with Code-Lite. DeWayne Thomas, one of the Code-Lite object-oriented gurus, will be coming in periodically to help the group along. Since the team is so small, they have rotated facilitating at each meeting, but when DeWayne is there, he will take on that role and provide some extra guidance about the process, as well as later evaluations of design and coding.

THE PROJECT PLAN

The complexity of controlling traffic in Chapel Hollow stems from the ever-changing nature of intersections, corridors, and vehicle volumes. Reusable objects should make it easier to accommodate growth without losing control over the software. The project development segments reflect this view of the system. The analysis started with a simple intersection. Once that was understood, the concepts were enhanced for a more complex intersection. Finally, the team intends to model a zone, which is a group of intersections acting in coordination so that traffic moves smoothly through a corridor. In addition to describing the intersections, Frank has outlined the CRC techniques used in each segment.

Segment 1: Simple Intersection

The simple intersection is referred to as "semi-actuated," meaning that there are detectors on one of the streets in the intersection that record the presence of a vehicle waiting for the light to change, or, to use the jargon, "waiting to be serviced." It is said to have two phases, meaning that there are two combinations of light settings: one that allows movement on the main street, and one that allows movement on the side street.

Type: Simple, semi-actuated, two phases—major thoroughfare crosses minor street
Goal: Understand coordination and control of an intersection
Techniques: Brainstorming, candidate class lists, role plays of scenarios for simple intersection

Segment 2: Complex Intersection

The next segment expands the CRC card set and makes any changes necessary to carry out role play for more complex intersections. The team has decided that if they can role play a set of CRC cards for a simple intersection and reuse them for a complex intersection, then they should be able to use the same cards with any scenarios they come up with for altering the basic factors such as phasing, or number of streets and signal heads. However, when we pick up the project team's story in a minute, they are in the midst of working on the complex intersection.

Type: Complex, fully actuated, four phases—major thoroughfare with turning lane crosses minor street
Goal: Determine ability to add complexity to intersections
Techniques: Role plays of scenarios for complex intersections, CRC cards, hierarchy chart

Segment 3: Zone Control

The last segment deals with the problem of including multiple intersections in a zone so that all of the lights can be timed. Right now there are only two zones in town that are critical to the traffic at peak times, and neither one of them has timed lights. Traffic control at intersections is the "hot spot" at the heart of the system. Activating zones with progressive lights will be a very concrete source of relief to the increasing number of commuters, and the team wants to be sure the analysis for the complex intersection can be extended easily to accomodate zones.

Type: Zoned corridor of variety of intersections, major thoroughfare crossing minor streets

Goal: Determine ability to coordinate multiple intersections

Techniques: Role plays of scenarios for complex intersections, CRC cards, hierarchy chart

TRAFFIC MANAGEMENT CONCEPTS

You have already heard some of the important vocabulary we will be using in this chapter. An "intersection" is a place where some number of streets cross. An "actuated" intersection refers to a crossing where one or more of the lanes have been equipped with a detection device that knows when a car is waiting in the lane. "Semi-actuated" means that only some part of the intersection has been equipped with detectors. In our case, the first project segment involves an intersection in which there are detectors on the minor street, but no detectors in the main street. An intersection with more than two roads crossing might have several streets actuated, but not all, and still be called semi-actuated. "Fully actuated" intersections have detectors for all of the traffic streams.

Figure 9-1 shows a number of different intersections at grade. This means that there are no overpasses, so all of the traffic movement must be coordinated in such a way that every lane is serviced. The CRC card set for the system should work, that is, a role play should progress smoothly, no matter which intersection is involved. Hence, the intersections provide the team with a basic set of scenarios. For each intersection type, there will be additional scenarios that test for different combinations of traffic flow and vehicles waiting to be serviced.

The use of detectors helps the system time the lights and override default times to service waiting vehicles. Every combination of red/green, permitting some cars to move and prohibiting motion in other directions is called a "phase." For example, in a two-way intersection like the one shown in Figure 9-2, there might be two phases. Each phase involves a set of timed intervals with a total cycle length that is the elapsed time between the start of the cycle (fresh green, for example) and the end of the cycle (end of red). Phases prevent "conflicting streams" of traffic from colliding. In some cases, phases are controlled

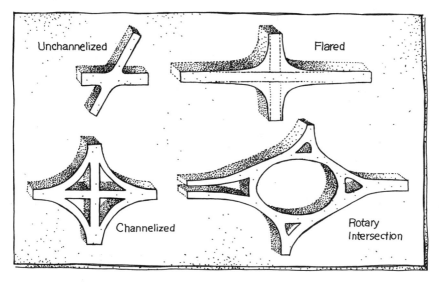

Figure 9-1 **Intersections at Grade**

by lights for every possible movement pattern; in others, signals work in combination with known right-of-way laws. Note that the length of the intervals in a phase may vary, but the phasing of all signal faces for the intersection must have the same cycle length, or you are going to have some collisions!

Some additional terms you will need to know are "detector," "signal head," "signal face," and "light." The detector can be any sort of device that senses the presence of a vehicle. Usually this is a metal detector, which is why bicycles made of light metals or alloys may leave a rider waiting for a long time. The "signal head" is the entire box that holds the traffic lights. It may have any number of "signal faces" depending on how the intersection is designed. A "signal face" consists of "lights," usually red, green, and amber, but there may also be turning lights. All of these instruments are used to move "traffic streams" or lines of moving vehicles.

You will recognize all of this vocabulary in the core class list and role-play assignments for the CRC card set developed by the team prior to the arrival of DeWayne Thomas shown in Figure 9-3.

As you can see, in a small group it is difficult to anticipate role assignments that minimize actors collaborating with themselves. This is where holding up the CRC card "in play" can help the group keep track of which class is client and which is server.

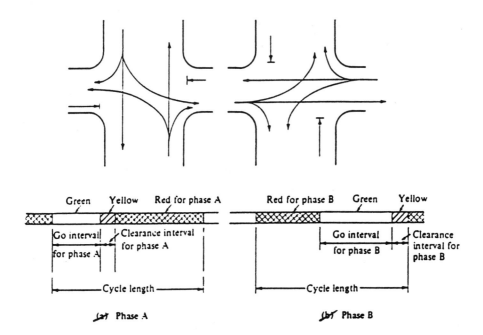

Green   Yellow   Red for phase A   Red for phase B   Green   Yellow

Go interval | Clearance interval   Go interval | Clearance
for phase A | for phase A   for phase B | interval for
                                                              phase B

Cycle length   Cycle length

(a) Phase A   (b) Phase B

Figure 9-2 **A Two-Phase Signal System**

Source: Traffic and Highway Engineering, Second Edition by Nicholas J. Garber and Lester
A. Hoel is copyright © by PWS Publishing Company, a division of International Thomson
Publishing Inc.

Core Class	Role Player
Intersection	Joe
TrafficLight	Ellen
Detector	Frank
IntervalManager	Joe
PhaseTimer	Ellen
SignalFace	Ellen
IntervalTimer	Frank
PhaseManager	Frank
Timer	Joe

Figure 9-3 **Role-Play Assignments**

ROLE PLAY: THE FIRST ENACTMENT

DeWayne Thomas suggested that Frank let the project team work on its own to come up with a set of CRC cards. He wanted them to establish a baseline analysis of the system which he could review looking for ways to improve the conceptualization of classes without hand-holding through the basic trial-and-error of finding classes, an activity that the Chapel Hollow staff were certainly better equipped to do by themselves.

Frank began the meeting with a brief overview of the project plan. Joe explained some of the basics of traffic control and Ellen presented the CRC card set. When they were through, DeWayne asked the team to role play the CRC card set for him so that he could see how the collaborations looked "in action." The CRC card set included the following classes:

Intersection (preliminary)	
Know phase plan	
Know current phase	PhaseManager
Know state of detectors	
Initiate phase change	IntervalManager
Set phase time	PhaseTimer

PhaseManager (preliminary)	
Know phase plan	

Detector (preliminary)	
Notify if vehicle present	Intersection

IntervalManager (preliminary)	
Know interval plans	
Adjust intervals	SignalFace, IntervalTimer

SignalFace (preliminary)	
Know TrafficLight status	
Set TrafficLight (on/off)	TrafficLight

TrafficLight (preliminary)	
Know on/off status	
Know color	
Set on/off	

Timer (preliminary) Subclass: IntervalTimer, PhaseTimer	
Set time	
Countdown time	
Notify when zero	Intersection, IntervalManager

PhaseTimer (preliminary) Superclass: Timer	
Notify when zero	Intersection

IntervalTimer (preliminary) Superclass: Timer	
Notify when zero	IntervalManager

The team did several role plays, for both two-phase and four-phase intersections, to demonstrate that the CRC cards could handle both basic and more complex scenarios. To give you a sense of the approach they used, let's look at a portion of the role play where a vehicle arrives at a four-phase intersection during the red interval of the phase and wants to be serviced for a left-hand turn. Notice that the actors do not comment on the rationale for their collaborations during the role play. This can be difficult, but already assuming the role of facilitator, DeWayne reminded them that it would be easier to evaluate the logic behind the CRC card set if the role play went uninterrupted.

"Let's respect the line between enactment and assessment," he told them. "You are not using the role play to search for responsibilities and collaborations at this point, so let it run from start to finish. Everyone has something to write notes on, right?" The team nodded in confirmation and began the role play:

> DETECTOR: Intersection, there is a vehicle over me waiting for service.
>
> INTERSECTION: I have Detector indicating a vehicle waiting. PhaseManager, what phase are we in?
>
> PHASEMANAGER: We are in Phase B allowing movement on the cross street.
>
> INTERSECTION: Looking at my current phase conditions, I see that this phase has just begun. I cannot change the phase right away, but as soon as the time is up, I will initiate a phase change.
>
> PHASETIMER: Intersection, I am at zero.
>
> INTERSECTION: IntervalManager, adjust your intervals.
>
> INTERVALMANAGER: I will adjust the intervals. SignalFace#1, set your lights to Red. SignalFace#2, set your lights to Green. IntervalTimer, tell me when 45 seconds is up.
>
> INTERVALTIMER: OK.
>
> SIGNALFACE#1: TrafficLight#1 and TrafficLight#2, set yourselves off. TrafficLight#3, set yourself on.
>
> SIGNALFACE#2: TrafficLight#2 and TrafficLight#3, set yourselves off. TrafficLight#1, set yourself on.
>
> (Each TrafficLight responds OK.). . .

ASSESSMENT: EVALUATING THE ROLE PLAY

Listening to the quick role play, DeWayne noticed that the team had made a mistake common to newcomers to the object-oriented perspective, one that often remained unchanged in a lot of "experienced" designers. The Intersection and the IntervalManager classes suffered from what some people call the "god class complex." Instead of breaking down the procedural picture into parts and allocating work out to classes using encapsulation to hide information and behavior, the team had created a set of "worker" classes and "god" classes that were modeled on a functional hierarchy similar to a structure chart with transaction center modules.

"What you should aim for are classes that can do their jobs with as little dependency on other classes as possible," DeWayne explained. "The Intersection class, for instance, needs to know about phases, so you want to give that behavior to the Intersection rather than create a 'manager' class that coordinates for the Intersection class. Intersection should have the knowledge required to make the decision about which phase to 'service' (go green) next. Without delegating behavior to a manager who knows more than Intersection, Intersection looks at its own body of knowledge and, when appropriate, requests that a Phase activate or deactivate itself."

Frank pointed out that this meant that Phase also needs to encapsulate all of its behavior and knowledge. When it receives a message from Intersection, it knows what it needs to know to activate. This would include the minimum green time interval and amber time interval. "Maybe it even needs to know whether it needs to be included in a sequence, whether there is a vehicle waiting. Maybe Detector collaborates with Phase instead of Intersection."

Ellen suggested that if they were going to do this, the Phase class should collaborate with the PhaseTimer. "This way," she said, thinking out loud, "there can be as many phases as we need at an intersection, dependent upon the number of streets and special lanes."

This sounded good to DeWayne, but it also reminded him that he wanted to ask about the choice of two types of timers. Joe was helpful here, pointing out that a timer was a timer, a mechanism that counted down to zero. On the basis of this, the group decided to drop the idea of an abstract timer class. "This is really a false abstraction," Frank observed. "DeWayne is right. We have two instances of the same class, not an abstract class and two subclasses."

Before they could go on, the team decided that they needed to write a new CRC card for Intersection to see what the effect would be on the old set of cards. Intersection now had the following behavior and knowledge:

Intersection (revised)	
Knows phases and their sequencing	
Knows which phase(s) need(s) servicing	
Terminates active phase	Phase
Activates inactive phase	Phase

As soon as they tried to write the CRC card for Phase, they came up against the problem of what to do with the initial collaborators with the preliminary versions of the Phase, TrafficLight, and SignalFace classes. DeWayne pointed out the effect of better use of encapsulation in describing Phase and Intersection. He suggested that they step back from the problem for a minute and try to think about the traffic control application in a more abstract way.

"We want classes that are both smart and dumb," DeWayne continued. "They are smart because they do all of their job, if possible, based on their own behavior and knowledge, but dumb because they should not need to know anything about the other classes.

How can we look at the problem of vehicles moving through the intersection and the traffic lights in terms of a class with good encapsulation?"

Joe took a stab at the problem. "Even though I am not a computer person," he interjected tentatively, "I am beginning to catch on to the way you think, DeWayne. These signals and all that are really mechanical systems. What is at the bottom of it all are the lanes of traffic. Let's call 'em traffic streams. Cars move or don't move in response to seeing a light, but from the point of view of coordination of phases, what matters is, can they move or not?"

This gave Ellen the idea of a TrafficStream class. "The way it works is that the TrafficStream knows if it needs servicing and then collaborates with the SignalFace when the Phase activates it. Look what happens if you encapsulate all the vehicle information and stop/go signal behavior in TrafficStream."

Ellen wrote out a new CRC card for Phase and a card for TrafficStream. Looking them over, the team agreed that they had successfully allocated all of the behavior of Interval-Manager and PhaseManager while eliminating the coordinator or godlike behavior of the old collaborations.

Phase (revised)	
Know which TrafficStream(s) involved	
Know minimum green time	
Know minimum amber time	
Know if it needs servicing	TrafficStream
Activate TrafficStream (go green, go red)	TrafficStream
Report minimum green time elapsed	Timer, Intersection
Notify when needs servicing	Intersection

TrafficStream (revised)	
Knows its lights	
Knows if it is red or green	
Knows if it needs servicing	Detector
Goes green	SignalFace
Goes red	SignalFace
Notifies if it needs servicing	Intersection

Ellen liked this solution. "We can add anything we want as a TrafficStream instance," she exclaimed. "If Joe wants to install pedestrian signals, that is going to be another instance of TrafficStream. We don't care about the physical nature of the lane, the traffic, or even the kind of SignalHead and combinations of lights, arrows, words, etc. From the point of view of the system, we have a TrafficStream that is governed by a SignalFace. Look how this clarifies the SignalFace CRC card. Whether we have a Walk/Don't Walk sign or a set of lights, it is all the same behavior."

SignalFace (revised)	
Knows its lights	
Sets lights (on/off)	

The CRC cards for Timer and Detector remained the same, except that Frank wanted the Detector to both know and report if a vehicle is present. He explained, "That's in case we want to poll for that information when we do the design. In the role play, I would suggest we stick with the idea that the Detector reports (that's what it does), but in the implementation we might poll (that's how it does it)."

The team was pleased with the cards. DeWayne had earned his consulting fee, steering them towards a more effective use of classes. Encapsulation meant a lot more now that they saw how it helps refine class collaborations instead of echoing a procedural command model.

ENACTMENT TWO: VERIFYING THE CARDS

Ellen sketched a four-phase, fully actuated intersection on the board. It involved six streams of traffic indicated on the diagram by the letters "t/s" and a number. In this case, Main, the major street, had four streams while Maple, a minor street, had only two. The intersection is shown in Figure 9-4. In this intersection, each phase has a minimum transition to red (amber time) of 10 seconds. Phase 1 has a minimum green time of 30 seconds. All other phases have a minimum green time of 40 seconds. The phasing of traffic streams (red/green) is shown in Figure 9-5. Note that t/s stands for TrafficStream on the map and in the table. We will continue to use the convention during the role play.

The team chose a scenario in which a vehicle on Maple headed south wants to make a left-hand turn on Main. The current phase is Phase 2, and, according to the table in Figure 9-5, only t/s 3 and t/s 4 are green; all others are red. In other words, traffic is flowing on Main and waiting on Maple. Joe pointed out that this was the important thing, and

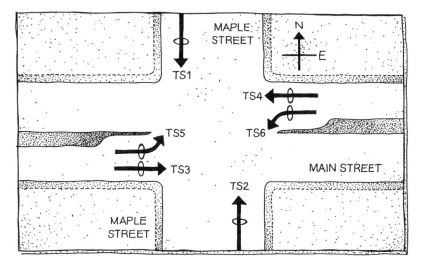

Figure 9-4 **The Model Intersection**

Phase 1	Maple N/S		
		ts1	green
		ts2	green
		ts3	red
		ts4	red
		ts5	red
		ts6	red

Phase 3	Main E+T		
		ts1	red
		ts2	red
		ts3	green
		ts4	red
		ts5	green
		ts6	red

Phase 2	Main E/W		
		ts1	red
		ts2	red
		ts3	green
		ts4	green
		ts5	red
		ts6	red

Phase 4	Main W+T		
		ts1	red
		ts2	red
		ts3	red
		ts4	green
		ts5	red
		ts6	green

Figure 9-5 **Traffic Stream Phases of the Model Intersection**

that the absence of a turning lane on Maple meant that, from the point of view of the Intersection, the fact that the vehicle will turn left is irrelevant. That movement will be governed by the regulations for right-of-way, not the SignalFace settings.

Before listening to the role play, it may be helpful to see the entire set of revised CRC cards, as developed in the previous discussion. On the CRC cards, the team has included responsibilities for Detector to notify TrafficStream that a vehicle is present, for Traffic-Stream to notify Phase that it needs service, and for Phase to notify Intersection that it needs service. The reason for including this sequence is to encapsulate behavior so that, should TrafficStream change (for example, to include pedestrian streams), Phase is not affected. The number of possible Phases, in turn, and how they work does not need to be known by Intersection. Later on, during Design, the coder may decide to use a polling implementation rather than reporting, but, for the duration of the role play, the team will follow the reporting pattern.

Intersection (final)	
Knows Phases and their sequencing	
Knows which Phase(s) need(s) servicing	Phase
Tells green (active) Phase(s) to terminate service (go red)	
Tells red (inactive) Phase(s) to open service (go green)	

Phase (final)	
Knows its TrafficStreams	
Knows its minimum green time interval	
Knows its minimum yellow time interval	
Initiates TrafficStream movement (go green, go red)	TrafficStream
Knows if it needs servicing	TrafficStream
Reports when minimum green time elapsed	Timer, Intersection
Notifies if needs service	Intersection

TrafficStream (final)	
Knows its lights (bulbs)	
Knows if it is red or green	
Knows if it needs servicing	Detector
Goes green	SignalFace
Goes red (amber time from Phase)	SignalFace
Notifies if it needs servicing	Intersection

Detector (final)	
Notifies if vehicle is present	TrafficStream
Knows if a vehicle is present	

SignalFace (final)	
Knows its Lights	
Sets Lights (on/off)	

Timer (final)	
Sets time	
Counts down time	
Notifies when zero	

DETECTOR: TrafficStream 1, a vehicle is present.

TRAFFICSTREAM 1: OK, I'll record the request for service and notify Phase.

PHASE: OK, I see that I must be active to meet the demand for service. I'll notify Intersection so that I am in the queue for being active.

INTERSECTION: I see that Phase 1 wants servicing. According to the sequence in my Phase Plan, I can initiate Phase 1 next, but not until the active Phase reports minimum green time has elapsed.

DeWayne interrupted the role play here. He wanted the team to see that this same basic scenario would repeat for as many TrafficStream and Phase combinations as there are possible combinations of vehicles arriving and requests for service being communicated.

"As long as the minimum green time for the current Phase has not elapsed, this part of the role play can be repeating. But for now, let's keep it simple and work with this one request."

Joe agreed with DeWayne and, looking again at his card, said, "As Intersection, I can deal with any number of requests because I have my plan for servicing the Phases. At any given point in time, I can consult that, see who needs servicing, see what phase I am in and what phase can be next, and all of that. How I do it is irrelevant at this point. That's internal logic—how, not what. What I am going to do is decide."

> PHASE 2: OK, let's get going. Intersection, my minimum green time has elapsed.
> INTERSECTION: I'll check my plan and the sequence of phases. Looks good. I can activate Phase 1. Phase 2, terminate. Phase 1, open service.
> PHASE 2: OK.
> PHASE 1: Ready to open service according to my Phase Plan. I'll notify the appropriate TrafficStreams. In this case, that would be t/s 3, t/s 4, t/s 5 and t/s 6 go red; t/s 1 and t/s 2 go green. Timer, count down.
> TRAFFICSTREAM: In each case, I'll tell SignalFace to go amber to red or to go green. By the way, in the case of t/s 5 and t/s 6, the state is already red, so I will ignore the message.
> SIGNALFACE: I'll set the lights.

Everyone agreed that the new CRC cards worked more effectively than the old set. They ran through a number of scenarios, but it was going to be impossible to cover all of the combinations of demands and phases, so they selected those that were the most important (the "hot spots"). For instance, before going on to a new situation, DeWayne suggested that they play out the first scenario, with the assumption that the phase times out before another demand for service is made.

> TIMER: Time has elapsed for Phase 1. Phase, I am at zero.
> PHASE: Intersection, minimum green time has expired.
> INTERSECTION: I have no demands for service. I'll check the sequencing. The default setup is Phase 2 active (servicing the larger street). Phase 1, terminate service. Phase 2, open service.
> PHASE 1: OK, service terminated.
> PHASE 2: Ready to open service. I'll notify TrafficStream according to the phase plan.
> TRAFFICSTREAM: I'll tell SignalFace unless I am already set correctly, in which case I ignore the message.
> SIGNALFACE: I'll set the lights.

Satisfied with the cards, the team concluded the meeting. DeWayne asked them to think about the problem of zones for the next session. If the cards could accommodate this probable extension, he felt that the project would be ready to move on to tackle design and coding.

USING ROLE PLAY TO EXTEND THE SYSTEM

DeWayne began the meeting with a short go-around. He asked each member of the team to comment on something they had learned so far about object-oriented analysis. This gave everyone a breather, and also gave DeWayne a chance to fulfill his role as facilitator and consultant. Code-Lite had promised Frank not only a CRC card analysis, but also a team that would have a good grounding in OO basics. He finished the discussion with a short review of class hierarchies, objects, and instances. "I keep holding us back from jumping into design," DeWayne explained, "but I also want you to see that the CRC role play is laying groundwork which helps the designer make informed choices."

Once the group had warmed up, DeWayne introduced the final segment for analysis: corridors and zones. "We now need to add the classes needed to manage sets of intersections," DeWayne began. "We want to reuse the classes we have already mapped out, but we may also discover that they need to be revised."

"Corridor and Zone are the obvious class candidates, but I think that they are aliases," Frank suggested. "Corridor and zone are synonyms for a situation in which several Intersections are set to have the same cycle length and timed to initiate movement of a traffic stream in a progressive pattern. Look at this," he said, passing around a copy of the diagram shown in Figure 9-6. "What we try to do is coordinate the phases at the intersections in a zone so that a platoon of vehicles starting at one end of the zone can reach the other end of the zone with a minimum of delay. We use these Time–Space Diagrams to see how to stagger the phases and the split of the lights."

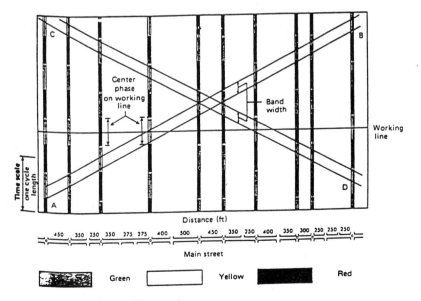

Figure 9-6 ***Typical Traffic Zone Time–Space Diagram***
Source: Transportion and Traffic Engineering Handbook, 2nd ed, by Homburger, © 1982.
Reprinted by permission of Prentice-Hall, Inc., Upper Saddle River, New Jersey.

"At 4:00 P.M. we could initiate a Time-of-Day Plan that would optimize the Zone that includes these lights on Main and minimize vehicle delay. When we allow this progression, we may end up with a stack of vehicles on the side streets waiting to be serviced—for example, on Elm or Maple. Some delay for those small streets is not a problem. We control this by changing the rules for responding to those detectors. The Time-of-Day plan sets up phase lengths that are not altered to accommodate demand on the minor approaches."

"I'll be Zone," Ellen volunteered, starting a new CRC card. "I am putting 'initiate Time-of-Day plan' as one of my responsibilities, with Intersection as my collaborator."

Joe looked over the Intersection CRC card to decide whether or not to add a new responsibility to respond. It looked as if he did not have to change anything. The responsibility "knows phases and their sequencing" could include knowing the cycle length.

The team began the role play:

ZONE: It is now 4:00 P.M., so I'm going to initiate the time-of-day plan for rush hour by telling Intersection a new set of Phase plans and sequences.

INTERSECTION: I am adjusting the sequencing and notifying Phase.

PHASE: I'm not sure what to do. Looking over my responsibilities, I don't think that I need to do anything!

Joe looked again at the Intersection CRC card and suggested that the only effect of adding a Zone class would be to alter the cycle length. This change would cause an Intersection to make an adjustment to the sequencing of phases. For instance, a phase that was skipped because there was no demand for service might be included (go green) in coordination with the rest of the corridor, but only the Intersection needs to know this logic. The Phase will not need to know anything. When the Intersection tells the Phase to terminate or open service, to go green or go red, Phase does not care why.

The team was pleased. The CRC cards for the individual intersections would work regardless of the coordination of intersections by the time-of-day plan. Frank silently applauded himself for the choice of an object-oriented approach. Adding zones might look like a small change from the point of view of the CRC cards, but doing so with a minimum of system revision will be saving him a lot of time and money as the town grows and more corridors are defined.

Zone (final)	
Knows Time-of-Day Plan	
Initiates Time-of-Day Plan	Intersection

The final set of CRC cards was written up and approved as ready for design. The new card, Zone, was added.

LOOKING AHEAD

The next step in the project is going to be the application of the information on the CRC cards to specific design issues related to the implementation of the traffic system.

In the next two chapters, we provide a preview of the coding process for three languages: Smalltalk, C++, and Java. Three recognized programming experts join us in demonstrating how they would implement from the same set of CRC cards, those for the complex traffic intersection. Although this may seem to be a big jump, it will help you to see the strength of CRC as an analysis technique that establishes a strong object-oriented foundation for design and implementation. Finally, the transition from CRC cards to a formal methodology is discussed in the last chapter of the book.

Chapter 10

Implementing CRC in Smalltalk

The objective of this chapter is to show how the CRC analysis for the traffic intersection is used to actually build a Smalltalk software implementation. Our emphasis is on showing what we actually did to build the system, so we don't just show you the code (although fully working code is included). We show you the iterations we progressed through—the why and how of developing a working Smalltalk system.

For those who haven't used Smalltalk, we've included a brief introduction to the programming environment. We then show how a Smalltalk designer might review the analysis, and what changes would be suggested for the unique features of Smalltalk. The balance of the chapter focuses on the implementation of a prototype simulation, along with all the relevant code. Finally, we have some suggestions for where to go for more Smalltalk learning, information, and assistance.

THE SMALLTALK PROGRAMMING ENVIRONMENT

Before we look at how the CRC cards are used with Smalltalk, let's review Smalltalk itself. If you are already familiar with Smalltalk, you can skip to the next section. Although we implemented our simulation using the capabilities of the IBM VisualAge Smalltalk programming environment, we used features which are common to most other Smalltalk dialects as well. Smalltalk as a programming environment has four central components: the language, the supplied class hierarchy, browsers, and the system engine. These components are seamlessly integrated and work together to make a powerful, productive, and fun programming experience.

First of all, Smalltalk is a programming language. The Smalltalk language is often called a "pure" object-oriented programming language because everything in Smalltalk is an object. Smalltalk objects communicate with each other using messages, which trigger executing code stored in methods. Methods are written as either instance or class methods. Every object has a class. So, for example, if an instance of class **TrafficLight** called *aTraffic-Light* were sent the message to change to red, the code would look as follows:

```
aTrafficLight goRed.
```

Note that the receiver of the message, *aTrafficLight,* precedes the message, *goRed.* In this case, the message "goRed" is sent to the instance stored in a variable named *aTraffic-Light.* This code snippet would cause the code written for the instance method named "goRed" stored with the class of *aTrafficLight* to be executed.

The second component of Smalltalk is the supplied class hierarchy, which provides many classes that simplify coding tasks. The Smalltalk base classes include support for keeping collections of things, iterating through code, evaluating Boolean expressions, performing operations with numbers, implementing multiprocessing applications, and creating user interfaces. Other classes can be added as needed, and many are sold by vendors. For example, features are available for IBM Smalltalk which add classes that perform tasks such as accessing databases, performing transactions, distributing objects, communicating over networks, and integrating with other environments such as Lotus Notes, CICS, and the World Wide Web. For this prototype, we used features available from base classes which are available in almost all vendors' versions of Smalltalk.

The third component of the Smalltalk environment is a set of user interfaces called "browsers." Browsers allow programmers to quickly locate code that needs editing, make the changes, and test. For example, it is easy to view the code in a method and click on an action to show a list of all messages sent by that method. From this list, the list of all implementers of methods corresponding to those messages can be found. In this way, it is easy to trace back through the other methods used by a method, to propagate changes, and to reuse existing code. Similarly, it is easy to trace all senders of a message, all references to a class or global variable, and so on. The browsers can also be used to describe code. This can be done by associating comments with methods or classes, by grouping methods into categories, and by differentiating public and private methods. Complementing the browsers are integrated debuggers, inspectors, and workspace logs which simplify testing and debugging. Several Smalltalk environments now also include visual programming browsers and user interface builders.

Most professional programmers install a code management library as an integrated feature of their browsers. The "Envy" code management library, used by IBM and available for other Smalltalk variants, is the one we use. This code management library allows code to be easily shared among developers, keeps related classes together in collections called "applications," manages the configurations needed to run the code on various platforms and feature sets, and automatically maintains backup copies of every method and class changed during development. A good code management library is indispensable to the success of any complex programming endeavor.

The fourth component is the Smalltalk engine, which consists of an image and a virtual machine. The image is a binary file that contains the executable code. The virtual machine interprets the bytes stored in the image to actually run the code. Smalltalk can be thought of as an interpreted language, which is useful because in any text area in the programming environment a snippet of code can be selected and executed, to begin a test, display the state of an object, or perform almost any other action. In actuality, almost all modern Smalltalk implementations perform some degree of compilation when storing methods. Some Smalltalk implementations even compile the code down to bytes that can be directly executed by the microprocessor.

SMALLTALK CODING GUIDELINES

There are some simple but powerful coding conventions used throughout the Smalltalk community that make everyone's code more readable, maintainable, and reusable. In general, the convention can be summarized as follows: Methods should be short enough to fit on one screen; names of classes, variables, and methods should be descriptive and written out in full; multiple words in names should be separated using capital letters between the words; and no underscores should be used. When these conventions are followed, it is easier to navigate and understand both your own code and that of others. The book *Smalltalk with Style* by S. Kublics (1995: Prentice Hall) is the best detailed guide to accepted coding practices.

Smalltalk is well suited to rapidly creating powerful applications. However, there is a fairly steep learning curve at the very beginning. Especially for programmers coming from other languages, learning Smalltalk syntax can be a bit challenging. But once the basic syntax of the language is understood, and familiarity with the browsers and the supplied class hierarchy is achieved, Smalltalk can be used to rapidly implement complex systems.

Naming Conventions

In Smalltalk, the use of proper naming by all developers is critical to the overall quality of the entire programming environment. Writing code which does not match expected naming conventions will frustrate fellow Smalltalk programmers whenever they work with your code. Fortunately, the naming conventions for Smalltalk are fairly straightforward.

Classes always start with a capital letter. Method names (selectors) always start with a lowercase letter (with very few exceptions). Complex names are made by concatenating words, without an underscore, and capitalizing the first letter of each word starting with the second word. Words are rarely truncated or abbreviated (with exceptions for only the most obvious words). For example, a good class name might be **TrafficStream.** A method implemented on **TrafficStream** might be **needsService.** In contrast, bad names are **Trafficstream, Traffic_Stream,** and **ndssrvc.**

For methods with multiple arguments, the words between arguments do not start with capitalization. For example, use **servicePhase:fromDetector:** not **servicePhase:FromDetector:** because the "F" in "From" should not be capitalized. With acronyms, only the first letter of the acronym is usually capitalized to highlight the separation of the next word in the complex selector; for example, use **transformToTcpIpFormat** instead of **transformToTCPIPFormat.**

USING CRC CARDS WITH SMALLTALK

The data in the CRC cards can be almost directly mapped to implementation classes written in Smalltalk. That is, since each CRC card represents the behavior of an object participating in the intersection solution, this behavior can be written in Smalltalk to implement the solution. The design phase for this type of problem can be very short: just enough to provide an understanding of the basic structure of the classes. Prototype implementation can begin almost immediately.

As a result of the time spent by the team developing the CRC card analysis, everyone on the team is comfortable with the scope, complexity, and terminology of the traffic intersection solution. As the team developed the CRC cards, it created a special language to communicate team concepts. The traffic solution has been documented in the language of the group. Developing CRC cards is an analysis activity and looks at the solution in the abstract. Now, during the design phase, the information in the CRC cards is applied to a specific programming approach: Smalltalk. That is, an analysis for an object-oriented system is "implementation-neutral," whereas the design is "implementation-specific."

During the design and prototype portion of the project, the CRC cards are changed so that they give a description of the implementation. Sometimes, design and development are done as two separate steps; however, in object-oriented programming the design is frequently done by developing a prototype along with the design documentation.

DESIGN APPROACH

The first job of the designer is to understand the solution described by the CRC cards. For Smalltalk, this is usually done by sketching out the classes and instances in a design specification, then building a prototype. The design and prototype are then refined over several iterations.

Let's return to our case study. First, the analysis information was read and discussed with the analysis team. Using the CRC cards and examples, the basic scope and terminology of the problem was explored. Several hand-drawn diagrams were created to show the object instances interacting and how the classes were structured.

The rough diagrams were then converted to more formal diagrams (see Figure 10-1 and Figure 10-2, later) and approved by the analysis team. Next, a first pass was made at creating class definitions. (In Smalltalk it is easy to quickly create and experiment with classes.) After the basic framework of classes was in place, a small part of the solution was selected, designed, implemented, and tested. When that piece was done, another small part of the solution was then selected, implemented, and tested. As complex areas were uncovered during the implementation of each small piece, coding was interrupted to revisit the project-wide design, and perhaps rework the earlier pieces to fit the new thinking. Eventually, the entire prototype was implemented. Subsequent iterations simply added new features.

This approach to developing the prototype mimics a more general "iterative process" used to develop large software projects with Smalltalk. Using this process, the entire software project evolves over several iterations of introducing new parts of the solution. At the end of each iteration, it is important to make sure that the code written thus far is stable and cohesive. The partial system should be suitable for presentation to management or customers as a demonstration of the team's progress.

In large projects, an iteration can last from four to six weeks, with weekly checkpoints to keep everyone on track. Likewise, when many programmers are working simultaneously, everybody's code should be merged together at least once a week. An example set of iterations might be:

Iteration 1: Complete Proof of Concept Prototype
Iteration 2: Complete Product Framework
Iteration 3: Complete Function Set One
Iteration 4: Complete Function Set Two
Iteration 5: Ship Customer "Beta" Package
Iteration 6: Ship Final Package

The intersection prototype in this chapter could be considered the first iteration of developing the complete traffic intersection solution. We don't actually control real traffic light control boxes in real time, but we create a software prototype of such a system in operation.

Analysis versus Program Design

The analysis, including the CRC cards, provides the starting point for the design and is used to verify that the design and implementation solve the right problems. In general, the analysis describes what the solution does and the design describes how it is done. There are two reasons to do a design. First, the design is used to describe how you are going to build the solution so it is easier to build. Second, the design describes the solution you built so it is easier to maintain.

For small software projects using Smalltalk, informal designs work well. The environment is well suited for building prototypes, so a general design can be quickly refined through prototyping and iterative development. For large or complex projects, most any of the popular object-oriented design methodologies discussed elsewhere in this book can be adapted for use with Smalltalk. If the team is not experienced with using a design methodology, it is probably best to have an expert available to mentor the team through the first project. Since object-oriented systems usually evolve during implementation, it is also a good idea to assign someone the responsibility of ensuring that the design and the code remain consistent. At the end of the project, the design should describe the system that was actually built!

Going from Analysis to Design and Code

We initially used two design diagrams to describe the intersection solution before beginning implementation: a class structure diagram and an instance interaction diagram. The class structure diagram shows the static relationship among the classes in the system. The instance interaction diagram shows the flow of control among instances operating in a specific use case.

We also had to decide on the naming system to be used for the classes and methods in the traffic light system implementation. For this project, the prefix **Tls** (Traffic Light System) is used on all Smalltalk classes to identify the "foundry" where the classes were created. This helps avoid name conflicts with other classes used in similar projects or alternative implementations. For example, class **Intersection** is created later as class **TlsIntersection.** Likewise, any methods added to base classes are prefixed with "tls." For example, if a method in the Traffic Light System called *isOpen* were to be added to class Object, it would be added and referenced as method *tlsIsOpen.*

Class Structure Diagram

The class structure diagram shown in Figure 10-1 was developed directly from the CRC cards produced by the analysis team. This drawing shows each class described by the CRC cards. A class is represented by a box with three sections. The top section shows the class name. In a more complex diagram, the middle section of each box would show the attributes of the class, which are then implemented as instance variables in Smalltalk. The bottom section would show the messages understood by the class. The lines show the relationships between the classes. The text on each line describes the relationship. Relationships are directional; in this diagram, the text associated with each line is positioned near the start of the relationship and can be indicated by arrows as well. For example, the diagram shows that a **TrafficStream** instance will "request service from" a **Phase** instance. The boxes show classes but represent the relationships among all instances of those classes.

Instance Interaction Diagram

The instance interaction diagram shown in Figure 10-2 describes specific instances interacting for a particular use case. The interaction shown is for the use case of a phase

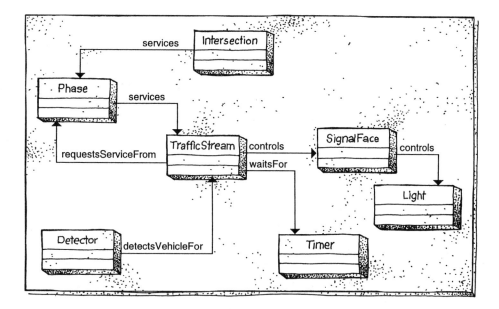

Figure 10-1 **Class Structure Diagram (before Prototype Implementation)**

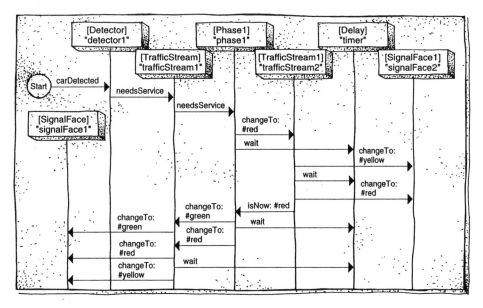

Figure 10-2 **Class Structure Diagram**

change. The circled word "Start" on the left is the starting point, and interactions continue with messages toward the top of the diagram occurring before messages toward the bottom of the diagram. The boxes at the top represent instances of specific classes, with the class in brackets and the name of the instance in quotes. The quoted name is just used for convenience when discussing the diagram. For example, after starting, the instance of **Detector** called "detector1" receives a "car detected" message. This causes the detector to send the message "car detected" to the instance of **TrafficStream** called "trafficStream1." The interactions continue as **SignalFace** "signalFace1" changes from green to yellow to red.

Design Enhancements

The traffic team designing the Chapel Hollow CRC cards did a pretty good job. There are always implementation-dependent changes which are uncovered during the design and development of a prototype, and this one is no different. It is almost always true that more responsibilities have to be added to the analysis classes for the details of making the code work. In the case of the traffic system, the added responsibilities centered around the **TlsPhase** class.

When we browsed the Smalltalk class hierarchy looking for existing classes which could be reused, we found that the existing **Delay** class could be used instead of **Timer.** Therefore, we changed the CRC cards to rename the **Timer** class to **Delay,** and reworded its responsibilities to correspond to those already provided by **Delay.**

The class **TrafficStream** was changed so that it informs its phases that it needs service, rather than talking to the intersection. This simplifies the interactions among the classes. Each **Phase** then notifies the **Intersection** that it needs service. The **Intersection** only needs to know about phases, rather than having to know about both **Phase** and **TrafficStream** (as was implied by the analysis cards). Since one **TrafficStream** can be serviced by more than one **Phase,** all phases which can service a **TrafficStream** are notified by the traffic stream when it needs service. Likewise, when a **Phase** is queried by the intersection as to whether it needs service, it must poll its waiting traffic streams to see if it still needs to be serviced. By the time a phase is queried, it is possible that another phase has already taken care of the waiting vehicles. In the CRC analysis the intersection had to know everything about phases and their traffic streams. That seemed to violate the encapsulation of the knowledge about traffic streams in phases. In Smalltalk it is easy to distribute this knowledge and have the various classes interact smoothly.

Finally, the **Light** class was eliminated, and lights are now treated as *attributes* of the **SignalFace.** Lights have no attributes, and no behavior beyond being on or off. All of these changes are shown in Figure 10-3, the revised class structure diagram.

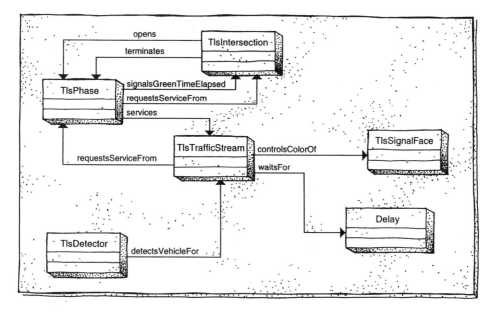

Figure 10-3 **Class Structure Diagram (after Initial Prototype)**

CONSTRUCTING CLASSES

Creating the initial set of classes was done using the revised CRC cards from the design session. One class was created for each class described by a CRC card, except for the class **Timer.** Since the base IBM Smalltalk class hierarchy includes the **Delay** class, we don't need to create the **Timer** class. This is one of the nice things about Smalltalk: often, what you need is already there! As you develop several applications in the same area, you'll often find existing classes you can reuse, subclass, or extend.

As each class was created, a guess at possible instance variables was made. The instance variables needed were derived from the responsibilities shown in the CRC cards. For example, the CRC card for class **Intersection** shows a responsibility "knows phases and their sequencing"; based on this information, the instance variable *phases* is added to class **TlsIntersection.** It seemed that the instance variable *phases* should be an instance of the **OrderedCollection** class, already provided in the base Smalltalk hierarchy. An ordered collection can keep the phases in the same order the intersection will rotate through to service them.

After the instance variables were added to the classes, "getter" and "setter" methods were generated for each instance variable. These methods are sometimes called "accessor" methods. When the phase's "setter" method is generated, we named the argument as *anOrderedCollection*, indicating that the argument to be assigned to the instance variable should be an ordered collection.

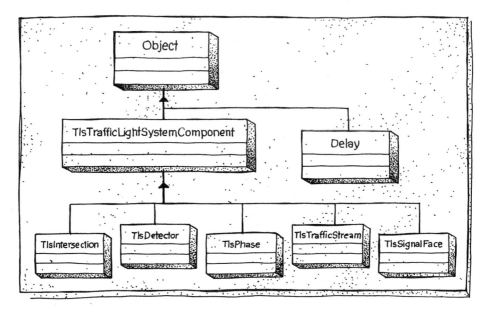

Figure 10-4 **The Traffic Light System Smalltalk Class Hierarchy**

The class hierarchy for the traffic light system is shown in Figure 10-4. This is a structure diagram showing the inheritance relationships among the classes. The little triangle under class **Object** and class **TlsTrafficLightSystemComponent** indicates that the line is an inheritance relationship. For example, in this diagram, class **TlsIntersection** inherits attributes and behavior from class **TlsTrafficLightSystemComponent,** and class **TlsTrafficLightSystem-Component** inherits attributes and behavior from class **Object.**

In the first pass, you might be tempted to create all new classes as subclasses of **Object.** However, for the prototype, each instance will need a log to write out its activity as the intersection goes through its cycles. To accommodate the code needed for testing and debugging, it helps to create one common abstract superclass. We called it **TlsTrafficLight-SystemComponent.** This class is used to hold behavior common to all other classes in the system. This includes support for assigning names to instances (used in debugging and the log), and behavior needed to log events in a text workspace. A log is an instance of **EtWork-space,** which is provided in the base Smalltalk hierarchy to display a simple window for text output. Using this kind of an abstract superclass will simplify testing and debugging not only during development, but for the life of the code. This is true even if the behavior provided by the abstract superclass is not needed in the production application.

CONSTRUCTING METHODS

After the classes were created, the prototype was extended to create a complete solution by building one small portion at time. The work started with class **Detector,** as it is the object which starts a phase change (see Figure 10-2). After the **Detector** was working, the methods for the other classes were developed by using the CRC cards to walk through the interactions among the classes. The methods for each class were then implemented as needed to fix bugs and complete the working system.

The complete prototype was built using four tests. The first test just ran a single detector reporting events to the log. It was used to get the log code working and was a good way to get started without diving into too much complexity. The second test ran a simple intersection of two traffic streams and two phases. The third test ran a complete intersection similar to the one defined in the specification, but with very rapid timing so that the testing could go more quickly. Finally, the fourth test ran the specific intersection used in the CRC analysis. The following sections discuss these tests in further detail.

The traffic system code is stored in the code library in an application called **TlsTraffic-LightSystemApp.** The test methods in the following discussion are written as class methods in the class **TlsTrafficLightSystemApp.**

FIRST TEST: IMPLEMENTING THE DETECTOR

Class **Detector** was implemented first. Writing the detector involved two complexities. First, each detector needs to be set up to run in the background and periodically send a "needs service" message to its traffic stream. Second, we needed a way to log each event to watch the system operate and confirm that it works. The log was done first. The log was implemented by adding instance variables *log* and *name* to class **TlsTrafficSystemComponent.** A log is an instance of a workspace—in this case, class **EtWorkspace.** A workspace is a text window such as a simple text editor. The *name* is a string added before each method printed in the log; it can be used during inspection of instances to identify which instance is which.

After the log is initialized, messages can be added to it by a simple line of code. For example:

```
self show: 'Vehicle detected.'.
```

This would result in a message in the log as follows:

```
75 secs - Detector2: Vehicle detected.
```

Since all classes in this system are subclasses of class **TlsTrafficSystemComponent,** once the log was set up for **Detector,** the same code could be reused for all other classes. The second part of creating the **Detector** class was to set it up to periodically detect a vehicle. In the actual system, this would be done by interfacing with the detector loops in the road. For the prototype, the detector was set up with a test method so detection automatically happened periodically. This test method was written to fork a block to execute in a separate Smalltalk process from the rest of the system. Since Smalltalk has extensive support for preemptive multitasking within the executing image, this was not difficult. As we'll see in the following sections, using multiple processes simplifies coding in several important places. The test method in class **TlsDetector** is:

```
TlsDetectors>>#testDetectionEvery: aMillisecondCount

    "Detect a vehicle every few milliseconds until the log is
closed..."
    "Fork the following block so it executes in the background"
    [
        [log shell isDestroyed] whileFalse: [
            (Delay forMilliseconds: aMillisecondCount) wait.
            self vehicleDetected.
            self show: 'Vehicle detected.'.
            self isVehiclePresent: false.].

    ] forkAt: (Processor userBackgroundPriority).
```

The block around all the code is used to fork the process in the background priority, as shown in the last line of code. Now reading top down, the *whileFalse:* block will execute until the log window for the detector is closed (i.e., until the log's window shell is destroyed). Each time the body of the while loop executes, the process will delay for the specified time, detect a vehicle (*self vehicleDetected*), send a message to the log, and finally reset the variable that says that a vehicle was detected. For more complex simulations, random numbers could be used to set the interval time using the base class **EsRandom.**

During testing, the *vehicleDetected* method did nothing. Later, code was added to send the "vehicleDetected" message to the detector's traffic stream. To test the detector and log code, class method *test1* was written in class **TlsTrafficLightSystemApp.** The code for this method is:

```
TlsTrafficLightSystemApp class>>#test1

    "Test the system"

        (TlsDetector new) log: (EtWorkspace new open);
            name: 'Detector1';
            testDetectionEvery: 1000.
```

This code creates a new detector, assigns an open workspace as its log, sets the name of the detector, and starts the test. The result is that a workspace opens and the message "Vehicle Detected" is displayed every 1000 milliseconds.

SECOND TEST: A SIMPLE INTERSECTION

We used the first test to get familiar with the traffic classes, and to set up the framework for logging events. This was simply a good place to get started! The next test built the code to run a simple intersection consisting of two phases.

During this stage of coding, each class was implemented by going through each CRC card and editing its corresponding class to implement the listed responsibilities. The instance interaction and structure diagrams were used to supplement the information in the CRC cards. Initially, each responsibility was implemented as a method which consisted only of a comment. In the next pass, the methods were extended to add the code implementing the behavior described by the responsibilities on the CRC cards. While we were implementing some of these methods, requirements for additional methods came to light. This often happens and could lead to the creation of additional methods in the current class, to extending a collaborating class, or to the addition or modification of instance variables.

In general, responsibilities on the cards that read "knows about x" are usually implemented as "setter" methods for an instance variable. Most instance variables were defined in the earlier pass. The goal for this second test was to build the framework of a basic structure of the interacting objects.

For example, the CRC card for Intersection has the responsibility "knows which phases need service." In class **TlsIntersection,** this is implemented by adding the instance variable *phasesNeedingService*, and the method *addPhaseNeedingService:* with the argument a phase. When a new instance of a **TlsIntersection** is created, it is initialized. During initialization, the instance variable *phasesNeedingService* is set to a new instance of class **OrderedCollection.** The method *addPhaseNeedingService:* can therefore expect the instance variable to have been initialized properly already. The original code for the *addPhaseNeedingService:* method is:

```
TlsIntersection>>#addPhaseNeedingService: aPhase

   "Add a phase to the end of the line that needs service"
   "If the phase is already on the list, do not add it again"

   (phasesNeedingService includes: aPhase) ifFalse: [
      phasesNeedingService addLast: aPhase].
```

Later, as the prototype develops, we will extend this method. After all the responsibilities were implemented, the second test case on class **TlsTrafficLightSystemApp** was written. This was:

```
TlsTrafficLightSystemApp class>>#test2

"Test the system with a simple intersection of two streams and
two phases"
```

```
| log intersection detector1 phase1 trafficStream1 detector2
phase2 trafficStream2 |

   log:= self EtWorkspace new open.

   intersection := (TlsIntersection new) name: 'Intersection';
         log: log.

   trafficStream1 := (TlsTrafficStream new) name:
'TrafficStream1';
         isRed: true;
         log: log.

  phase1 := (TlsPhase new) name: 'Phase1';
         intersection: intersection;
         minimumGreenTime: 5;
         minimumYellowTime: 1;
         trafficStreams: (OrderedCollection with:
trafficStream1);
         log: log.

  trafficStream1 phase: phase1.

  detector1 :=(TlsDetector new) name: 'Detector1';
         log: (EtWorkspace new open);
         trafficStream: trafficStream1;
         testDetectionEvery: 1000;
         yourself.

   trafficStream2 := (TlsTrafficStream new) name:
'TrafficStream2';
         isRed: true;
         log: log.

  phase2 := (TlsPhase new) name: 'Phase2';
         intersection: intersection;
         minimumGreenTime: 2;
         minimumYellowTime: 1;
         trafficStreams: (OrderedCollection with:
trafficStream2);
         log: log.

  trafficStream2 phase: phase2.
```

```
detector2 :=(TlsDetector new) name: 'Detector2';
        log: (EtWorkspace new open);
        trafficStream: trafficStream2;
        testDetectionEvery: 4000;
        yourself.
```

```
intersection phases: (OrderedCollection with: phase1 with:
phase2);
        phasesRed: (OrderedCollection with: phase1 with:
phase2).
```

```
intersection startServicingPhases.
```

This code starts by creating a log, which is a single open workspace used by the intersection as well as the phases and traffic streams. For this test, the detectors send so many messages that they each get their own workspaces rather than cluttering up the main workspace. After the log is created, the intersection, phases, traffic streams, and detectors are created.

The first traffic system phase is created with the following code:

```
phase1 := (TlsPhase new) name: 'Phase1';
      intersection: intersection;
      minimumGreenTime: 5;
      minimumYellowTime: 1;
      trafficStreams: (OrderedCollection with:
trafficStream1);
        log: log.
```

Here, the phase is assigned a name, a log, and an intersection; has its transition times set; and is assigned to a collection of traffic streams. After the phase is created, it is assigned to its traffic streams with *trafficStream1 phase: phase1*.

After all the detectors, traffic streams, and phases are created, the intersection is set up with its phases:

```
intersection phases: (OrderedCollection with: phase1 with:
phase2);
  phasesRed: (OrderedCollection with: phase1 with: phase2).
```

There is no need to initialize the intersection to indicate that there are no green phases and no phases needing service, since these are the default conditions.

Finally, the intersection is started with *intersection startServicingPhases,* and processing starts. Since the *startServicingPhases* method was not listed as a responsibility, it was added after the test was written. At this point, the prototype begins to drive the design rather than the CRC cards and design diagrams. The *startServicingPhases* method contains the main loop for running the intersection. The loop runs until the intersection is stopped for some reason. Whenever a phase needs service, a phase is serviced. To make it easier to test, the loop runs in a background process. To support these new requirements, an *isStopped* instance variable was added to the intersection and initialized to **false.** The message "stop" can be sent to the intersection to set this instance variable to true. A *whileFalse:* block is used to iterate over the intersection's phase changes.

A Smalltalk semaphore was used to determine when a phase might need service. Class **Semaphore** is a class available in the base class hierarchy that can be used either to synchronize multiple processes or to serialize access to a shared resource. For the prototype, we used two instance methods on semaphore: *wait* and *signal*. When a semaphore receives the "wait" message, the sending process is blocked until the semaphore receives the "signal" message from another process.

The instance variable *somethingHasChangedSemaphore,* added to class **TlsIntersection,** is initialized to be a new instance of class **Semaphore.** This semaphore is signaled whenever a phase reports that the minimum green time has elapsed and when a new phase needs service. In other words, the semaphore is signaled whenever something changes that may result in a phase change. When the semaphore is signaled, the phases are checked to see if a phase change should occur.

Before we continue, let's go back and change the method *addPhaseNeedingService:* to signal the semaphore. The change is highlighted in bold below:

```
TlsIntersection>>#addPhaseNeedingService: aPhase

    "Add a phase to the end of the line that needs service"
    "If the phase is already on the list, do not add it again"

    (phasesNeedingService includes: aPhase) ifFalse: [
        phasesNeedingService addLast: aPhase.

        "Now signal that something has changed"
        somethingHasChangedSemaphore signal. ].
```

All phases for an intersection are stored in an ordered collection. When a phase requests service, it is serviced in the order of the collection of phases, which is not necessarily the order in which the request for service was received. This is done by keeping an index of the last phase serviced, and walking that index through the collection of phases, checking each phase to see if it needs service. After the last phase in the collection has been checked, the index is reset to point back to the start of the collection. The instance variable *lastPhaseServicedIndex* is used to hold the index. The instance variable is initialized when phase servicing starts.

So, the code for instance method *startServicingPhases* in class **TlsIntersection** is:

```
TlsIntersection>>#startServicingPhases

    "This is the main loop for the intersection
    Whenever something has changed, service the next phase
if needed."

[ "Fork this block in the background "
  [ isStopped ] whileFalse: [

    "Wait until something changes"
    somethingHasChangedSemaphore wait.

    "Service the next phase in order"
    self serviceNextPhase

] ] forkAt: Processor userBackgroundPriority.
```

Now let's examine the *serviceNextPhase* method. This method checks to see if there is some work to do; if so, it finds the next phase to service, terminates the currently open phase, and then opens the next phase. If there are no phases to service, then the method returns right away. If the current phase is still open and its minimum green time has not elapsed, it is entitled to be open and so the method returns right away.

If a phase change is possible, then the next phase to service is found using the method *findNextPhaseToService*. This method iterates through the phases in service order, starting with the last one serviced, to find the next phase to service. The *findNextPhaseToService* method could be changed to implement a different priority scheme, such as one used to coordinating the timing of many intersections.

The selected phase is then removed from the list of phases needing service. If it is not open already, the currently open phase is terminated, and the selected phase is added to the list of phases entitled to be opened and opened. The phase will remain entitled to be open until its minimum green time expires. So, the code to service the next phase is:

```
TlsIntersection>>#serviceNextPhase

    "Service the next one on the queue if any "
    | nextPhase nextPhaseIndex |

    phasesNeedingService isEmpty ifTrue: [ ^nil ]. "Leave if
nothing to do"
    phasesEntitledToBeOpen notEmpty ifTrue: [ ^nil ]. "Leave if
another phase still green"

    nextPhase := self findNextPhaseToService.
```

```
nextPhase isNil ifTrue: [ ^nil ]. "Leave if nothing to do"

phasesNeedingService remove: nextPhase.

nextPhase isOpen ifFalse: [
    phasesTerminated remove: nextPhase.

    phasesOpen copy do: [ :phase |
      phasesOpen remove: phase.
      phase terminate.
      phasesTerminated addLast: phase.].

    phasesEntitledToBeOpen addLast: nextPhase.
    phasesOpen addLast: nextPhase.
    nextPhase open. ].
```

At this stage of testing, the phases did not actually control the lights, but simply wrote to the log "Phase opened" and "Phase terminated." As the next test was developed, control of the lights was added.

THIRD TEST: A FULL INTERSECTION

The third test extends the prototype to actually show the lights changing and to support an intersection with six traffic streams and four phases. This simulates a typical intersection with four straight lanes of traffic plus two left-turn lanes, where one left-turn lane stays green longer than the other.

Let's first look at controlling the lights in the phase. In the original design, when a phase was open it would cycle its traffic streams to green, and when it was terminated it would cycle its traffic streams to red. However, this design could lead to situations where a traffic stream would be changed to red at the end of one phase, and then immediately change back to green at the beginning of the next phase. To avoid this, the implementation was changed so that each phase knows both the traffic streams to set green and the traffic streams to set red at the start of a phase, and also knows to do nothing at the end. Now a traffic stream will stay green if it is going to be green in the next phase as well. Therefore, class **TlsPhase** was changed to add two instance variables: *trafficStreamsToMakeRed* and *trafficStreamsToMakeGreen*.

The second test method was then changed to add code to initialize these instance variables as follows:

```
phase1 := (TlsPhase new) name: 'Phase1';
  log: log;
  intersection: intersection;
```

```
minimumGreenTime: 5;
minimumYellowTime: 1;
trafficStreamsToMakeGreen: (OrderedCollection with:
trafficStream1);
trafficStreamsToMakeRed: (OrderedCollection with:
trafficStream2).
```

When a phase is opened it is sent the "open" message. The *open* instance method of **TlsPhase** tells its "traffic streams to make red" that they should go red, waits for them all to go red, then tells its "traffic streams to make green" to go green. Since a traffic stream controls how long it takes to change from green to red (i.e., going from green to yellow to red), the phase must wait until all streams go red before it changes any streams to green. It does this by forking several processes so all red traffic streams start to go red at (roughly) the same time, then it waits for all the streams to signal that they have gone red. Again, a semaphore is used to synchronize the processes.

The code for the *open* method follows. At the top of the method, there is a check to see if anything at all needs to be done, the method returns without doing anything. The phase then opens, forks processes to set some traffic streams to red, waits for them to complete, forks some processes to set some traffic streams to green, waits for them to complete, delays for the minimum green time, and tells the intersection that its minimum green time has passed.

```
TlsPhase>>#open

  "Tell my red streams to go red and my green streams to go
green"
  | areAnyInNeed completionSemaphore signalCount toMakeRed
toMakeGreen |

  "Check to make sure a traffic stream still needs service"

  areAnyInNeed := false.
  completionSemaphore := Semaphore new.

  trafficStreamsToMakeGreen copy do: [ :eachStream |
    eachStream needsService ifTrue: [
        areAnyInNeed := true ]].

  "If no stream needs service, then do not go green and let the
next phase go"
  areAnyInNeed ifFalse: [
      intersection minimumGreenTimeElapsedForPhase: self.
      ^self ].
```

```
    self show: 'Opening'. "Write message to log"
    isOpen := true.


"Fork to change lights to red"
(toMakeRed := trafficStreamsToMakeRed copy) do: [ :eachStream |
 [eachStream goRed.
 completionSemaphore signal ] forkAt: Processor
userBackgroundPriority ].


 "Wait for all to finish changing to red"
 1 to: toMakeRed size do: [ :i |
    completionSemaphore wait ].


 "Fork to change lights to green"
 (toMakeGreen := trafficStreamsToMakeGreen copy) do:
  [ :eachStream |
    [eachStream goGreenWithPhase: self.
    completionSemaphore signal ] forkAt: Processor
   userBackgroundPriority ].


 "Wait for all to finish changing to green"
 1 to: toMakeGreen size do: [ :i |
    completionSemaphore wait ].

"When my minimum time is elapsed, tell the intersection."
[(Delay forSeconds: minimumGreenTime) wait.
    intersection minimumGreenTimeElapsedForPhase: self
    ]forkAt: Processor userBackgroundPriority.
```

When the intersection receives the "minimumGreenTimeElapsedForPhase:" message, it removes the phase from the list of phases entitled to be green and signals that "something has changed." This will cause the next phase in order waiting to be serviced to be opened, and the whole process repeats.

FOURTH TEST: THE SPECIFIED INTERSECTION

The fourth test implements the timing schedule specified in the analysis, and extends the detector scheme to support the detection schedule the analysts specified. For example, phase 1 is constructed using the following code snippet:

```
"MapleNorth+MapleSouth Phase"

greenStreams := OrderedCollection
            with: (trafficStreams at: 1)
```

```
            with: (trafficStreams at: 2).
redStreams := (OrderedCollection new) addAll: trafficStreams;
            removeAll: greenStreams;
            yourself.
phase := (TlsPhase new)name: 'MapleNorth+MapleSouth';
        log: log;
            intersection: intersection;
            minimumGreenTime: 30;
            minimumYellowTime: 10;
            trafficStreamsToMakeGreen: greenStreams;
            trafficStreamsToMakeRed: redStreams;
            yourself.

phases at: 1 put: phase.
```

To support the detection requirement, the *testDetectionAt:* method added to class **TlsDetector** code is used; the parameter is an array of second counts to cause detection. The code to use the detector is:

```
(TlsDetector new) name: 'MainEastDetector(dts3)';
        log: log;
        trafficStream: (trafficStreams at: 3);
        testDetectionAt: #(75 232 302 345 495).
```

In this case, a vehicle will be detected at 75, 232, 302, 345, and 495 seconds into the test. The code for test case four is shown as "Smalltalk Test Method Four" at the end of the chapter. The output log from running this test is shown following the code.

Saving the Prototype

Smalltalk provides several ways to save code. Recall that the code is developed by updating an "image" containing all the executing code as well as a pointer to the source code. The source code itself is stored in a code library or source file. During development, the code is saved by saving the image. If a code library is used, the code can be saved by exporting it into a binary format that can be imported to another code library. When the code is exported, it maintains its version and edition information, making it more easy to use and manage when it is imported into another code library.

Finally, the most simple and portable mechanism is to "file out" the code in a source file. Filed-out code can be modified using any text editor. The file can then be "filed in" to recreate the classes to add or update the classes in the image. When it is filed back in to an image which runs with a code library, all the classes and methods are recreated with new editions.

REUSING COMPONENTS

The key to reusing components is to find them and understand them. A large quantity of reusable Smalltalk code exists, but it is often buried in the heart of applications and environment tools. In Smalltalk, most applications and system tools are shipped with source code to help promote reuse. Normally, code is reused by finding it with the browsers and reading the code to see how it works. In some cases, design documentation is available to help promote reuse.

There are two ways to reuse Smalltalk code. The first is very common, but is not generally considered "reuse" in the object-oriented sense: source code can be cut from one method or class and pasted into another. In this case, the programmer assumes ownership of the copied code. The risk in this technique is that fixes to the original classes will not be propagated to the target class. In some cases, there may also be copyright issues which must be addressed.

Second, an existing class can be subclassed. The subclass can extend the code from the superclass as needed. This gives complete reuse and often allows programmers to create new applications and features by writing very little code. The risk with this approach is that the superclass can be redesigned or modified in the future in a way that affects the subclass. This reuse approach works best when the superclass is either very stable, or is owned by the same organization where it is reused. Either reuse approach is reasonable, as long as you are cognizant of the risks involved.

The intersection prototype provides several potential reuse opportunities for the future. First, someone who wanted to create a similar pattern of forking processes and joining them after they are complete could cut and paste the source code to replicate this behavior. Second, an intersection with different behavior could be easily written by creating subclasses of the classes in the traffic light system application. For example, an intersection which supports platoons of cars traveling between intersections could be implemented by creating a subclass of class **TlsIntersection** and overriding the *findNextPhaseToService* method. Likewise, additional instance variables could be added to the new class as needed. These modifications could be made without changing anything in the original intersection code!

TIPS AND RESOURCES FOR FURTHER STUDY

One of the best resources is on-line: the Internet newsgroup *comp.lang.smalltalk*. The helpful people in this newsgroup are a great source of information, language tips, and further pointers. Fortunately, book stores are increasingly well stocked with titles on Smalltalk, design patterns, and object-oriented design methodologies. For Smalltalk style, we particularly like Kublic's book *Smalltalk with Style*. On IBM Smalltalk, read David Smith's *IBM Smalltalk: The Language* (Addison-Wesley), and Shafer and Herndon's *IBM Smalltalk Programming for Windows and OS/2* (Prima). For ParcPlace/Digitalk, read *The*

Smalltalk Developer's Guide to VisualWorks (SIGS) by Tim Howard. The definitive early reference is by Goldberg and Robson: *Smalltalk-80: The Language* (Addison-Wesley), although you will now find many of the particulars implemented differently.

Smalltalk Express, an excellent version of the language, is available for download at no charge from ObjectShare/ParcPlace at http://www.objectshare.com. It includes excellent on-line documentation and demonstration files, and is based on the no longer sold Smalltalk/V. This is an excellent learning tool, although we would not recommend it for commercial applications. The book closest in syntax to Smalltalk Express is LaLonde's *Discovering Smalltalk* (Addison-Wesley).

Nothing beats having an experienced person around when embarking on a new endeavor. This is particularly true given the sophistication of the Smalltalk environment. If you have the resources to find good mentoring and training, the initial learning process will be greatly facilitated. And, just as with any programming language, you've got to jump into the water before you can swim. We hope the traffic light system can help your stroke!

THE CODE: SMALLTALK TEST METHOD FOUR

```
TlsTrafficLightSystemApp>>#test4

  "Test the system
  This test has an intersection with four phases, and matches
the input specification:
      1  MapleNorth+MapleSouth - 10 sec
      2  MainEast+MainWest - 10 sec
      3  MainEast+MainEastLeftTurn - 10 sec
      4  MainWest+MainWestLeftTurn - 5 sec
There are six traffic streams
      1  MapleSouth
      2  MapleNorth
      3  MainEast
      4  MainWest
      5  MainWestLeftTurn
      6  MainEastLeftTurn  "

  | log intersection detectors phases trafficStreams
redStreams greenStreams phase |

  log:= EtWorkspace new open.

  intersection := (TlsIntersection new)  name: 'Intersection';
                      log: log.
```

```
    trafficStreams := Array new: 6.
    trafficStreams at: 1 put: ((TlsTrafficStream new) name:
'MapleSouth(ts1)';
                            isRed: true;
                            log: log;
                            yourself).
    trafficStreams at: 2 put: ((TlsTrafficStream new) name:
'MapleNorth(ts2)';
                            isRed: true;
                            log: log;
                            yourself).

trafficStreams at: 3 put: ((TlsTrafficStream new) name:
'MainEast(ts3)';
                            isRed: true;
                            log: log;
                            yourself).

    trafficStreams at: 4 put: ((TlsTrafficStream new) name:
'MainWest(ts4)';
                            isRed: true;
                            log: log;
                            yourself).

    trafficStreams at: 5 put: ((TlsTrafficStream new) name:
'MainEastLeftTurn(ts5)';
                            isRed: true;
                            log: log;
                            yourself).

    trafficStreams at: 6 put: ((TlsTrafficStream new) name:
'MainWestLeftTurn(ts6)';
                            isRed: true;
                            log: log;
                            yourself).

    phases := Array new: 4.

    "MapleNorth+MapleSouth Phase"
    greenStreams := OrderedCollection with: (trafficStreams at:
1)
                with: (trafficStreams at: 2).
    redStreams := (OrderedCollection new) addAll: trafficStreams;
        removeAll: greenStreams;
        yourself.
```

```
     phase := (TlsPhase new) name:
'MapleNorth+MapleSouth(p1)';
                log: log;
                intersection: intersection;
                minimumGreenTime: 30;
                minimumYellowTime: 10;
                trafficStreamsToMakeGreen: greenStreams;
                trafficStreamsToMakeRed: redStreams;
                yourself.

   phases at: 1 put: phase.

   "MainEast+MainWest"
   greenStreams := OrderedCollection with: (trafficStreams at:
3)
       with: (trafficStreams at: 4).
   redStreams := (OrderedCollection new) addAll: trafficStreams;
       removeAll: greenStreams;
       yourself.
   phase := (TlsPhase new)
       name: 'MainEast+MainWest(p2)';
       log: log;
       intersection: intersection;
       minimumGreenTime: 40;
       minimumYellowTime: 10;
       trafficStreamsToMakeGreen: greenStreams;
       trafficStreamsToMakeRed: redStreams;
       yourself.

phases at: 2 put: phase.

"MainEast+MainEastLeftTurn"
greenStreams := OrderedCollection with: (trafficStreams at: 3)
       with: (trafficStreams at: 5).
redStreams := (OrderedCollection new) addAll: trafficStreams;
       removeAll: greenStreams;
       yourself.
phase := (TlsPhase new)name: 'MainEast+MainEastLeftTurn(p3)';
                log: log;
                intersection: intersection;
                minimumGreenTime: 40;
                minimumYellowTime: 10;
                trafficStreamsToMakeGreen: greenStreams;
                trafficStreamsToMakeRed: redStreams;
                yourself.
```

```
      phases at: 3 put: phase.

      "MainWest+MainWestLeftTurn"
      greenStreams := OrderedCollection with: (trafficStreams at: 4)
            with: (trafficStreams at: 6).
      redStreams := (OrderedCollection new) addAll: trafficStreams;
            removeAll: greenStreams;
            yourself.
        phase := (TlsPhase new) name:
      'MainWest+MainWestLeftTurn(p4)';
                  log: log;
                  intersection: intersection;
                  minimumGreenTime: 40;
                  minimumYellowTime: 10;
                  trafficStreamsToMakeGreen: greenStreams;
                  trafficStreamsToMakeRed: redStreams;
                  yourself.

      phases at: 4 put: phase.

      (trafficStreams at: 1) phasesToNotifyForService:
          (OrderedCollection with: (phases at: 1)). "MapleN"

      (trafficStreams at: 2) phasesToNotifyForService:
          (OrderedCollection with: (phases at: 1)). "MapleS"

      (trafficStreams at: 3) phasesToNotifyForService:
          (OrderedCollection with: (phases at: 2) with: (phases
      at: 3)). "MainE"

      (trafficStreams at: 4) phasesToNotifyForService:
          (OrderedCollection with: (phases at: 2) with: (phases
      at: 4)). "MainW"

      (trafficStreams at: 5) phasesToNotifyForService:
          (OrderedCollection with: (phases at: 3)). "MainET"

      (trafficStreams at: 6) phasesToNotifyForService:
          (OrderedCollection with: (phases at: 4)). "MainWT"

      (TlsDetector new) name: 'MapleSouthDetector(dts1)';
              log: log;
            trafficStream: (trafficStreams at: 1);
            testDetectionAt: #(10).
```

```
(TlsDetector new) name: 'MapleNorthDetector(dts2)';
        log: log;
      trafficStream: (trafficStreams at: 2);
      testDetectionAt: #(243).

(TlsDetector new) name: 'MainEastDetector(dts3)';
        log: log;
      trafficStream: (trafficStreams at: 3);
      testDetectionAt: #(75 147 232 302 345 495).

(TlsDetector new) name: 'MainWestDetector(dts4)';
        log: log;
      trafficStream: (trafficStreams at: 4);
      testDetectionAt: #(222 303 340 504).

(TlsDetector new) name: 'MainEastLeftDetector(dts5)';
        log: log;
      trafficStream: (trafficStreams at: 5);
      testDetectionAt: #(148 301).

(TlsDetector new) name: 'MainWestLeftDetector(dts6)';
        log: log;
      trafficStream: (trafficStreams at: 6);
      testDetectionAt: #(45 304) .

intersection phases: phases copy asOrderedCollection;
        phasesTerminated: phases asOrderedCollection.

  (trafficStreams at: 4) vehicleDetected.
  intersection startServicingPhases.

^intersection
```

Output from Smalltalk Test Four

1. Detection Log
0 secs - MainWestDetector(dts4): Vehicle detected.
10 secs - MapleSouthDetector(dts1): Vehicle detected.
45 secs - MainWestLeftDetector(dts6): Vehicle detected.
75 secs - MainEastDetector(dts3): Vehicle detected.
147 secs - MainEastDetector(dts3): Vehicle detected.
148 secs - MainEastLeftDetector(dts5): Vehicle detected.
222 secs - MainWestDetector(dts4): Vehicle detected.
232 secs - MainEastDetector(dts3): Vehicle detected.

243 secs - MapleNorthDetector(dts2): Vehicle detected.
301 secs - MainEastLeftDetector(dts5): Vehicle detected.
302 secs - MainEastDetector(dts3): Vehicle detected.
303 secs - MainWestDetector(dts4): Vehicle detected.
304 secs - MainWestLeftDetector(dts6): Vehicle detected.
340 secs - MainWestDetector(dts4): Vehicle detected.
345 secs - MainEastDetector(dts3): Vehicle detected.
495 secs - MainEastDetector(dts3): Vehicle detected.
504 secs - MainWestDetector(dts4): Vehicle detected.

2. Phase Change Log

0 secs - MainEast+MainWest(p2): Opening
0 secs - MainWest+MainWestLeftTurn(p4): Minimum yellow time is: 10 seconds.
0 secs - MainWest+MainWestLeftTurn(p4): Minimum green time is: 40 seconds.
0 secs - MainEast+MainEastLeftTurn(p3): Minimum yellow time is: 10 seconds.
0 secs - MainEast+MainEastLeftTurn(p3): Minimum green time is: 40 seconds.
0 secs - MainEast+MainWest(p2): Minimum yellow time is: 10 seconds.
0 secs - MainEast+MainWest(p2): Minimum green time is: 40 seconds.
0 secs - MapleNorth+MapleSouth(p1): Minimum yellow time is: 10 seconds.
0 secs - MapleNorth+MapleSouth(p1): Minimum green time is: 30 seconds.
0 secs - MainEast+MainWest(p2): Open
0 secs - Intersection: ---Phase Change Complete----------
40 secs - MainEast+MainWest(p2): Terminated
40 secs - MapleNorth+MapleSouth(p1): Opening
50 secs - MapleNorth+MapleSouth(p1): Open
50 secs - Intersection: Waiting: MainWest+MainWestLeftTurn(p4)
50 secs - Intersection: ---Phase Change Complete----------
80 secs - MapleNorth+MapleSouth(p1): Terminated
80 secs - MainEast+MainWest(p2): Opening
90 secs - MainEast+MainWest(p2): Open
90 secs - Intersection: Waiting: MainWest+MainWestLeftTurn(p4)
90 secs - Intersection: ---Phase Change Complete----------
130 secs - MainEast+MainWest(p2): Terminated
130 secs - MainWest+MainWestLeftTurn(p4): Opening
140 secs - MainWest+MainWestLeftTurn(p4): Open
140 secs - Intersection: ---Phase Change Complete----------
180 secs - MainWest+MainWestLeftTurn(p4): Terminated
180 secs - MainEast+MainWest(p2): Opening
190 secs - MainEast+MainWest(p2): Open
190 secs - Intersection: Waiting: MainEast+MainEastLeftTurn(p3)
190 secs - Intersection: ---Phase Change Complete----------

230 secs - MainEast+MainWest(p2): Terminated

230 secs - MainEast+MainEastLeftTurn(p3): Opening

240 secs - MainEast+MainEastLeftTurn(p3): Open

240 secs - Intersection: Waiting: MainEast+MainWest(p2)

240 secs - Intersection: Waiting: MainWest+MainWestLeftTurn(p4)

240 secs - Intersection: ---Phase Change Complete-----------

280 secs - MainEast+MainEastLeftTurn(p3): Terminated

280 secs - MainWest+MainWestLeftTurn(p4): Opening

290 secs - MainWest+MainWestLeftTurn(p4): Open

290 secs - Intersection: Waiting: MapleNorth+MapleSouth(p1)

290 secs - Intersection: ---Phase Change Complete-----------

330 secs - MainWest+MainWestLeftTurn(p4): Terminated

330 secs - MapleNorth+MapleSouth(p1): Opening

340 secs - MapleNorth+MapleSouth(p1): Open

340 secs - Intersection: Waiting: MainEast+MainEastLeftTurn(p3)

340 secs - Intersection: Waiting: MainEast+MainWest(p2)

340 secs - Intersection: Waiting: MainWest+MainWestLeftTurn(p4)

340 secs - Intersection: ---Phase Change Complete-----------

370 secs - MapleNorth+MapleSouth(p1): Terminated

370 secs - MainEast+MainWest(p2): Opening

380 secs - MainEast+MainWest(p2): Open

380 secs - Intersection: Waiting: MainEast+MainEastLeftTurn(p3)

380 secs - Intersection: Waiting: MainWest+MainWestLeftTurn(p4)

380 secs - Intersection: ---Phase Change Complete-----------

420 secs - MainEast+MainWest(p2): Terminated

420 secs - MainEast+MainEastLeftTurn(p3): Opening

430 secs - MainEast+MainEastLeftTurn(p3): Open

430 secs - Intersection: Waiting: MainWest+MainWestLeftTurn(p4)

430 secs - Intersection: ---Phase Change Complete-----------

470 secs - MainEast+MainEastLeftTurn(p3): Terminated

470 secs - MainWest+MainWestLeftTurn(p4): Opening

480 secs - MainWest+MainWestLeftTurn(p4): Open

480 secs - Intersection: ---Phase Change Complete-----------

520 secs - MainWest+MainWestLeftTurn(p4): Terminated

520 secs - MainEast+MainWest(p2): Opening

530 secs - MainEast+MainWest(p2): Open

530 secs - Intersection: ---Phase Change Complete-----------

Chapter 11

Implementing CRC
in C++ and Java

We began coding the Complex Traffic Intersection in C++ by establishing some clear requirements for the finished product (the creation of our Java applet is outlined later in the chapter). Because this is a first round of implementation, we planned to build an architecture around the CRC cards that would be as easy as possible to modify and update through later iterations in the design process. Where possible, we aimed to preserve the structural relationships identified in the cards. We also wanted to hide the underlying implementation details such as the user interface and the C++ application framework, so that the same basic architecture could be smoothly ported to different environments.

Though portability is not an overall concern for this particular project, we wished to be able to test the basic architecture without a large investment in I/O gadgetry, and without having to extensively rewrite each class as the user interface became more fully developed. The goal is an implementation that can be easily attached to frameworks ranging from a pure character-based interface (used in the first round of testing scenarios to validate the concepts) to a graphical user interface suitable for developing new scenarios and demonstrating the workings of the system.

As we first reviewed the CRC cards, we noted that this was a fairly typical project: even in detailed sets of cards, there is very little information to guide an actual implementation. Simply "translating" the CRC cards into C++ is not an option. Although the cards are useful for locating operations within the system, they provide only loose guidelines with respect to object construction, parameters for member functions, and location of data members. Many important design decisions are not addressed at all in the cards, including the types of data members; the circumstances under which objects are created; where to use pointers, references, and locally constructed objects; how to coordinate the activities of objects; and input/output strategies.

DEVELOPING C++ SYSTEMS

A plan of action we have found useful when developing from CRC cards is working "top-down." In successive layers of detail, start with a relatively direct transcription of the cards, and then fill in the implementation components. Our goal early in design is to hide code and data structures. If this is done well, it will be possible to change the implemented code structure independently of the object-oriented design architecture. We have found that this process is facilitated by recursively iterating through four specific stages of design:

Developing the class interface
Designing constructors (the public implementation)
The private implementation
The I/O framework

A quick overview of each design step, and of our recommended coding standards, is in order before we jump into the details of the C++ code itself. We'll follow the implementation process from the Traffic Intersection CRC cards, as it actually progressed through each of these four iterative stages.

Class Interface Design

Typically, the responsibilities listed on CRC cards cannot be directly translated into member functions. Function names, parameters, and some return information must be identified. An easy trap to fall into at this stage is to identify function parameters with the actual data elements specified on the CRC cards. In practice, it is usually better to invent new classes to encapsulate method parameters. Each method requiring parameters has one argument which is an object of a new "parameter" class. That way, one doesn't have to worry about implicitly exposing data elements, and later changes to the parameters can be easily accommodated by adjusting the parameter class definition. In some cases, such parameters will actually not represent new classes at all, but will be implemented as "typedefs" (alias names) for some other class or built-in type.

This is also the time to decide what standards will be used for names in the design. The importance of selecting good names cannot be overemphasized. Good names are not selected in isolation, but should reinforce each other by being used consistently. Names should reflect function not form. If any other information is encoded in the name, it should be information about how the name can be used (scope, class derivation possibilities, variable or constant, etc.), rather than what its static type is. Advanced C++ programmers like to refer to this naming style as "Hungarian" notation, for amusing reasons not necessary to detail here!

These are our tips for C++ class interface development, which we will detail shortly, as we show the code for the Traffic System:

Develop the public section of class definitions from CRC cards
Define additional classes to manage parameters and return types
Use names that emphasize object scope and capabilities (not
　　structure)
Keep built-in C++ types invisible

Designing Constructors

Although C++ supports data hiding through the use of public and private keywords, the lines of demarcation do not entirely coincide with those that the higher-level model of the CRC cards would suggest. For example, constructors are generally public and used frequently throughout applications whenever objects are created and destroyed. But the interface that the constructors represent usually cannot be identified directly from the CRC cards. Decisions about constructors imply a particular implementation, since they identify what is required in order to create an object. As a result, they also have an impact on when and where objects can be created. As the implementation progresses, constructors are frequently added and altered. But to start that process, we must make some initial judgments about how objects of various classes will work together. We find it useful to sketch out a likely set of constructors early in the process and then refine them as we move more deeply into the implementation. The goal in designing a good set of constructors is to support object creation in useful contexts, without revealing too much about the inner workings of the class. As with the interface to other public functions, we typically create parameter classes to encapsulate the information being passed to the constructor. Our tips for public implementations of constructors are implemented in the C++ code later in the chapter, and can be summarized here:

Objects with constructor parameters need class definitions
Do not use constructors for Public Interface operations!
Declare regular member functions, called from the constructor if
　　necessary

Private Implementation

Many issues must be settled to completely implement a C++ design. In particular, this includes identifying and coding data types and algorithms that will enable each class of objects to perform its particular duties. Even as we arrange the model suggested by the CRC cards into a working implementation, we must continue vigilantly to encapsulate anything which might later need to be changed. The implementation that emerges should thus be highly object-oriented, to the point that there is essentially no visible use of built-in C++ data types, and no explicit attachment to anything that is not implied by the model represented on the CRC cards. Ideally, this implementation remains one step removed from issues of user-interface design, database requirements, and other environmental constraints. Resist the temptation to "switch to C," even if it looks as if it will give you a quick performance boost. The places where performance cannot be improved sufficiently through a better (and still encapsulated) design occur only in very specialized domains. If you have to do something to an object, make sure it's an operation the object can perform, rather than unpacking the object's structure. It's always better to redesign an interface than to unpack an object's structure within the application code. We have some suggestions for doing all this, again summarized in a list with the details shown later as the code unfolds:

> Define data elements
> Use type names that suggest object *use*
> Keep member functions short and clear
> Declare local types to implement classes (some types are classes,
>   and some are simple type definitions)
> Avoid built-in C++ data types
> Resist the temptation to "switch to C"

I/O Frameworks

C++ derives advantages and disadvantages from its relative independence from particular implementation environments. Unlike Smalltalk or Java, the language comes with no standard high-level machinery for performing input and output operations, or creating persistent data. The advantage, for a well-crafted C++ program, is a high degree of portability to environments with widely different characteristics. The disadvantage is that unless the program is well crafted, it can become mired in a sticky quagmire of implementation-dependent I/O code. For a variety of reasons we will explore in depth later, there is an often-irresistible temptation to make I/O and the rest of the application environment visible, rather than treating it as the implementation detail it really is. The main guidelines for developing these I/O frameworks are as follows:

> Application frameworks should be invisible (except at the lowest
>   levels)
> Use classes dependent on "outside" information, for database
>   and I/O
> Keep the number of classes reaching out to a minimum

C++ Coding Guidelines

A variety of coding standards exist for C++, and there are many schools of thought about the perfect style. In practice, the most important job of a coding standard is to enable a programmer to quickly see the essential features of the code. As a result, it matters less *what* the standard is than *how consistently* it is adhered to. In the code presented in this chapter, we used some basic principles which have served us quite well on many projects of this size. For those who would like a more detailed discussion of C++ coding standards, we suggest consulting both *Taligent's Guide to Designing Programs: Well-Mannered Object-Oriented Design in C++* (Addison-Wesley) and the coding standards page of the Ellemtel Company, found at http://web2.airmail.net/~rks/ellhome.htm. The core standards we enforced in the traffic implementation cover naming, data types, classes, and a few miscellaneous items:

Naming

Class names and methods start with uppercase letters. Data elements begin with 'f_', while local variables have no prefix and begin with lowercase letters. Global variables begin with the prefix 'the' (as in 'theEventQueue'); where supported, we prefer to place global variables in namespaces. In general, prefixes indicate the scope of a name rather than its type. To the extent it is important, type is usually easily deduced from the name's usage, whereas scope is not. Functions whose names begin with "Create" return pointers to heap objects whose deletion is the responsibility of the caller. Functions whose names begin with "Get" that return pointers return a "borrowed" pointer; the caller may use it and then discard it.

Types

C++ basic types (including those defined in the ANSI Standard Library) are never used directly, with the exception of the bool type. They are either encapsulated in a wrapper class, or hidden behind a typedef (alias name) so that their purpose rather than their structure is indicated in the name. Pointer and reference marks in declarations (* and & respectively) are separated by white space from both the type and the name, for the simple reason that it makes them more visible.

Classes

Public sections always come first, because they usually contain what one is looking for. If the private section contains functions and data, the functions are listed first. There is at most one public, protected, or private section. In-line function definitions are never written in the class definition, but are always placed in the header file below the class definition. Constructors always have member initialization lists, and all data members must appear in each list.

Odds and Ends

Header files are always safety-wrapped with #ifndef/#endif to avoid problems with multiple inclusion. Overloaded operators are used sparingly. Our rule of thumb is that an expression involving the overloaded operator must appear to do the same thing even if each operand type is replaced with a built-in type. If there is no similar built-in type, we use named functions instead. Pointers to members are never used explicitly. Pointers are required to act as if they have at most one level of indirection. If they must be used at all (which we discourage), pointers to pointers must be wrapped in a smart pointer class with suitable access functions.

CREATING THE TRAFFIC SYSTEM CLASS INTERFACE

Our first task was to specify the interface of the classes that correspond to the CRC card collaborations and responsibilities. Though those were well worked out on the cards, they could not simply be copied line for line into C++. We noted at once the following essential operations:

Intersection handles requests for Phase and Timer service
Phase handles requests for TrafficStream service
TrafficStream handles requests for Detector service

Even at this basic level, we found ourselves having to make an implementation decision: whether to use a polling model, in which the Intersection checks regularly for new requests, or to use a callback model, in which the requesters such as the Phase send messages of their own whenever a new request is necessary. Our initial approach was to prefer a polling arrangement because that would better support a single-tasking implementation. However, we also tried to structure the solution so that moving to a message-driven callback model would require making as few public interface changes as possible.

One of the perils of large C++ projects is arranging class dependencies so that changes tend to ripple through the application. Typically, such dependencies are managed by putting each class definition into its own header and creating a corresponding code file for the implementation. This works to a certain extent, but it is inadequate by itself. Where possible, we also try to manipulate classes that are passed as parameters or returned from functions as pointers or references, so that incomplete class definitions can suffice and the whole header file for the parameter class need only be included in the code module. A variety of such strategies exists, employing techniques such as "handle" classes or abstract base classes (see *Design Patterns* by Gamma et al., Coplien's *Advanced C++*, or Meyers's *Effective C++*).

Including the header files in this case would work physically, but it can lead to extensive compilation dependencies that greatly reduce the usefulness of modularizing the program in the first place! The whole point, after all, is not to have to "recompile the world" when low-level modifications are made. In the example code that follows, for instance, we can change the structure or member functions of a PhaseRequest at will, and only the classes that actually call its member functions will have to be recompiled. If we actually included the PhaseRequest header file, then each time we made a change to the PhaseRequest, every class that includes the Intersection header would also have to be recompiled, even if they make no use of the PhaseRequest callback function at all.

```cpp
// Incomplete class definitions in place of header files

class PhaseRequest;          //  What Phase sends to Intersection
class TimerRequest;          //  What Timer sends to Phase
class TrafficStreamRequest;  //  What TrafficStream sends to Phase
class DetectorRequest;       //  What Detector sends to TrafficStream
class SignalSetting;         //  What Phase sends to TrafficStream
class TimerSetting;          //  What Phase sends to Timer

// Class definitions from CRC Cards

class Intersection
{
  public:
    void Activate();      // Start Intersection
    void Receive( const PhaseRequest & request );
                          // Callback from Phase
};

class Phase
{
public:
  void Activate();        // Enter phase (adjust TrafficStreams)

  void Receive( const TrafficStreamRequest & request );
                          // Callback from TrafficStream
  void Receive( const TimerRequest & timer );
                          // Callback from Timer

  PhaseRequest & GetLastRequest();
                          // Polled from Intersection
};

class TrafficStream
{
public:
  void Activate( SignalSetting & style );
                          // Allow traffic movement

  void Receive( const DetectorRequest & request );
                          // Callback from Detector

  TrafficStreamRequest & GetLastRequest();
                          // Polled from Phase
};
```

```
class Detector
{
public:
  DetectorRequest & GetLastRequest();
                        // Polled from TrafficStream
};

class SignalFace
{
public:
  void SetTo( SignalSetting & ss );
  SignalSetting & GetSignalState() const;
};

class Timer
{
public:
  void SetTime( TimerSetting & time );
                        // Prepare timer for activity
  void Start();         // Start timer
  TimerRequest & GetLastRequest();
                        // Poll for timer state
};
```

Part of specifying the interface required us to pass information through various member functions. In order to make the code robust, one should always attempt to code everything in the way that is most likely to keep the details invisible. In this case, even though the CRC cards made it clear what was to be passed, we chose to package each set of member function parameters and return values in its own class. This eliminated any inadvertent exposure of implementation details through the structure of a parameter list or return types. Each of those classes would get their own CRC cards in a more elaborate system, but we can skip that step in this simple case.

We tried to be consistent in naming the methods. Each class has a method to set it in motion called "Activate." Where we suspect that objects of the class would have to be stopped by a message, we also put in a "Deactivate" function. Unlike the other classes, Timer and SignalFace do not generate their own state internally, so they have a complete set of methods to allow another object to adjust their state. In keeping with our coding standard for such functions, these all have the format "SetSomething." The callback functions all have the name "Receive," selected where necessary through the regular C++ function overloading rules by the parameter type that the function is intended to handle.

PUBLIC IMPLEMENTATION OF CONSTRUCTORS

One of the nasty pitfalls of C++ is that not every "public" component of a class is actually part of its object-oriented interface. This is not simply a question of "visibility"—designating a parameter as a reference or value parameter, or writing the body of a function in-line makes those implementation details visible. But they are still logically private. On the other hand, constructors are quite public, both physically and logically. Yet from the standpoint of object-oriented design, they are still implementation details!

The particular goal of what we are calling "public implementation" is to detail the interface that will be used to create each kind of object in our program. It is here that we wonder about how to construct an object, and make some preliminary decisions about where and how the objects of each class are likely to be used—whether they are to be stack- or heap-allocated, whether they will require copying, whether copying them should be disallowed entirely, and what they need to know in order to be properly initialized.

Having a suitable set of constructors has a major influence on how the parts of an application can work together, and these decisions are thus not isolated and encapsulated in the way that the data elements and member function bodies are. CRC cards give us only the vaguest of guidelines for this purpose, yet treating constructor design as a pure implementation detail often results in brittle, "hard-wired" applications that are harder to evolve as the analysis and design continue. Instead of leaving constructor design to the last minute, we should carefully design the interfaces that will be used to build objects, so that we can fully specify how to use each object before we get into the issue of how it will perform each of its required tasks.

A reasonable set of constructors can often be sketched out by writing tentative lines of application code. For example, here is the application we arrived at to test the intersection classes, using a simple command-line interface:

```
const IntersectionConfigurationKey IXKEY_MAIN_MAPLE =
"Main+Maple";

int main()
{
  Intersection MainAndMaple =
      IntersectionConfiguration(IXKEY_MAIN_MAPLE);
  MainAndMaple.Activate();
  return 0;
}
```

The Intersection constructor uses an IntersectionConfiguration object to initialize itself, as illustrated in Figure 11-1. In order to hide details about where that configuration information comes from, class IntersectionConfigurationKey encapsulates the source of that information. In a full-blown application, this class might provide methods to allow the name of the intersection to be looked up as either a file or a database record. Or we could

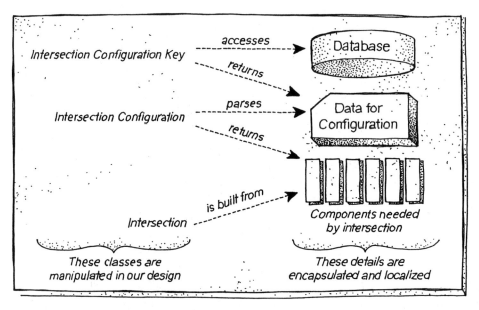

Figure 11-1 **The IntersectionConfiguration C++ Object Model**

simply leave it as a type definition for a character string. In either case, the Intersection-Configuration remains essentially the same if we decide to load it from a different source, and the Intersection itself is completely indifferent.

We add constructors wherever a class needs to be built from parameter information. Some of these classes will also later need default and copy constructors. Controlling the use of constructors is important, and one should never write either a default or copy constructor "just because"—the decision to allow copying or default initialization must be a deliberate part of the design process. Once one has mastered C++ syntax, it is easy to add new constructors or to alter any aspect of the class interface. The hard part, as usual, is staying clear about why one is doing so.

Here is how we started to fill in constructors for the basic CRC card classes:

```
// Constructor Parameter Classes

class IntersectionConfiguration;
class PhaseConfiguration;
class TrafficStreamConfiguration;
class DetectorConfiguration;

// Class definitions with Constructors
```

```
class Intersection
{
public:
  Intersection( IntersectionConfiguration & ic );
  // Other interface as before
};

class Phase
{
public:
  Phase( PhaseConfiguration & pc );
  // Other interface as before
};

class TrafficStream
{
public:
  TrafficStream( TrafficStreamConfiguration & tsc );
  // Other interface as before
};

class Detector
{
public:
  Detector( DetectorConfiguration & dc );
  // Other interface as before
};

class Timer
{
public:
  Timer();
};
```

Even though constructors and destructors are syntactically paired, destructors are not specified here because they are never invoked explicitly in application code. We can add or remove them at will when (and if) they prove necessary.

PRIVATE IMPLEMENTATIONS IN THE TRAFFIC SYSTEM

Most C++ compilers include sophisticated tools, and we could compile the code we just wrote in an effort to detect inconsistencies. The compiler could help with problems such as unmatched parameter names or missing class declarations. In fact, each stage of coding should be followed by compiling. We can't link the application (owing to missing function implementations), but it's very useful to know as early as possible if there is interface inconsistency. Once these problems are resolved, we can flesh out the class definitions and supply implementations of member functions until compilation is error-free.

We should start in what is often the most useful place: by sketching out the data structures that each CRC card suggested would be necessary. Once again, as with the member function parameters, this requires us to invent a certain number of new classes in order to avoid making implementation decisions too early. It also forces us to make some decisions about where certain information will be located.

TrafficStreams

The biggest decision revolved around where to locate the list of TrafficStreams that each Phase would manipulate. The CRC cards called for the TrafficStreams to be known by the Phase. However, each Phase needs to have exactly the same set of TrafficStreams. A Phase will determine the state for each TrafficStream, by passing a set of SignalSettings to the Activate method of each TrafficStream.

Practically, we have two alternatives: (1) create a list of TrafficStreams in each Phase; or (2) get the list of TrafficStreams from somewhere else. Since creating a different list of TrafficStreams for each Phase would make it hard to coordinate Detectors and SignalFaces through the TrafficStreams, we preferred the second alternative. But that leaves us with the further question of which class will be responsible for building the list of TrafficStreams and making it available to the Phases. Since the set of TrafficStreams is physically an attribute of the (real-world) Intersection, we chose to put that responsibility in the Intersection class (Figure 11-2).

This is an important decision in the Traffic System, since the CRC card analysis suggests that Intersections do not know anything about TrafficStreams. As a result, it is particularly important to verify that the Intersection does nothing with the TrafficStreams except use them to initialize the Phases. Failing to respect such design decisions as one makes otherwise sensible adjustments to the class structure is an insidious form of "ignoring the analysis," especially as C++ provides no syntactic way to prevent such errors!

Various other decisions need to be made about the Traffic implementation. To support notification of Phases by their TrafficStreams, it was desirable to make each TrafficStream aware of all the Phases in which it is active so that they could be notified when some service is required. It is the responsibility of the Phase to add itself to this list via a method of TrafficStream, so we invented the AddRespondingPhase method. The Phase parameter is passed as a pointer, in keeping with a common C++ convention that pointers are passed (instead of references) to functions that plan to store the pointer beyond the duration of that method. This permits a callback from the Stream to the Phase so the Intersection may correctly select future Phase sequences.

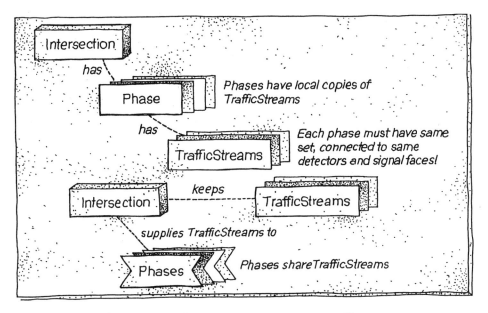

Figure 11-2 **Modeling the Implementation: Intersection, TrafficStreams, and Phases**

List and Queue Services

A decision was made to encapsulate the actual numbers of Phases, TrafficStreams, Detectors, and SignalFaces composing the system. Thus, the Intersection has a Queue of Phases and a List of TrafficStreams; the Phase uses the Intersection's List of Traffic-Streams and keeps its own List of SignalSettings; and the TrafficStream has a List of Detectors and a List of SignalFaces. Although these lists are redundant in the event that there is only one Detector or SignalFace (as is the case in the prototype application), putting them in place early makes it much easier to add or remove objects later without having to reimplement the containing class.

In the actual implementation, the C++ Standard Template Library (STL) was used to provide the underlying list and queue services. Even though the STL is on its way to becoming "standard" C++, all that status implies is that those components should be treated the same way we treat built-in types in the language: we keep them completely encapsulated and out of our design. Thus, our List of TrafficStreams *uses* an STL List for its implementation, but it is not simply identical to that list. If we keep that detail encapsulated, we preserve our flexibility in the event of later design changes that might, for instance, make a customized collection more suitable than the stock STL List.

The Timer

One final decision involves the Timer. Since we want to preserve some generality in this class, we will have the TimerSetting manage which object receives the callback so we can derive new TimerSetting classes later that will handle callbacks to Phase, Traffic-Stream, and whoever else might need to use such a timer. Thus, we don't have an explicit reference of whom to notify when the Timer has run its course, but use the TimerSetting as an intermediary for that purpose.

The Intersection Class

We'll explore the implementation of the Intersection class, and later of the Phase class, to illustrate the process of development. Unfortunately, there is not enough space to examine every detail of the implementation, since even this short application ends up with many lines of code. A complete set of files suitable for study and compilation by many popular PC C++ compilers is available from the authors through the Addison-Wesley Web site. Here is the class definition for the intersection class:

```cpp
// Header file: intrsect.h
// Intersection class

#ifndef INTERSECTION_H_
#define INTERSECTION_H_

// Component declarations and definitions

class PhaseQueue;
class PhaseRequest;
class IntersectionConfiguration;
class TrafficStreamList;
class DisplayDevice;

// Class definition

class Intersection
{
  public:
    Intersection( IntersectionConfiguration & ic );
    ~Intersection();

    void Activate();                    // Start Intersection
    void Receive( const PhaseRequest & request );
                                        // Callback from Phase

  private:
    PhaseQueue          * f_phases;
```

```
    TrafficStreamList       * f_streams;
    bool                      f_terminate;
};
```

```
#endif /* INTERSECTION_H_ */
```

The nontrivial data elements in the Intersection class are stored as pointers and allocated dynamically from heap memory. There are two reasons for this. First, it eliminates a compiler dependency: When we have to change the representation of the PhaseQueue or TrafficStreamList, none of the classes that depend on Intersection need to be changed. This kind of isolation can be very important in large applications. Second, we want to encapsulate the knowledge about how to set up an intersection in the IntersectionConfiguration class. Rather than have the Intersection know all about how to build a PhaseQueue or Traffic-StreamList, we place that knowledge in the IntersectionConfiguration and have it build the objects. This is a common way to isolate dependencies on database or I/O environments.

The creation of the two data elements is the responsibility of the IntersectionConfiguration; however, destroying them becomes the responsibility of the Intersection itself. Therefore, class Intersection has a destructor to perform that work.

Here is a complete implementation of the Intersection class, relying on some functions from the Phase class. As is typical in a well-developed Object-Oriented C++ program, the methods are all small and rely heavily on services of helper classes. Our usual rule of thumb is that if a member function requires more than about 15 lines of code, we need to encapsulate more of the operation. Typically, member functions are less than six lines. The key principle is to make sure that a reader can comprehend the function easily.

```
// Code File: intrsect.cpp
// Intersection class

// Interface definition

#include "intrsect.h"

// Implementation dependencies

#include "ixconfig.h"    // IntersectionConfiguration def.
#include "phaseq.h"      // PhaseQueue definition
#include "phasereq.h"    // PhaseRequest definition
#include "trafflst.h"    // TrafficStreamList definition

// Member Function Definitions

Intersection::Intersection
                  ( IntersectionConfiguration & ixconfig )
  : f_streams(0), f_phases(0), f_terminate(false)
```

```
  {
    f_streams = ixconfig.CreateTrafficStreamList(this);
    f_phases = ixconfig.CreatePhaseQueue(this);
  }

Intersection::~Intersection()
{
    delete f_streams;
    delete f_phases;
}

void Intersection::Activate()
{
    PhaseIterator active_phase = f_phases->Initial();

    while ( !f_terminate )
      {
      active_phase->Activate();
      active_phase = f_phases->GetNextActivePhase(active_phase);
      }
}

void Intersection::Receive( const PhaseRequest & request )
{
    f_terminate = request.IsTerminate();
}
```

The Phase Class

The final Phase class interface, with a pair of small in-line functions, looks like this:

```
// Header File: phase.h
// Phase class

#include "tmrset.h"        // TimerSetting definition
#include "phasereq.h"      // PhaseRequest definition

#include <bool.h>          // obsolete with ANSI C++
#include <time.h>          // for time_t definition
#include "bstring.h"       // sort-of-ANSI string class

typedef string PhaseName;
class SignalSettingList;
class PhaseConfiguration;
class TrafficStreamList;
```

```cpp
class TrafficStreamRequest;
class TimerRequest;
class Intersection;

// Class definition

class Phase
{
  public:

    Phase( PhaseConfiguration & pc );
    Phase( const Phase & ph );
    ~Phase();

    void Activate();     // Do Amber and Red transitions

    bool IsActive() const;

    void Receive( const TrafficStreamRequest & request );
                    // Callback from TrafficStream
    void Receive( const TimerRequest & timer );
                    // Callback from Timer

    bool NeedsService() const;

    PhaseRequest & GetLastRequest();
                    // Could be polled from Intersection

  private:

    // Helper functions

    void AddPhaseToStreamRequestList();
            // notify streams if this is a "green" phase
    void DoTransition();
            // turn lights to amber as needed
    void DoActive();
            // turn lights to red and green per f_settings

    // Data elements

    enum ActiveStateType { InActive, InTransition, Active };
            // Active state constants for f_active
```

```
    TrafficStreamList * f_streams;
                                // shared from Intersection
    SignalSettingList * f_settings;
                                // target stream settings
    TimerSetting        f_min_green;
    TimerSetting        f_min_amber;
    Intersection      * f_intersection;
                                // Used to send PhaseRequest
    PhaseName           f_name;
    ActiveStateType     f_active;
    PhaseRequest        f_last_request;
};

// Inline function definitions

inline PhaseRequest & Phase::GetLastRequest()
{
  return f_last_request;
}

inline bool Phase::IsActive() const
{
  return f_active != Inactive;
}
```

The Intersection and Phase classes contain the first uses of C++ basic types: the bool and string types defined in the ANSI draft standard. However, the string is used only to provide a new type name: PhaseName. It is our experience that this kind of "type hiding" greatly increases the flexibility of later designs by reducing dependency on the implicit characteristics of the built-in type. This flexibility does not come without a price, however. The essential trade-off is that although the design intent and use of the element becomes clearer, it may be more tedious to verify that the type can be used in a particular place. We might wonder later, for instance, if a PhaseName object supports the C++ iostream output operator; using the "string" class directly (at least if the programmer is familiar with the standard types) provides an immediate answer. But that is a small price to pay for a design that discourages implicit assumptions about the properties of data elements.

C++ OO DESIGN PRIORITIES

The Phase class illustrates quite well what hides behind the scenes of a typical C++ class. The first set of member functions is the constructors. Since the f_settings member is dynamically allocated and Phase objects may be copied, we need to supply a copy constructor and a destructor. Our coding standard also requires us to provide an assignment operator in this case. Since we do not anticipate assigning Phases, we have declared the assignment operator in the private section of the class without implementing it (though the implementation would be trivial).

Here we start to get a picture of the gruesome details lying behind the scenes. The PhaseConfiguration initializes a lot of data elements in the Phase. If we had to make each of these elements a separate parameter to the constructor, we would rapidly lose sight of the design we are trying to implement. Initializing the Phase from the PhaseConfiguration requires us to break the PhaseConfiguration apart into its components. This sort of activity should be confined to constructors and assignment operators. Elsewhere, if we need to do something with the PhaseConfiguration, we should create a method or helper class to do it. Failing to do so leads rapidly to "reverting to C"—giving up on interface/implementation distinctions and writing line after line of tangled code to make sure that each piece is where we need it.

```cpp
// Code File: phase.cpp
// Phase class

// Interface definition

#include "phase.h"

// Implementation dependencies

#include "phconfig.h"    // PhaseConfiguration definition
#include "tstrmreq.h"    // TrafficStreamRequest definition
#include "timer.h"       // TimerRequest, Timer definitions
#include "ssetlist.h"    // SignalSettingList definition
#include "trafflst.h"    // TrafficStreamList definition
#include "intrsect.h"    // Intersection definition

// Member Function Definitions

Phase::Phase( PhaseConfiguration &pc )
  : f_streams(pc.GetTrafficStreamList()),
    f_settings(pc.CreateSignalSettingList()),
    f_min_green(pc.GetMinGreen()),
    f_min_amber(pc.GetMinAmber()),
    f_last_request(0, false),
    f_intersection(pc.GetIntersection()),
    f_name(pc.GetName()),
    f_active(Inactive)
```

```
{
  f_min_amber.SetPhase(this);
  f_min_green.SetPhase(this);
  AddPhaseToStreamRequestList();
}

Phase::Phase( const Phase & p )
  : f_streams(p.f_streams),
    f_settings(new SignalSettingList(*p.f_settings)),
    f_min_green(p.f_min_green),
    f_min_amber(p.f_min_amber),
    f_last_request(0, true),
    f_intersection(p.f_intersection),
    f_name(p.f_name),
    f_active(Inactive)
{
  f_min_amber.SetPhase(this);
  f_min_green.SetPhase(this);
  AddPhaseToStreamRequestList();
}

Phase::~Phase()
{
  RemovePhaseFromStreamRequestList();
  delete f_settings;
}
```

Member Functions

The AddPhaseToStreamRequestList, and its partner RemovePhaseFromStreamRequest-List(), are used to facilitate notifying a phase when it needs service. If a car is detected in a "red" TrafficStream, that TrafficStream will notify all the Phases in which it might be green so that one of them can request service. Since creating these request lists is a nontrivial operation that is repeated in two separate constructors, we have made it a private helper function:

```
void Phase::AddPhaseToStreamRequestList()
{
  SignalSettingListIterator ssli;
  TrafficStreamListIterator tsli;

  for ( ssli = f_settings->Begin(), tsli = f_streams->Begin();
       tsli < f_streams->End();
       ++tsli, ++ssli )
```

```
    {
    if ( *ssli == SignalFace::sf_green )
        {
        tsli->AddRespondingPhase( this );
        }
    }
}

void Phase::AddPhaseToStreamRequestList()
{
  SignalSettingListIterator ssli;
  TrafficStreamListIterator tsli;

  for ( ssli = f_settings->Begin(), tsli = f_streams->Begin();
      tsli < f_streams->End();
      ++tsli, ++ssli )
    {
    if ( *ssli == SignalFace::sf_green )
        {
        tsli->RemoveRespondingPhase( this );
        }
    }
}
```

The NeedsService member function determines whether any TrafficStreams that are green in this Phase have a need for service. In this implementation we need to poll each TrafficStream for its needs.

```
bool Phase::NeedsService() const
{
  SignalSettingListIterator ssli;
  TrafficStreamListIterator tsli;

  for ( ssli = f_settings->Begin(), tsli = f_streams->Begin();
      tsli < f_streams->End();
      ++tsli, ++ssli )
    {
    if ( ! tsli->IsActive() &&
        *ssli == SignalFace::sf_green &&
        tsli->NeedsService() )
      return true;
    }
  return false;
}
```

The Activate member function initiates a transition from green to red on appropriate traffic streams. This is done in two parts; first, the Transition state turns the traffic streams amber, and then the active state changes the lights to red and green. The private helper functions DoTransition and DoActive are introduced simply to make the Activate function simpler. The progress between these two states is tracked in the f_active data member, and coordinated by the Timer object, which passes notifications back to the Phase through its Receive(TimerRequest) member function. The Receive function is also used to forward termination requests to the Phase and Intersection. We'll go on to discuss the Display::DrawActivePhase function in the next section.

```
void Phase::Activate()
{
  if ( IsActive() )
    return;

  if ( f_last_request.IsTerminate() )
    return;
  else          // clear last request
    f_last_request = PhaseRequest( 0, false );

  DoTransition();
}

void Phase::DoTransition()
{
  f_active = Transition;              // Transition state

  // Set the amber lights (could be a helper function)

  SignalSettingListIterator ssli;
  TrafficStreamListIterator tsli;

  bool need_amber = false;

  for ( ssli = f_settings->Begin(), tsli = f_streams->Begin();
      tsli < f_streams->End();
      ++tsli, ++ssli )
    {
    if ( tsli->IsActive() && *ssli == SignalFace::sf_red )
      {
      need_amber = true;
      tsli->Activate( SignalFace::sf_amber );
      }
    }
  theDisplay.DrawActivePhase( this );   // See I/O section!
```

```
  // Set timer request for the minimum amber time

  if ( need_amber )
    {
    theTimer.SetTime( f_min_amber );
    theTimer.Start();
    }
  else
    // simulate timer request if didn't need amber stage
    Receive( TimerRequest( TimerRequest::ReachedTarget ) );
}

void Phase::DoActive()
{
  f_active = Active;

  // Set the red and green lights

  SignalSettingListIterator ssli;
  TrafficStreamListIterator tsli;

  for ( ssli = f_settings->Begin(), tsli = f_streams->Begin();
      tsli < f_streams->End();
      ++tsli, ++ssli )
    {
    tsli->Activate( * ssli );
    }
  theDisplay.DrawActivePhase( this );   // See I/O Section

  // Set a timer request for the minimum green time

  theTimer.SetTime( f_min_green );
  theTimer.Start();
}

void Phase::Receive( const TrafficStreamRequest & ts )
{
  f_last_request = PhaseRequest( ts.GetStream(), true,
                            f_last_request.IsTerminate() );
}

void Phase::Receive( const TimerRequest & tr )
{
  if ( tr.GetType() == TimerRequest::ReachedTarget)
```

```
      {
      if ( f_active == Transition )      // done with transition
        {
        DoActive();                      // move to active state
        }
      else if ( f_active == Active )     // done with phase
        {
        f_active = Inactive;
        }
      }
  else if ( tr.GetType() == TimerRequest::Terminate )
    {
    // notify intersection that we're done
    f_last_request = PhaseRequest( f_last_request.GetStream(),
                          f_last_request.IsNeedService(),
                          true );
    f_intersection->Receive( f_last_request );
    }
}
```

The Intersection and Phase classes rely on several other classes to perform their work, which will not be discussed here. In the next section we will look at several extensions to the Phase, Intersection, and Detector classes which are necessary for input and output.

THE TRAFFIC SYSTEM I/O FRAMEWORK

Most people learn C++ "backwards." Depending on the environment their compiler supports and their project at hand, they will start off building on top of iostreams (or even the old C stdio library) or deriving new bits and pieces from the Microsoft Foundation Classes (MFC), from the Object Windows Library, or from some other class library. This approach encourages one to treat the underlying application framework and I/O environment as if they have the same design importance as the CRC card analysis of the application.

At its best, this approach leaves a lot of rusty machinery in full view of later maintainers. At its worst, it will lead to the same kind of rupture in vocabulary, architecture, and vision that would typically occur when structured programming analyses get nailed to data structures and functions. The results can be particularly sordid when the Microsoft Foundation Classes are used. Like other application frameworks, MFC is strongly tied to its own peculiar object model, but it goes further and dangles public structures and data members in front of the programmer like bait. We strongly recommend against making MFC, or any I/O library, a publicly visible part of your application architecture.

User Interactions

The right way to take on I/O issues is to figure out where we want users to interact with our model, and then create interface classes that will hide the details of that interaction from the model itself. This is much better than squeezing the model into the approach mandated by some purchased library. Discussions of the CRC cards that start off with, "Okay, that will be the Document and this will be the View" should set off alarm bells.

In the Traffic Intersection, input interactions with the outside world take place in two primary areas: stored information and user interaction. The stored information that the application relies on is the configuration of the intersection, which is accessed through the IntersectionConfiguration. The user interaction happens through the Detector. In addition, the Timer class provides contact with the outside world (or at least with something outside the model) by determining when a Phase must change state.

Output consists of reporting what state the Intersection is in. The class with the closest connection to information we might wish to display is the Phase, but the actual settings of traffic streams are contained in the SignalFaces. Some experimentation is often required to find the proper fit. We ultimately elected to have the Phase initiate output and delegate some of the reporting to the TrafficStreamList.

In designing the I/O system, we follow the same strategy we did before: work out an architecture, and chisel away at the hard parts until the pieces are small enough to handle easily. One of the decisions we want to put off until the very end is whether the program will run in console mode or under a GUI. The GUI ends up not much harder to build if one remembers that it is an implementation detail, not a structural principle. (The author's source code for this section includes both an MFC version of the program and a console version, which differ only in low-level implementation details.)

The basic inputs to the console mode prototype are the following:

An intersection configuration file indicating the static parameters of each of the traffic streams and phases (used by IntersectionConfiguration)

A list of detector events, indicating the time and traffic stream on which they occur (used by Detector via its helper, EventManager)

The output will be a list of events in time order, including both the detector events and the states of the signal faces as they change.

The rest of the implementation is just bookkeeping: We used the Standard Template Library reference implementation to supply basic collection components, and a string class that resembles a subset of the proposed ANSI standard string. In keeping with our coding standard, we did not use any built-in C types directly. We borrowed some type definitions from standard headers, including size_t for an array position, and time_t for a number of seconds.

Encapsulating Input

In the interests of space, we won't worry about how a Phase or TrafficStream gets built (or the PhaseQueue or TrafficStreamList, which in this implementation are the actual builders). Instead, we'll look at the Detector and Timer classes to see how a complete sequenced I/O structure can be incorporated, with scarcely a change to the simple interfaces we worked out earlier. We'll begin by looking at the Detector class to see how input gets into the system:

```
// Code File: detect.h
// Detector class

class Detector
{
  public:
    Detector( DetectorConfiguration & dc );
    ~Detector();

    void Detect();                  // Interface for I/O device

  private:
    Detector( const Detector & dt );         // disallowed
    void operator = ( const Detector & dt);  // disallowed

    DetectorRequest f_last_request;
    TrafficStream * f_stream;                // shared;
};
```

There's hardly a trace of the I/O system in this final version, other than the callback method named Detect. Things get more interesting when we look at the class implementation:

```
// Code File: detect.cpp
// Detector class

// Interface definition

#include "detect.h"

// Implementation dependencies

#include "traffic.h"
#include "events.h"

// Member Function Definitions
```

```
Detector::Detector( DetectorConfiguration & dc )
  : f_stream(dc)
{
  theEventQueue.AddDetector( this );
}

Detector::Detector( const Detector & )
  : f_stream(0)
{
  theEventQueue.AddDetector( this );
}

Detector::~Detector()
{
  theEventQueue.RemoveDetector( this );
}

void Detector::Detect()
{
  f_stream->Receive( DetectorRequest() );
}
```

The helper object called theEventQueue is a global source of events of type Event-Manager. In the console application, we let the Timer drive theEventQueue by calling a member function named FindEventsBetween. Inside that function, the occurrence of a detector event leads to theEventQueue calling the Detector's Detect method. Here is the implementation of the key Timer methods:

```
void Timer::SetTime( TimerSetting & ts )
{
  f_setting = ts;
  f_target_time = f_current_time + f_setting.GetTime();
}

void Timer::Start()
{
  bool ok = theEventQueue.FindEventsBetween
                        ( f_current_time, f_target_time );
  f_current_time = f_target_time;
  f_last_request = TimerRequest(TimerRequest::ReachedTarget);
  f_setting.Callback(f_last_request);      // goes to Phase
  if ( ! ok )
```

```
    {
    f_last_request = TimerRequest(TimerRequest::Terminate);
    f_setting.Callback(f_last_request);    // goes to Phase
    }
  return;
}
```

Encapsulating Output

Output requires us to do a greater variety of things and is thus a bit more complex. As we mentioned earlier, the Phase class became the key for controlling output. To initiate output of the Traffic Stream states, we call the DrawActivePhase method from a new Display-Manager class (see the earlier implementation of the DoTransition and DoActive methods).

The actual strategy for reaching back into the model for information to display can be seen in Figure 11-3. The DisplayManager is generic for both character mode and graphical interfaces, and it uses callback functions in various classes such as Phase and TrafficStream to have them hand over relevant parts of their private state for display. The actual work of output is done by a class called DisplayDevice. Here is the implementation of the DrawActivePhase function from the DisplayManager. The f_device data member is a DisplayDevice and is created along with the DeviceManager.

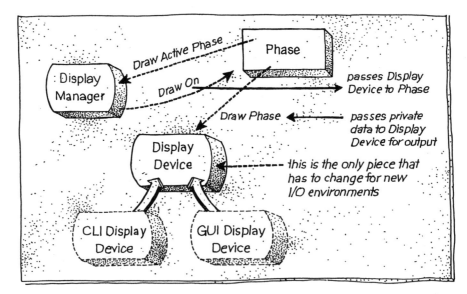

Figure 11-3 **Separating Output from the Essential Model**

```
void DisplayManager::DrawActivePhase(const Phase * phase) const
{
  f_timer->DisplayOn( f_device );
  phase->DisplayOn( f_device );
}
```

The DisplayOn methods, which are placed into the Timer, Phase, and TrafficStream classes, are used to hide implementation details from the display. Both the Timer and the Phase can supply private data directly to the DisplayDevice, which has a series of special member functions to format that data for output. To illustrate how this works (and its overall simplicity), here is the declaration and definition of the DisplayOn function for the Phase:

```
// code file: phase.h
// Phase class

class DisplayDevice;

class Phase
{
  public:
    void DisplayOn( DisplayDevice * dd ) const;
    // other interface is the same
};

// code file:  phase.cpp
// Phase class

void Phase::DisplayOn( DisplayDevice * dd ) const
{
  dd->DisplayPhase( f_name );
  for ( TrafficStreamListIterator tsli = f_streams->Begin();
      tsli < f_streams->End();
      ++tsli )
    {
    tsli->DisplayOn( dd );    // TrafficStream::DisplayOn()
    }
}
```

We eventually reach the bottom line of actual output in the DisplayDevice, and it is as easy as writing a "Hello World" program. Here is the DisplayDevice's DisplayPhase method definition:

```
void DisplayDevice::DisplayPhase( PhaseName name )
{
  cout << name << endl;
}
```

Even with some of the ugly details exposed, the C++ code is clear and straightforward. More importantly, it has kept the whole I/O system invisible to the other classes in the application. Although more complex applications or I/O systems might require additional classes to be involved, the results are easier to adjust and develop later if they are originally constructed in this top-down fashion. The discussion in this chapter covers the most important details of the finished application. The complete C++ implementation, both for 32-bit Windows using MFC and for a command line using iostreams, is available on the Addison-Wesley Web site.

MOVING TO JAVA

An experienced C++ programmer should have little trouble learning Java, and also should be able to easily convert small applications into Java code. The basic syntax is somewhat the same. The contribution Java makes is that it does not let risky practices carry over from the C++ world, in large part by including lessons from Smalltalk as well as industry experience maintaining older systems. We're fortunate that our C++ implementation of the traffic system didn't use poor practices such as overloading operators or pointers to pointers, for Java would not permit it. There are no pointers in Java, and in fact we find that most times none are necessary. We can never be left with wasted memory, marked as used but never referenced, because Java has a garbage collector working behind the scenes. The programmer never has to worry about these problems. Best of all, Java is inherently Web-enabled.

We're not going to enumerate all the features of Java in this book (for that, see *Core Java* by Gary Cornell and Cay Horstmann, the creator of the implementation discussed in this section). What we are going to do is show some of Java's capabilities to you by showing how the Traffic system could be simulated. We'll explain briefly the approach which would be taken by experienced Java connoisseurs. As we saw with both C++ and Smalltalk, there are some tricky issues not settled by the CRC cards. But in Java, it's even easier than it is in C++ to focus in on the application itself! Our approach in this section, therefore, is not to directly translate the C++ implementation into Java. We've focused on some of the unique strengths of Java, in particular on the ease with which graphical interfaces can be constructed. These aspects are emphasized over the details of intersection timing, for example.

The Java Approach to the Traffic System

A Java graphical applet seemed to be the best way of implementing the Traffic system. Java graphics are portable and standard, which means that every Java programmer knows how to paint a screen and how to handle events. The C++ implementation already does the text output; however, there seemed little point to implementing only that in Java. It would be an easy matter to add a text area on the bottom of the screen to hold the text output.

Our Java plan was to draw the intersection, the traffic lights, and the sensors, all as graphical objects. The traffic lights show up as three circles, one of which is filled with red, yellow, or green. The sensors are just squares. The user can click the mouse on a detector to "trip" it. This simulates a car driving over the detector. As a result, the lights change eventually. If you read the C++ implementation, you'll see that many inner details are different. For example, initialization is handled differently, as is the location of the GUI components.

The init method is called when the applet is first loaded, in order to set up the traffic streams and phases for the intersection.

The paint method is called whenever the surface of the applet must be repainted; that is, when it is first exposed, when a part of it has been temporarily obscured, or when the program calls the repaint method. In the paint method, we paint the outline of the road segments, and then we ask each traffic stream to paint itself.

In the mouseDown method, we trap mouse clicks onto the sensors. We let each of the phases have a look at the mouse click. If one of them accepts it, we turn the current color to yellow. The code which follows shows further detail on the scheduling of these events.

The elapsed method is called when a timer has elapsed. It updates the state and the color of the current traffic light, and asks each of the traffic streams if it needs servicing. Not all applets have an elapsed method; ours does since we set ourselves up for timer notifications by implementing the Timed interface.

The setColor method is a convenience function. It calls the setColor method of a phase, and receives from that method the time needed to schedule the next event. A zero is returned if that phase can stay on indefinitely. SetColor then launches a timer which will elapse at the given time, when it will call the elapsed method. Here's the main class of the intersection applet:

```java
public class Intersection extends Applet implements Timed
            // when loaded; set up streams and phases
{   public void init()
    {   ts = new TrafficStream[7];
        // not using ts0 entry for consistency with CRC cards
        ts[1] = new TrafficStream(XCENTER - WIDTH / 2,
            YCENTER - WIDTH / 2 - YSTREAM, XSTREAM, YSTREAM,
SignalFace.LEFT);
        ts[2] = new TrafficStream(XCENTER + WIDTH / 2 - XSTREAM,
            YCENTER + WIDTH / 2, XSTREAM, YSTREAM,
SignalFace.RIGHT);
        ts[3] = new TrafficStream(XCENTER - WIDTH / 2 - XSTREAM,
            YCENTER + WIDTH / 2 - YSTREAM, XSTREAM, YSTREAM, SignalFace.RIGHT);
        ts[4] = new TrafficStream(XCENTER + WIDTH / 2,
            YCENTER - WIDTH / 2, XSTREAM, YSTREAM,
SignalFace.LEFT);
        ts[5] = new TrafficStream(XCENTER - WIDTH / 2 - XSTREAM,
            YCENTER + WIDTH / 2 - 2 * YSTREAM, XSTREAM, YSTREAM,
SignalFace.RIGHT);
```

```
        ts[6] = new TrafficStream(XCENTER + WIDTH / 2,
            YCENTER - WIDTH / 2 + YSTREAM, XSTREAM, YSTREAM,
SignalFace.LEFT);

        phases = new Phase[5];
            // not using ts0 entry for consistency with CRC cards
        phases[1] = new Phase(30, 10);
        phases[1].addStream(ts[1]).addStream(ts[2]);
        phases[2] = new Phase(40, 10);
        phases[2].addStream(ts[3]).addStream(ts[4]);
        phases[3] = new Phase(40, 10);
        phases[3].addStream(ts[3]).addStream(ts[5]);
        phases[4] = new Phase(40, 10);
        phases[4].addStream(ts[4]).addStream(ts[6]);

        setColor(2, SignalFace.GREEN);
    }

    public void paint(Graphics g)
            // repaint road; ask streams to repaint
    { g.drawLine(0, YCENTER - WIDTH / 2, XCENTER - WIDTH / 2,
YCENTER - WIDTH / 2);
        g.drawLine(XCENTER - WIDTH / 2, YCENTER - WIDTH / 2,
XCENTER - WIDTH / 2, 0);

        g.drawLine(0, YCENTER + WIDTH / 2, XCENTER - WIDTH / 2,
YCENTER + WIDTH / 2);
        g.drawLine(XCENTER - WIDTH / 2, YCENTER + WIDTH / 2,
XCENTER - WIDTH / 2, 2 * YCENTER);

        g.drawLine(XCENTER + WIDTH / 2, 0, XCENTER + WIDTH / 2,
YCENTER - WIDTH / 2);
        g.drawLine(XCENTER + WIDTH / 2, YCENTER - WIDTH / 2, 2 *
XCENTER, YCENTER - WIDTH / 2);

        g.drawLine(XCENTER + WIDTH / 2, YCENTER + WIDTH / 2, 2 *
XCENTER, YCENTER + WIDTH / 2);
        g.drawLine(XCENTER + WIDTH / 2, YCENTER + WIDTH / 2,
XCENTER + WIDTH / 2, 2 * YCENTER);

        for (int i = 1; i < ts.length; i++)
            ts[i].paint(g);
    }
```

```
public boolean mouseDown(Event evt, int x, int y)
      // trap mouseclicks on sensors
{  for (int i = 1; i < phases.length; i++)
      if (phases[i].mouseDown(x, y))
      {  if (currentState == GREEN)
            setColor(currentPhase, SignalFace.YELLOW);
         else
            repaint();
         return true;
      }
   return false;
}

public void elapsed(Timer t)
      // update lights and check streams
{  if (currentState == GREEN_MIN) // end of minimum green phase
   {  boolean found = false;
      int j = currentPhase + 1;
      while (!found && j != currentPhase)
      {  j = j % phases.length;
         if (j == 0) j = 1;
         if (phases[j].needsServicing()) found = true;
         else j++;
      }
      if (found)
         setColor(currentPhase, SignalFace.YELLOW);
      else
         currentState = GREEN;
   }
   else if (currentState == YELLOW) // end of yellow phase
   {  setColor(currentPhase, SignalFace.RED);
      boolean found = false;
      int j = currentPhase + 1;
      while (!found)
      {  j = j % phases.length;
         if (j == 0) j = 1;
         if (phases[j].needsServicing()) found = true;
         else j++;
      }
      setColor(j, SignalFace.GREEN);
   }
}

private void setColor(int i, int color)
      //Get time from phase and set timer
```

```
{  int time = phases[i].setColor(color);
   if (color == SignalFace.GREEN)
   {  currentPhase = i;
      currentState = GREEN_MIN;
   }
   else if (color == SignalFace.YELLOW)
      currentState = YELLOW;
   repaint();
   if (time > 0)
      new Timer(this, time * 1000 / 10).start();
}

private Phase[] phases;
private TrafficStream[] ts;
int currentPhase;
int currentState;

private static int XCENTER = 160;
private static int YCENTER = 160;
private static int WIDTH = 120; // width of intersection
private static int XSTREAM = 4 * SignalFace.RADIUS;
private static int YSTREAM = 4 * SignalFace.RADIUS;
private static int GREEN_MIN = 1;
private static int GREEN = 2;
private static int YELLOW = 3;
}
```

Classes in the Java Traffic Applet

The first difficult choice we faced was where to locate the Intersection class itself. Intersection could be implemented as the "top" class, the one deriving from Applet. Alternatively, we could make Intersection the main data object of the Applet class. We decided to derive Intersection as a class from Applet. This enables it both to receive events directly and to initiate screen painting. We recommend following a similar approach for most Java applets.

Event handling is always important in a GUI program, and a majority of Java applications include a heavy interface component. In the Traffic applet, the events are repainting the screen, mouse button clicks, and timer notifications. Repainting is relatively simple, consisting of redrawing each of the traffic streams.

To implement timers, we use an approach discussed in detail in *Core Java* (see page 535 of the first edition). However, the *Core Java* timers give continuous ticks. We changed that to a single "elapsed" message, after which the timer dies:

```
interface Timed
{ public void elapsed(Timer t);
}

class Timer extends Thread
{ public Timer(Timed t, int i)
   { target = t; interval = i;
      setDaemon(true);
   }

   public void run()
   { try { sleep(interval); }
      catch(InterruptedException e) {}
      target.elapsed(this);
   }

   Timed target;
   int interval;
}
```

In applications such as this, timing can be somewhat confusing. In this implementation, an intersection can be in one of three states:

GREEN_MIN: the active phase is green for <= the minimum green time
GREEN: the active phase is green for > the minimum green time
YELLOW: the active phase is yellow

This state structure was not immediately apparent from the CRC cards. Although the CRC card talks about the "active phase(s)," there can only be a single active phase at any moment.

The timing events consist of the phase color change (the active-phase object knows how long that phase lasts) and a timer event initiated to report the end of that duration. Thus, there are timer events for the end of the minimum green time and the end of the yellow time. Note that each phase, not the intersection, determines these lengths. When the minimum green time has elapsed, then the intersection checks if any phase needs servicing—that is, whether the user has already clicked on one of the sensors.

When a mouse click comes, each phase looks at it. Each phase needs to determine if the click is inside the sensor of one of its traffic streams. If so, the phase remembers that it needs servicing. If the state of the intersection is GREEN, i.e., if the minimum green time has elapsed, then the phase is serviced immediately. Otherwise, the image is just repainted to fill in the sensor.

In this implementation, the only reason the Intersection object needs to hang on to the individual traffic streams is for screen painting. All other interaction goes through the phases. This is somewhat different than in the C++ implementation, but facilitates the GUI interactions with the mouse.

Now on to the other classes! The Phase is a nongraphical class which holds Traffic-Stream objects. A vector is used to hold them, because at construction time we don't know how many of them there are. Here is the class definition for Phase:

```
class Phase
{   public Phase(int theGreenTime, int theYellowTime)
    {   greenTime = theGreenTime;
        yellowTime = theYellowTime;
        tstreams = new Vector();
        needsSvc = false;
    }

    public Phase addStream(TrafficStream ts)
    {   tstreams.addElement(ts);
        return this;
    }

    public int setColor(int color) // returns the minimum time
in that color
    {   for (int i = 0; i < tstreams.size(); i++)

((TrafficStream)tstreams.elementAt(i)).setColor(color);
        if (color == SignalFace.GREEN)
        {   needsSvc = false;
            return greenTime;
        }
        else if (color == SignalFace.YELLOW) return yellowTime;
        else return 0;
    }

    public boolean needsServicing() { return needsSvc; }

    public boolean mouseDown(int x, int y)
    {   for (int i = 0; i < tstreams.size(); i++)
            if
(((TrafficStream)tstreams.elementAt(i)).mouseDown(x, y))
            {   needsSvc = true;
                return true;
            }
        return false;
    }
```

```
    int greenTime;
    int yellowTime;
    boolean needsSvc;
    Vector tstreams;
}
```

The methods of this class are "initiates Traffic stream movement" (which was called setColor), the "needsServicing" accessor, and the mouseDown pass-through that gives the mouse click to each traffic stream. Unlike the CRC card, this class does not "report when minimum green time elapsed." Rather, it reports the desired minimum green time to the Intersection (the result of setColor).

TrafficStream is just a container for a Detector and a SignalFace. It routes the paint, setColor, and mouseDown messages to these objects as appropriate. The Detector is a graphical object, drawn as a little rectangle on which the user can click to request service. To give feedback to the user, it changes appearance when clicked. Once the service has been granted (i.e., once the light turns green), the detector is turned off. For this reason, we added a reset method that is not present in the CRC card. Again, there is no "notifies if vehicle is present" function. If the mouse click is inside the square, and the detector isn't already on, then the mouseDown function returns true. That return value is percolated up to the Intersection object.

The SignalFace is a graphical object, rendering the traffic light and providing accessor methods for the color. It is true that all of the paint methods include many details on screen coordinates, but that is normal in most Java applets. Some advanced Java books contain suggestions on how this might be further modularized. The full code for the applet is available at the Addison-Wesley Web site.

POINTERS FOR MORE

Resources for C++ programmers trying to "do it right" abound, and a great deal continues to be written. For up-to-the-minute information, we're fond of the comp.lang.c++ moderated newsgroups, the comp.std.c++ standards discussion, and the frequently asked questions files located at Web site http://www.cerfnet.com/~mpcline/C%2b%2b-FAQs-Lite/. Beginners seeking a thorough treatment of the language would be well served by Bruce Eckel's book *C++ Inside and Out*. Anyone working in C++ should have a copy of the *C++ Annotated Reference Manual* by Margaret Ellis and Bjarne Stroustrup, as well as Stroustrup's *The Evolution of C++*. A good tutorial on some of the more advanced topics is Eckel's book *Thinking in C++*. Further background on the language and its peculiarities is contained in Stanley Lippmann's *The C++ Object Model*. For those seeking tips on what to do and what not to do, see Gamma et al.'s *Design Patterns*, James Coplien's book *Advanced C++*, and Scott Meyers's *Effective C++*. For style guidelines, the best is *Taligent's Guide to Designing*

Programs: Well-Mannered Object-Oriented Design in C++ (Addison-Wesley) and the coding standards page of the European company Ellemtel, found at http://web2.airmail.net/~rks/ellhome.htm.

For Java, you've had a brief introduction to one graphics-oriented approach to the Traffic Intersection. There are many other approaches to consider. For real fun, you could even think about a multiuser game where distributed Java applets represent users "driving" cars around the Web! Too bad that such fun is beyond the scope of this book. However, for more depth on Java, we recommend you read the book by the implementor of the traffic intersection: *Core Java* by Cay Horstmann (Prentice-Hall). Also excellent is *Java in a Nutshell* by Flanagan (O'Reilly), or the several books by members of the Sun development team, available exclusively from Addison-Wesley. For On-line communities, be sure to check the comp.lang.java newsgroup and the archive of Java resources on the Web at http://www.gamelan.com/. Most important for current applets and development kit enhancements is Sun's JavaSoft Web site at http://www.javasoft.com/. Finally, look at the Addison-Wesley Web site under the *CRC Card Book* pointer.

Chapter 12

Transition to Methodologies

We've just shown how CRC cards can be used as the basis for design and code in some popular languages. If you were naive, you might assume that with only the cards, you'll be able to build big systems. But you're smarter than that! There are good reasons why full-blown OO methodologies have a large market. CRC cards can help an analysis team establish a strong, fundamental model of classes, but there are a lot of other factors that come into play before the project is over. Even though we have shown you how CRC cards can directly inform programming decisions, in a large system, some complicated thinking and juggling of pools of detail will stand between the CRC card set and the final, delivered system. If your system is large, you are going to have to follow up the CRC card analysis with the use of a formal methodology. In this chapter, we will discuss this process and show you what our traffic control system might look like if we used some of the models that capture these additional complexities.

The discussion of methodologies is presented in seven sections. (1) First, we'll move on from extolling the virtues of CRC cards to show their potential limitations. (2) Then, we will explain just what constitutes a "methodology," and just what the best methodologies have to offer. (3) We'll introduce the Booch (Unified) method and (4) the Shlaer–Mellor method, and (5) show how the traffic control system CRC cards can be used to inform sample diagrams from each of these methods. (6) Finally, we will talk a little bit about CRC card software and (7) summarize the whole picture.

CRC CARDS HAVE LIMITS

First of all, it is important to acknowledge that CRC cards do not have enough notational power to document all the necessary components of a system. They cannot provide a detailed view of the data in objects; they do not specify implementation specifics; and they cannot provide an adequate view of the states through which objects transition during their life cycle. CRC cards provide only limited help in the aspects of design where strategic trade-offs must be made in order to factor functionality to different parts of the system. CRC cards alone provide almost no help in specifying things such as how users will give and receive data (interface design), interprocess communication functionality, algorithm design, data structures, performance, or resource utilization. For all of these things we are going to have to supplement or follow up the CRC card analysis with the use of some formal methodological tools.

The only exception to this is going to be a small system where the designer can extrapolate from the CRC card set and there are a limited number of additional factors to consider. We have shown you a prototype of this kind of activity in the translation of the CRC cards for the traffic control system into C++, Java, and Smalltalk. We did this by limiting the scale of the system. In large systems, it is clear that CRC cards are very useful early in the development life cycle. They can be used for design and coding in popular languages. But CRC cards do not offer enough detail to capture the multiplicity of views and the data necessary to fully implement large systems. For these purposes, what is needed is a robust, object-oriented development methodology.

WHY METHODOLOGIES ARE POWERFUL

A few years ago, there was a great deal of discussion in systems groups about "Business Process Reengineering" (BPR). The drive was to go beyond focusing on pieces of work in an organization, parts of its data, or systems supporting small sectors of activity. For this reason, BPR is an excellent approach, one that forces a company to take a look at overall activities and goals before developing systems. BPR forces us to work to make systems fit together so that the whole is, in fact, greater than the parts.

Object-oriented systems share this objective! Even if you carry over legacy systems, using an object-oriented approach to your overall systems support picture can yield the same global, fully coordinated results. Whether you implement all of your systems in one, object-oriented language or use another programming language, you can still use classes and collaboration as a foundation for analysis and structuring of your systems. You can even implement your object-oriented system in a non-object oriented language, albeit with more effort. Object orientation permits us to develop better systems beyond programming, extending most importantly to develop comprehensive requirements and analyses which include user participation while, at the other end of the life cycle, OO decreases maintenance and increases reuse of old software.

For this reason, it is important to recognize that the object-oriented approach is more than a development tool. It is a way of organizing our thinking about the world. What the OO approach gives us is a means for organizing our "biosystem," an ecosystem which cannot be seen as isolated from the life forms which surround it. Thus, the problem we are left with is in essence that of the complexity of life. In addition to knowing what classes we have and how they collaborate with other classes, we need to keep track of a wide range of contextual factors. We are going to need some formal, powerful notation system for this modeling problem.

So far, in this book, we have shown the basic foundation of object-oriented thinking: the analysis of classes, the class hierarchy, the responsibilities of each class, and the reliances among classes. These are the preliminary inputs toward the development of complex systems. The next steps toward a fully implemented system must add to this view by contributing: a more detailed mapping of use-cases (operations), subtypes and supertypes, object state transitions, and specific message templates (methods). Finally, with all of this information documented, the OO builder can construct constraint specifications and system meta-models. Only when all of this groundwork has been done can the final code be written for a large system.

Before we leave this introduction to go on and talk about methodologies, we want to remind you to keep in mind the SDLC mapped out earlier. Incre-cycling, the idea of repeating and augmenting, means that even though there are many details that need to be understood and modeled, the opportunity to prototype and firm up portions of the system, or sets of classes, as you go is still in force. Use the formal methodology to ensure precision, but do not fall back on a drawn-out and linear system development model.

Methodology Adoption Is a Must

In order to accommodate the detail and complexity of OO design, a methodology must be adopted. CRC analysis has been shown to be useful input to every methodology we know of, but it will not help you choose (or force you to choose) a specific methodology. Moreover, methodology debates can be as emotional as the choice of programming language (or whether you prefer Macs to PCs!). However, we can offer you some guidelines to help you understand what is involved in the use of the two most accepted object-oriented methodologies: Booch and Shlaer–Mellor. The work of other methodologists is gradually being incorporated into these two major approaches, including the work of Jacobson (use cases), Wirfs-Brock (collaboration graphs), and Rumbaugh. The details of this integration are beyond our current scope, but may be obtained from the various software tool vendors who support these approaches.

What is important about each methodology is the meaning of the terms and symbols it uses. The actual shape of a symbol, or the particular word chosen to express an idea, is really a matter of choice and should not distract you. We present in Figure 12-1 a summary of the terms used by Booch and Shlaer–Mellor for comparison. Figure 12-2 compares common relationship notation used by each. This comparison should be helpful as you read the separate sections on each methodology.

If we do the job of analysis well, our CRC cards can be used to build portions of methodology specifications. These full specifications can be used to generate the actual software classes and methods. That is exactly what robust object-oriented methodologies do: they allow you to capture information about the system, and to model it in a way that is useful to

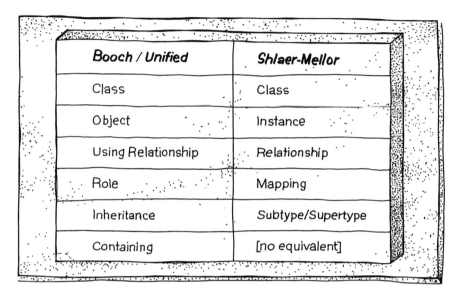

Figure 12-1 **The Vocabulary of the Methodologies**

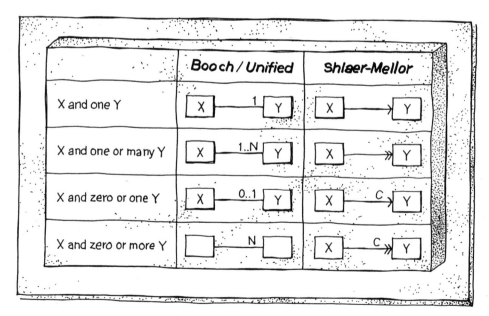

Figure 12-2 **Class Relationship Notations**

and even anticipates the way in which the final code will make use of analysis and design observations. This is the case for both the Booch unified method and the Shlaer–Mellor method. To give you a feel for how this works, after an all-too-quick overview of each methodology, we'll show how the Traffic case study looks when documented using a sample model from each notation method.

ONCE OVER THE BOOCH (UNIFIED) METHOD

The documentation set in the Booch method consists of six different diagrams for classes, objects, interactions, modules, processes, and state transitions. Taken together, these six diagrams define the application by documenting the classes and their interrelations, the structure of an object, and the collaborations between objects. Processes are allocated to objects which are called, naturally, processors. This defines the responsibilities of an object. Booch methodology supports the scheduling of processes, documents the valid states of each class, and, by extension, documents the valid states for the entire application system.

The Booch method consists of three steps: requirements analysis, domain analysis, and system design. These are defined as part of an iterative development life cycle; in other words, they are "mini"-cycles which produce small, but fully functional, pieces of the system each time through. The method itself does not address the issues of time or resource allocations to each iteration, but does define the deliverables for each step. Requirements analysis produces a "system function statement" and the "system charter," although this early stage may be considered as separate from the methodology.

Domain analysis delivers five documentation sets: class diagrams, inheritance diagrams, class specifications, object specifications, and object-scenario diagrams. The system design stage results in six deliverables: class-category diagrams, design class diagrams, class specifications, an architecture description, design object-scenario diagrams, and an executable release plan.

The stages of requirements analysis and domain analysis both benefit directly from CRC analysis techniques, particularly brainstorming and role play. The results of brainstorms can be used to create or enhance the system charter and the statement of system functionality. These documents are very useful as a form of contract with user management for the requirements they deem crucial.

CRC role plays result in completed class cards and hierarchies, which in the Booch method means that we have the content of the class diagrams, inheritance diagrams, class specifications, and object specifications. Since CRC role plays also insist upon realistic scripts for the "acting" of the team, the object-scenario diagrams of the Booch system need little effort to complete. (For those who wish to probe further, it is worth noting that Booch scenario diagrams are nearly identical to the use-case recording which is the focus of the methodology originally developed by Ivar Jacobson.)

Booch Domain Analysis

In agreement with the concepts of CRC card analysis, Booch domain analysis is concerned with identifying the central abstractions in the application area. These core classes serve as a starting point for discovering how the domain area actually works. Again, in accord with our discussion earlier, Booch concentrates here on the logical aspects of the system, without concern for implementation (language-specific) details. Once a CRC card analysis is completed, the results can be directly entered into a Booch design as classes and objects along with the appropriate specification. The Rational CRC software exports CRC analyses in Rational Rose "petal file" format, which is direct input for the Rose CASE tool. Transfer to other CASE tools may be accomplished via ASCII delimited files, if supported by the software.

The major notations used in Booch diagrams are relatively few, as shown in Figure 12-3. As an example, consider Figure 12-4, which provides the class diagram of a hydroponics gardening system. (Readers interested in more detail on the Booch methodology should be sure to consult *Object-Oriented Analysis and Design* [Addison-Wesley], upon which this discussion is based.) The class GardeningPlan includes an attribute "crop",

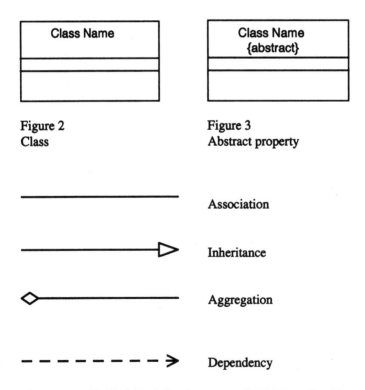

Figure 2
Class

Figure 3
Abstract property

Association

Inheritance

Aggregation

Dependency

Figure 12-3 **Unified Modeling Language (UML) Notation Elements**

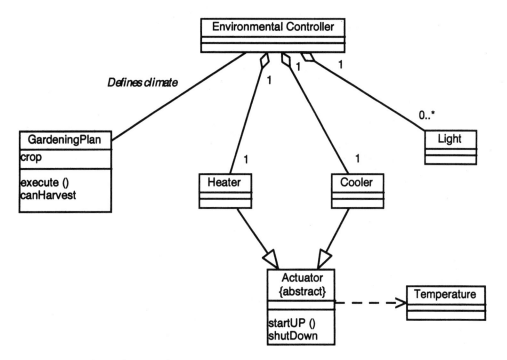

Figure 12-4 **Class Diagram for a Hydroponic Gardening System**
Adapted from: Object Oriented Analysis and Design with Applications, Second Edition
(Figure 5-5, page 181), © 1994 Benjamin-Cummings Publishing Company, Inc. Reprinted
by permission of Addison Wesley Longman, Inc.

and operations "execute" and "canHarvest". This class is associated with class Environ-
mentController, such that instances of the GardeningPlan define the climate that instances
of the controller modify. Heater and Cooler are shown as subclasses of Actuator, an abstract
class (noted by the "A" inside a triangle) which provides startUp and shutDown operations,
using the class Temperature.

As the Domain Analysis is developed (over a number of iterations), class specifications
are written. If you use CRC to find classes, you will see that most of the class specification is
already on the CRC card! The class specification includes a free text description of each class
responsibility, along with a list of the operations it will perform. The latter is the same as
the responsibilities listed on the CRC card analysis. If you plan to use Booch notation, you
should keep track of attributes on the back of the CRC card so that they are easy to find
when you list them as part of the class specification. The last item in the class specification
is a list of constraints, items which limit what actions the class should take. This has no
clear counterpart in CRC.

Role-playing the CRC cards has received a great deal of attention in this book, and the
Booch method includes a notational means for capturing role-play scenarios. These are
called "object-scenario diagrams" and show the set of operations that may occur in
response to a given script. Object-scenario diagrams delineate how objects collaborate to

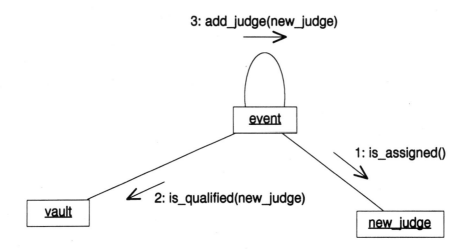

Figure 12-5 *Unified Modeling Language (UML) Collaboration Diagram*
Adapted from: Using the Booch Method: A Rational Approach, (Figure 5-1, page 57), ©
1994 Rational. Reprinted by permission of Addison Wesley Longman, Inc.

realize a use case. In other words, they perform the same function as the "collaborators" column on the right-hand side of the CRC card. The diagrams give one additional level of detail, which many also add to the CRC card: They are annotated with the name of the message sent to the collaborator. An example is shown in Figure 12-5.

The final element of Booch domain analysis is the development of a data dictionary, which is updated as work goes forward. This is said to be a comprehensive list of relevant "things," including all important classes, operations, and collaborations. In fact, the data dictionary serves as a complete index into every element in the analysis, and serves the same purpose later in the project as an index for the overall object architecture and implementation design.

Although the data dictionary is too advanced for the purposes of CRC analysis, we concur with its importance; the data-dictionary concept is familiar to structure analysts and database designers. The use of a dictionary ensures that a consistent vocabulary is used by all of the groups involved in the project. It also allows efficient lookup of random analysis elements as desired during reviews. And last, when details such as definitions are hidden, the data dictionary allows for a high-level textual overview of the system. Data dictionaries are difficult to maintain without CASE tool support.

Booch System Design

Following common usage (which is consistent with our view), the Booch method system design is seen as the enhancement of domain analysis into a working system implementation. The focus is on the implementation platform. The architecture necessary for a particular language is the key element. This corresponds to what we have shown in the chapters on implementing CRC card analysis in Smalltalk and in C++ and Java. The analysis is modified to create a series of reusable classes, with clear boundaries, internally cohesive collaborations, and efficient code. Although design is often language-specific, the Booch method discusses several approaches common to all OO code.

As systems grow, classes can be aggregated into categories. These are generally abstract classes said to be logically "close to the system boundaries." Class categories include the name of the abstract class, followed by the classes which make them up. An example is shown in Figure 12-6, in which you can find the GardeningPlan object shown previously within Figure 12-4, now listed as a class within the "Planning" category. The Booch "Top-Level Class Diagram" shown in Figure 12-6 is very similar to a class hierarchy chart.

In the Booch method, iterating through design, the class categories are used not only for the application domain classes, but also as a means of keeping the implementation classes separate from the domain. In other words, classes reused from the library for the user interface are not considered as part of the user application domain, and may be delineated separately.

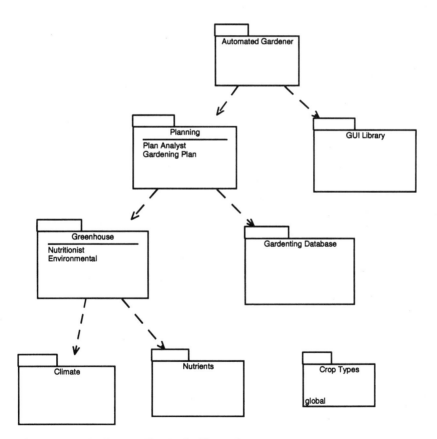

Figure 12-6 **Packages: The Main Class Diagram**
Adapted from: Object Oriented Analysis and Design with Applications, Second Edition
(Figure 5-7, page 183), © 1994 Benjamin-Cummings Publishing Company, Inc. Reprinted by permission of Addison Wesley Longman, Inc.

The Booch method has proven itself useful in the analysis and design of a wide range of object-oriented systems, using varied OO programming languages (Smalltalk, C++, ADA9x, and soon, perhaps even Java!). The method has become a key part of the emerging standards for object-oriented analysis and design methodologies, as an important guide for programmers during implementation. However, there is still debate about the best approach. A major segment of the OO practitioners argue for a more data-driven approach such as Shlaer–Mellor, which we examine next.

ONCE OVER THE SHLAER–MELLOR METHOD

For Steve Mellor and Sally Shlaer, the baseline of software development is a data-driven approach that looks first at information models and then at state and process models. The Shlaer–Mellor approach is described in detail in their books: *Object Lifecycles: Modeling the World in States* (1992) and *Object-Oriented Systems Analysis: Modeling the World in Data* (1988). The method was first developed for the analysis of real-time applications; however, it has since been utilized successfully in a wide variety of applications. These include corporate settings, manufacturing, telecommunications, finance, and government applications. The early definition of the method has been expanded to encompass a larger set of deliverables produced to standard guidelines. These are supported by tools sold by Shlaer and Mellor through their firm, Object Technology, in Berkeley, California, and by tools produced by other vendors.

Data-Driven Analysis

As we explained earlier in the chapter on managing projects, object-oriented methods reject the view of analysis and design as a linear process moving through cut-and-dried stages, one ending completely before the start of the next. The modified spiral SDLC, iterative and recursive, which we call incre-cycling, is a more realistic development approach. The Shlaer–Mellor methodology echoes this idea in its "recursive design" strategy. There are rules for the transformation of the analysis model into a system design through a series of recursions. The methodology is rigorous in its modeling, but flexible in its use of an evolving and changing representation of the real world. The rigor of the models makes the method somewhat difficult to learn but, because of that same rigor, repeatable.

Shlaer–Mellor sets a clear starting point for development: analysis must be driven by data. This data-driven approach is what distinguishes the method from Booch and other OO methodologies. The *information model*, the first step in the methodology, is the foundation for a description of the data, along with relationships and subtypes, that will look familiar to those who have worked with entity-relationship diagrams. The data mapping is done in conjunction with the definition of the objects (classes) and their responsibilities and collaborations. This is done before anything else. Shlaer–Mellor does not specifically rely on CRC cards, but teams struggling with the information model can use CRC analysis to unravel tricky class relationships, and can role-play them before completing their information model.

After the data is mapped and the objects have been defined, *state models* are created in order to show the life cycle of critical objects. These include notation for showing message connections (separated into asynchronous and synchronous), subsystems, and higher-level domains. These state models also include "bridges" as defined "visibility relationships" between domains. Domain definitions are established early in analysis and are defined on domain charts. Unless a project is very small, a single system is typically composed of more than one domain, as shown in the domain chart in Figure 12-7.

After the system is divided into domains, and domains are partitioned into subsystems, the overall project steps are inserted on a *project matrix* like the one shown in Figure 12-8. In this case, the system for train dispatch has been broken down into four

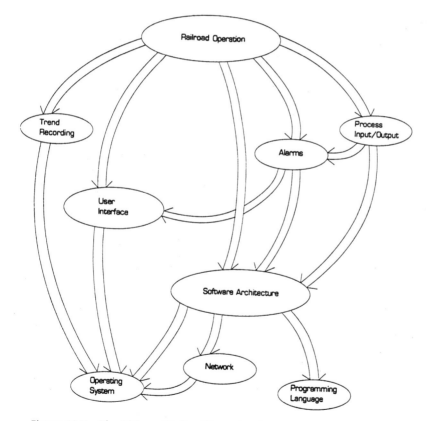

Figure 12-7 **The Shlaer–Mellor "Domain Chart"**
Source: *Object Lifecycles: Modeling the World in States* by Schlaer & Mellor, © 1991.
Reprinted by permission of Prentice-Hall, Inc. Upper Saddle River, NJ.

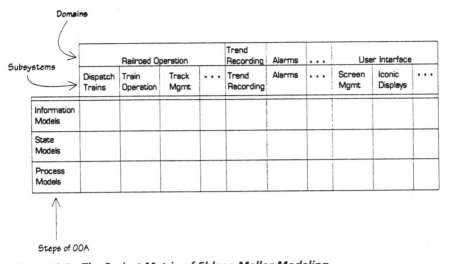

Figure 12-8 **The Project Matrix of Shlaer–Mellor Modeling**

Source: Object Lifecycles: Modeling the World in States by Schlaer & Mellor, © 1991.
Reprinted by permission of Prentice-Hall, Inc. Upper Saddle River, NJ.

domains with several subsystems. The project team can proceed by developing the three model sets, Information Models, State Diagrams, and Process Models for each domain.

The key to Shlaer–Mellor analysis is the emphasis on the critical role of information modeling. Linking CRC card techniques to Shlaer–Mellor, the team would enter all of the classes of objects discovered during CRC analysis on the information model diagram (Figure 12-9), along with their attributes and relationships. You can see that there would be duplication of effort if CRC cards were written for a trivial application and then rewritten on the information model. For this reason, if you choose the Shlaer–Mellor method, you may decide to use the CRC cards for only a portion of the system. Note also that the information model diagram must be accompanied by separate documentation for each component.

CRC card role play can also help the team understand the life cycle of the objects in the system in support of the creation of state diagrams. After the information model is complete, the state models can be started by using the results of the CRC role playing. Look for scenarios in which an incident causes an object (or class of objects) to change states, with an associated action which occurs when the object arrives at a new state. Figure 12-10 shows a state model for the train system. You can see that each of the states might match a scenario, or that the responsibilities used during a scenario provide the actions for the state model.

The last piece of the puzzle for Shlaer–Mellor is the way in which state models communicate via events. These relationships are captured using object communication models for each subsystem in the application domain. These *process models* can also be developed and tested using the role-playing techniques to understand the actions involved in a given

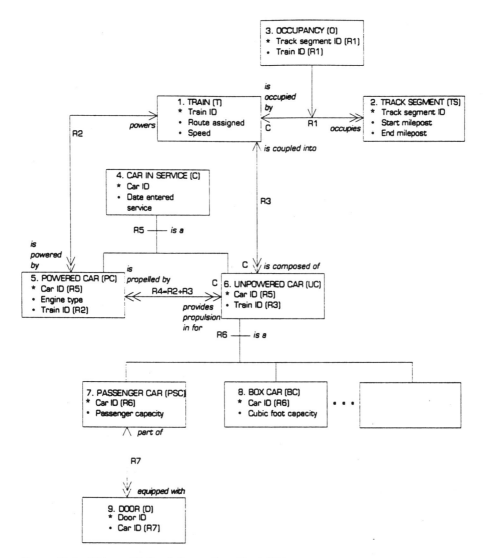

Figure 12-9   Shlaer–Mellor Information Model Diagram
Source: *Object Lifecycles: Modeling the World in States* by Schlaer & Mellor, © 1991.
Reprinted by permission of Prentice-Hall, Inc. Upper Saddle River, NJ.

action sequence. The model used to record this information is an *action data flow diagram*. For teams that are not using Shlaer–Mellor but who are used to structured techniques, this tool may help them analyze scenarios and map out role play, but they should beware of using it out of context. In Shlaer–Mellor the action data flow diagram supports a full set of data-driven models. Without this context, the action data flow diagram may lead to a functional orientation that is not useful in object-oriented development. Figure 12-11 shows an action data flow diagram for securing the arrival of an instance of the train class or a train object. This model supports item 3 of the state model shown in Figure 12-10.

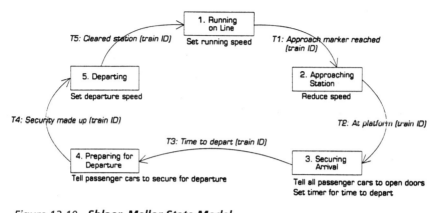

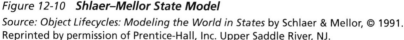

Figure 12-10 **Shlaer–Mellor State Model**
Source: *Object Lifecycles: Modeling the World in States* by Schlaer & Mellor, © 1991.
Reprinted by permission of Prentice-Hall, Inc. Upper Saddle River, NJ.

The last piece in the Shlaer–Mellor development cycle is *design definition*. A separate documentation set is used to capture this final perspective. One set of diagrams, class diagrams, describes the data contained as attributes, along with the operations (methods) of the class, parameters, and return values. Another diagram defines the flow of data and control within classes; another defines messages between classes (here we have the documentation for collaboration!); and still another defines inheritance relationships. This is a very detailed design notation which can be used directly to generate code. Be aware, however, that it does require considerable effort to complete. The argument in favor of this rigor and the effort it takes is that code generation can be done quickly and may even be automated. At the time of this writing, Object Technology has a tool that would automate this process in production.

Summing Up Shlaer–Mellor

One of the benefits of the Shlaer–Mellor method is the detailed map of the work products produced during OOA. A domain chart and product matrix, described earlier, are produced for the entire system. Subsystem communication models are produced for every subsystem, along with subsystem documentation of the models for information, object communication, and object access. These are supported at the subsystem level by various descriptive narratives, tabular data, and lists.

At the object level, a state model must be produced, along with supporting action data flow diagrams for each state, and process descriptions for every complex process of the relevant action. Many of the underlying concepts and notation are familiar to analysts who have worked with methodologies which supported Structured Analysis techniques.

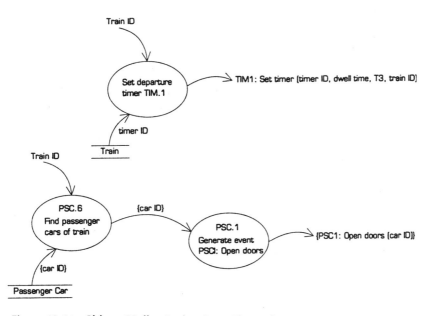

Figure 12-11 **Shlaer–Mellor Action Data Flow Diagram**
Source: Object Lifecycles: Modeling the World in States by Schlaer & Mellor, © 1991.
Reprinted by permission of Prentice-Hall, Inc. Upper Saddle River, NJ.

USING FORMAL METHODS FOR THE TRAFFIC CASE

Remember the traffic in Chapel Hollow? Using our techniques for brainstorming classes, and then role-playing the system, the team came up with a workable set of classes, their responsibilities, and their collaborations. It looked as if the flow of traffic through the town, with software controlled intersections, might actually get better instead of worse. At the end of the chapter, we saw the initial completed set of CRC cards created by the analysis team. That final set of CRC cards were used as the basis for our coding examples without too much trouble, but in a complex, large system, it is even more likely that, before generating code, the team would have to link the CRC card analysis to a formal method. To show how this works, we will use that same set of CRC cards to demonstrate how an initial design would look in the two methodologies just discussed.

Unified (Booch–Rumbaugh) Notation

The first thing that we will show are a number of diagrams from the Unified Booch–Rumbaugh notation. Look back at the end of the traffic system case study chapter for the full set of CRC cards we used to create these diagrams. The inheritance diagram is not included because there are no inheritance relationships among the six classes in the traffic system CRC card set. Figures 12-12 and 12-13 show sample diagrams in the Unified Booch–Rumbaugh notation.

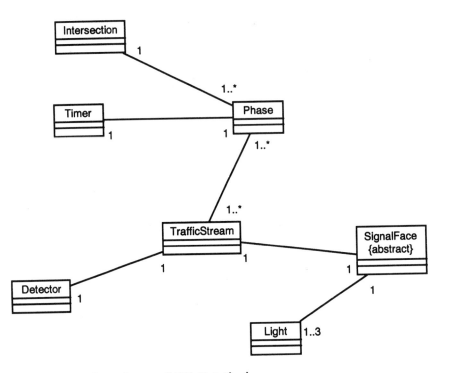

Figure 12-12 **Class Diagram (UML Notation)**

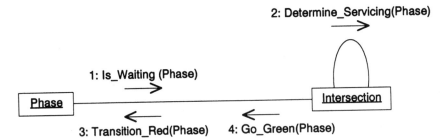

Figure 12-13 **Collaboration Diagram: Phase Demands Servicing**

Shlaer–Mellor Notation

Now, let's look at the same traffic system based on the same set of CRC cards and role play, but used as the basis for Shlaer–Mellor diagrams. In a full-blown version of the system, the methodology would call for a separate state model for each object and every state. We include only one model as an example, the state model for the action Go (Color) of a

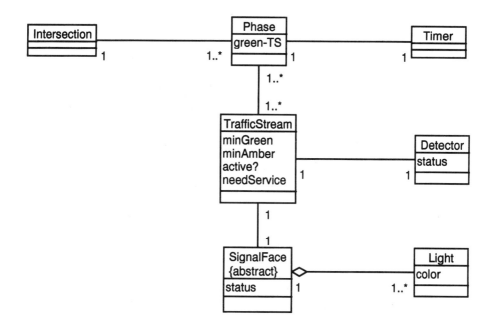

Figure 12-14 **Object Information Model (Information Structure Diagram)**

traffic light. Defining the details of the SignalFace class would be done during design, so, since our focus is analysis, we have not included that model in our figures. Figures 12-14 and 12-15 show sample models in Shlaer–Mellor notation.

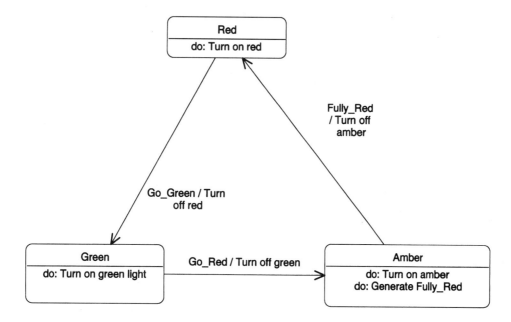

Figure 12-15 **State Model for SignalFace (Action: Go[Color])**

CRC CARD SOFTWARE

Software offers some advantages over manual systems, as we all realize! It can make revision easier, allow the CRC card set to be shared easily by people at distributed locations, and encourages the viewing of the analysis from different points of view (for example: by collaboration contracts, by hierarchy, by attributes, by super-class). An ideal tool would support both a graphical and a text display of its data. Use cases and collaborations would be best supported by hypertext-like links, so that you could jump to different views of the analysis easily.

Earlier in the book, we suggested that you use actual, physical, index cards and whiteboards during team brainstorms and role plays. There's something to writing on the cards, laying them out on the table, and passing them around to each other, that uniquely contributes to communication. If handwriting all the versions of cards isn't your thing and you do choose to use CRC card software right from the start, buy some card stock from a specialty supplier and run that in the laser printer so you'll have durable CRC cards to use at your meetings. Once you're done with role play and revision, the software may be able to take the CRC card set and feed it directly into a tool which supports the design methodology of your choice. This is exactly the case with Rational CRC, and we see signs that other software vendors will be following in the near future.

In sum, we see software as an asset to the capture of CRC card solutions, but not as a crucial element in using CRC cards for analysis. For this reason, we have included a short review of two software products on the market at the time we are writing (one commercial product and one shareware). As you know, keeping up with software products is difficult, so you will want to look at products yourself before deciding whether and what to buy.

Rational CRC

Rational CRC is a Windows-based tool which automates CRC card information. It is fully compatible with the approach to CRC card analysis discussed in this book. Rational CRC enables the analyst to include on each card links to parent classes and child classes, and thus to establish hierarchies. Individual cards can be printed, or cards can be printed in groups. The hierarchy graphs are particularly useful because they help the analysis team to visualize class interrelationships.

Rational CRC Class cards include responsibilities and collaborators. There is also room on the "back" of the card to record attributes. Following Wirfs-Brock, contracts can also be specified. A contract is a set of requests that a client can make of a server, defining a cohesive group of responsibilities. Contracts thus serve as a means of abstracting out similar responsibilities. Subsystems may be defined as sets of CRC cards which collaborate to fulfill a given collective set of responsibilities. The software represents them graphically as cards, displaying the external contracts along with the internal classes which carry them out.

The classes and subsystems defined in Rational CRC can be exported in "petal" format for import into the Rational Rose design tool. A class in the CRC software becomes a class in Rational Rose, along with the appropriate class category association if a subsystem was specified in the CRC software. CRC collaborations become Rose associations, and CRC attributes remain class attributes in Rose, although various details will be absent (such as the type, cardinality, and containment). These close connections to a methodology tool are unique to the Rational CRC product, and for those who intend to implement the Booch methodology it gives this product a competitive edge. The approach of deriving input for a methodology directly from CRC analysis is an important benefit which the close linking of Rose makes easier.

Other Tools

Shareware software tools are well-known for their ability to provide low-cost learning tools, even though they may have more bugs and fewer features compared to commercial tools. CRC software follows this pattern. We have found only one tool which we can recommend, CRC Tool. Version 1.2, the latest we worked with, has excellent printing features. Cards can be fed through a printer twice so that class attributes appear on the back, and various useful formatting options are available when printing CRC cards. Help is noticeably unhelpful in this version, and it is sometimes clumsy to change views of the analysis. Both problems will shortly be solved, according to the author, Stan Mitchell (stanm@compumedia.com). The tool does not currently export directly to a methodology tool; however, output in HTML and RTF formats is supported. At $30 for an individual license, and $200 for a site license, this is a reasonable, if limited tool.

Several other software tool vendors have good CRC products, available either as stand-alone components or as part of larger tool kits. InterSolv, vendors of the popular Excelerator II OOA&D, have a good CRC component (800-547-4000). Popkin Software and Systems recently released a CRC tool for System Architect, which can be used alone or with the System Architect Encyclopedia, and review of the beta copy we saw indicates this is worth looking over (800-732-5227). Gemstone software has a recently released CRC component which looks excellent. We expect most tool vendors will have a tool which supports CRC cards by the end of the year.

SUMMARY

In the previous two chapters we showed you how CRC cards could be used to create code, giving you the impression that CRC can be direct input to design. In this chapter, we have modified that implicit claim by showing you some of the limitations of CRC cards and some of the methods that take object-oriented development from a baseline of CRC analysis to detailed design diagrams. In other words, while endorsing the use of CRC cards for analysis, we honestly admit that the class cards can't show all the complexity necessary for large systems worked on by large numbers of people. For those situations, methodologies are necessary.

Building on this admission, we have shown you how systematic notation and documentation sets can be used to produce multiple, detailed views of systems and scenarios. To see this, we gave brief once-overs of the two most popular methodologies, the Unified (Booch–Rumbaugh) and the Shlaer–Mellor. Seeing the traffic case study in both notations gave you a feel for how they can be used. Finally, we reviewed automated support for CRC card analysis. Fortunately, at least one program also automates the generation of methodology documentation directly from the CRC card set, giving users a jump start.

This brings the book close to a close! If you started out new to classes and to CRC, and you think back to the start of the book, you've certainly come a long way. We hope you've learned "object think," and that you feel confident that you will get teams working to brainstorm classes and role-play systems. Those readers who already had some objects in their background have, we hope, gathered a few tips and tricks of the trade which they've "stolen" to use on their projects.

There are appendices to help you on your way out. The bibliography has the books we think are the most important, along with a few notes as to why. A "CRC Road Map" collects, in one place for easy reference, all the book's guidelines, tips and tricks.

We hope we have inspired some of you to learn a new OO programming language. Others, who work on big systems, will take our teamwork approaches into their groups while they consider one of the methodologies so necessary for large projects. We hope you will not only be building better systems, but will be working cooperatively and having more fun at work. We wish you the best of success as you embark into the world of classes, cards, and objects!

Appendix A

The CRC Road Map

All the tips, principles, and reminders are collected for quick review and reference!

CRC Team Guidelines (see Chapter 3)
Two is only company; ten is a crowd
Don't forget the user
Good analysts are good at making connections
A good designer is seen but not often heard
Choose your facilitator with a keen eye for quality

Brainstorming Principles (see Chapter 3)
All ideas are potential good ideas
Think fast and furiously first, ponder later
Give every voice a turn
A little humor can be a powerful force

Four-Step Approach to Brainstorming (see Chapter 3)
Step 1: Review brainstorming principles
Step 2: State session objectives
Step 3: Use a round-robin technique
Step 4: Discuss and select

Candidate Class Sources (see Chapter 3)
Read over all requirements documents
Look carefully at reports
Conduct interviews
Examine documentation, files, etc.

Selecting the CRC Team (see Chapter 3)
Pick a team open to change
No more than six people:
    Domain experts (1–2)
    Analysts (1–2)
    Experienced OO designer
    Facilitator and leader

CRC Warm-up Tips (see Chapter 3)
Give everyone a chance to participate early on
Take time to let the group get comfortable with each other
Avoid technical details; do not jump ahead
Set clear objectives and expectations

CRC Brainstorming Tips (see Chapter 3)
Have complete requirements resources on hand
Be sure the objective is clear
Don't censor ideas; record them
Don't get sidetracked by details prematurely

Opportunities for Collaboration (see Chapter 4)
Use scenarios and role play
Use the class hierarchy
Dependencies are collaboration clues
Identify clients, servers, and contracts

Identifying Hierarchies (see Chapter 4)
Look for "kind-of" relationships
Do not confuse "kind-of" hierarchies with "part-of" relationships
Name key abstractions
Look for frameworks

Core Class Selection Tips (see Chapter 4)
Start with classes for which there is consensus
Evaluate candidates against project scope
Distinguish attributes from classes
Look out for phantoms and ghosts, surrogates and aliases
Get ready to assign responsibilities
Take advantage of frameworks and patterns

Responsibility Allocation Tips (see Chapter 4)
Focus on "what," not "how"
Don't overload; factor out new classes instead
Take advantage of polymorphism: the same name for the same
   behavior
Take advantage of inheritance: hierarchies show class
   relationships
Take advantage of abstract classes: generalize common behavior

Responsibility Detection Pointers (see Chapter 4)
Brainstorm first, refine later
Think simple, factor out complexity
Use abstraction to advantage
Don't marry one solution; play the field first

Collaboration Tips (see Chapter 4)
Hierarchy signals collaborations
Identify clients and servers
Collaborations complement responsibilities
Add collaboration as you see connections between classes
Collaborators are pathways tested through scenarios

CRC Hierarchy Tips (see Chapter 4)
Explore "kind-of" relationships
Name key abstractions
Separate mixed classes where necessary
Place super/subclass sets in hierarchies
Look for reusable behavior (frameworks and patterns)

Role-Play Warm-up Tips (see Chapter 5)
Warm-up time is never wasted
Warm-up for every session
Inspire confidence
Don't get too serious too fast

Facilitating the Warm-up (see Chapter 5)
Introductions
Games
Interactive exercises
Light-hearted brainstorms
Formal go-arounds

Enactment Guidelines (see Chapter 5)
Identify and summarize scenarios (use agenda)
Assign roles to actors (distribute CRC cards)
Initiate scenario
Correct minor errors
Take assessment notes
Act out multiple scenarios

Assessment/Revision/Enactment Cycle (see Chapter 5)
"Go-around" comments
Identify problem points
Create problem-solving priority list
Change or confirm CRC cards
Identify scenarios to repeat or completed!

The Basic Steps of CRC Role Play (see Chapter 6)
Step 1: Create list of scenarios
Step 2: Assign roles
Step 3: Rehearse scenarios
Step 4: Correct CRC cards and revise scenarios
Step 5: Repeat steps 3 and 4
Step 6: Perform final scenarios

Role-Play Scenario Basics (see Chapter 6)
Concentrate on "must do" first
Develop "can do if" to handle contingencies
Record "might do" to test flexibility
Explore exceptions last
Frequently assess

Role-Play Session Pointers (see Chapter 6)
Clarify goals and objectives
Make sure team members are comfortable
Promote new ideas, encourage discovery
Confusion is rarely permanent

Running an Effective Role Play (see Chapter 6)
Stick to the scenario
Limit the time
Always warm up
Separate acting from analysis
Assess the results

Scenario Reminders (see Chapter 6)
Look for reusable frameworks
Try out "no problem," "must do" scripts first
Separate out conditional scenarios from "must do" scenarios
Develop "might do" scenarios that test for flexibility

Role-Play Reminders (see Chapter 6)
Always start with a warm-up
Enact and assess one scenario at a time
Add and revise but do not digress; hold discussion until
    assessment
Identify active classes by raising cards
It's OK to have fun

Using the Incremental SDLC to Manage (see Chapter 8)
Develop large systems in small steps
Manage iteration and maintain focus
Measure your progress
Update estimates and plans fast and frequently
Remember reuse
Teams should focus on work; work should focus on teams
Management commitment must be strong

Pilot Project Guidelines (see Chapter 8)
Nurture a cohesive team
Provide abundant support
Make early completion a priority
Work with a reasonable scale
Take advantage of opportunities for user interface

Start-up Guidelines (see Chapter 8)
Start now, but start small
Collect data right from the beginning
Make the training investment up front
Plan a coherent training ladder
Develop a core of experts
Use your experts to spread knowledge

Legacy Integration Guidelines (see Chapter 8)
Do not throw out working software
Create dynamic links to call non-OO code
Reuse responsibilities and the code that supports them
Parts wrappers can protect legacy code

OO Process Measurement Start Points (see Chapter 8)
Person-days per class
Classes per person
Person-days per incre-cycle
Incre-cycles per project
Percent classes reused
Percent frameworks/patterns developed

Appendix B

Bibliography

A highly selective list of a few books which we think are the best:

Booch, Grady: *Object-Oriented Analysis and Design with Applications* (1994: Benjamin-Cummings/Addison-Wesley).

With many examples in C++ of the Booch methodology output, this is the book which helped ensure its popularity. Very useful, although with the field changing so rapidly, and the coming Unified Notation (bringing together Booch, Rumbaugh, and Jacobson), you should check for a replacement title expected shortly after we go to press.

Butler, C. T. Lawrence, and Amy Rothstein: *On Conflict and Consensus,* 2nd Edition (1991: Food Not Bombs Publishing).

This is an excellent and succinct handbook on Formal Consensus decision making. Unlike current management vogue, instead of focusing on mythical "efficiency," this method focuses on the process itself and the quality of the outcomes. Hard to find in bookstores, it may be ordered for $10 from the publishers: 295 Forest Avenue #314, Portland ME 04101, 800-569-4054.

Coad, Peter: *Object Models: Strategies, Patterns, & Applications* (1995: Prentice-Hall PTR).

Through five case studies, shows 148 object stategies, 31 ready-to-use templates, and shareware which can be used for on-line modeling.

Goldberg, Adele, and Kenneth Rubin: *Succeeding with Objects: Decision Frameworks for Project Management* (1995: Addison-Wesley).

Great detail and practical advice on the managerial complications of OO development, including training and measurement.

Jacobson, Ivar: *Object-Oriented Software Engineering* (1992: Addison-Wesley).

Details the use-case approach to scenario building, a structured technique which focuses on recording all detail, not the discovery technique we discussed.

Pree, Wolfgang: *Design Patterns for Object-Oriented Software Development* (1995: Addison-Wesley).

Even though it draws examples from the C++ world, this thoughtful book gives insight into the design of frameworks using a "hot-spot" approach we find helpful. Especially useful in conjunction with the Coad book.

Shlaer, Sally, and Steve Mellor: *Object Lifecycles: Modeling the World in States* (1992: Prentice-Hall).

Applies data-driven techniques to user domain analysis, using a language-independent notation. The authors include a discussion on generating code through recursive design strategies.

Shlaer, Sally, and Steve Mellor: *Object-Oriented Systems Analysis: Modeling the World in Data* (1988: Prentice-Hall).

The original bible for the data-driven approaches, this title is in need of updating. However, it remains the most detailed summary of this useful approach to object-oriented analysis and design.

Taylor, David: *Object-Oriented Technology: A Manager's Guide* (1993: Wiley).

This is a classic already, as easily the clearest introduction to OO terminology and concepts for the neophyte.

Taylor, David: *Business Engineering with Object Technology* (1995: Wiley).

It's amazing how much information the author can convey in less than 200 pages. This follow-up to his earlier book places more emphasis on analysis and the development process.

Wirfs-Brock, Rebecca, Brian Wilkerson, and Lauren Wiener: *Designing Object-Oriented Software* (1990: Prentice-Hall PTR).

The most detailed explanation of the responsibility-driven design approach upon which the CRC card analysis technique is based. An excellent book to use in conjunction with our tips, tricks, and pointers.

Index